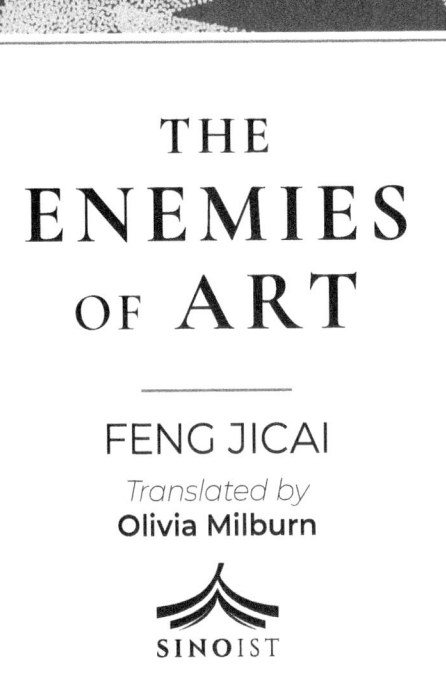

Published by Sinoist Books (an imprint of ACA Publishing Ltd)
London - Beijing

info@alaincharlesasia.com ☎ +44 20 3289 3885
www.sinoistbooks.com

Published by Sinoist Books (an imprint of ACA Publishing Ltd) in arrangement with People's Literature Publishing House

Author: Feng Jicai **Translator:** Olivia Milburn **Editor:** Matthew Keeler

Original Chinese Text © 艺术家们 (*yishujiamen*) 2020, People's Literature Publishing House/Feng Jicai, China

ALL RIGHTS RESERVED. NO PART OF THIS PUBLICATION MAY BE REPRODUCED IN MATERIAL FORM, BY ANY MEANS, WHETHER GRAPHIC, ELECTRONIC, MECHANICAL OR OTHER, INCLUDING PHOTOCOPYING OR INFORMATION STORAGE, IN WHOLE OR IN PART, AND MAY NOT BE USED TO PREPARE OTHER PUBLICATIONS WITHOUT WRITTEN PERMISSION FROM THE PUBLISHER.

English Translation text © 2023 ACA Publishing Ltd, London, UK. A catalogue record for *The Enemies of Art* is available from the National Bibliographic Service of the British Library.

This novel is entirely a work of fiction. The names, characters and incidents portrayed in it are the work of the author's imagination. Any resemblance to actual persons, living or dead, events or localities is entirely coincidental.

Hardback ISBN: 978-1-83890-552-1
Paperback ISBN: 978-1-83890-551-4
eBook ISBN: 978-1-83890-553-8

Sinoist Books is honoured to be supported using public funding by Arts Council England.

THE ENEMIES OF ART

FENG JICAI

TRANSLATED BY
OLIVIA MILBURN

SINOIST BOOKS

FOREWORD

I've always wanted to write this novel, which makes use of both my brush and my pen. I am not intending to be obscurantist here. I wanted to use a pen to write about the extraordinary endeavours and very different destinies of a group of painters; I wanted to use a brush to write the perception that only painters have. Although these painters are purely fictional, they are my contemporaries. I know what they think and how they feel, where they reached their peaks and where they pitched into the troughs of their era, when they fell into confusion, and the weight of idealism and human nature upon their palettes.

Artists consume fireworks, but because their work is to create eternal aesthetic lives, they are a group of extraordinary people in their thinking, feeling, imagination and even psychology. This forced me to use another set of pens and ink, different from when writing novels of local colour. I wanted to write about a completely different group of characters with their own distinctive lives, which involved yet another kind of pen and ink.

I don't shy away from criticism. This is necessary to explore the truth of life.

I also don't shy away from being an idealist and an aesthete. My ideals come from my heart, and my aestheticism rejects hypocrisy.

I know that half of my readers are my contemporaries and half are younger than me. I believe that my contemporaries will share my feelings; I hope that readers younger than me, as they vicariously experience the good luck and bad of the characters in this book, can come to understand artists and understand me.

Feng Jicai
May 2020

PREFACE
ON THE ARTIST

In the development of human art history, there have been two giant steps: one is the move from spontaneous art to conscious art; the second is from conscious art to artistic consciousness. The latter one is due to the emergence of artists. Since then, art has become extremely complicated.

The job of an artist is to personalise art. Creativity has come to mean originality. There is no transcendence in art, only difference, and the successful reveal themselves through thousands of differences. The personal charm of each individual artist has become the soul of his art. Therefore, mediocrity and shallowness are regarded as garbage, and any kind of tradition of copying is regarded as theft: both are the elimination of art. But as to how to turn personal charm into personalised art – each artist has their own secrets.

Through their hard work, they create a new world. This world is not a copy of the real world. Wisdom shines everywhere, talent overflows everywhere; colours are their own language, all sounds are spiritual, and all spaces leave room for the imagination. Everything in art is moving from nothing to something. Each protagonist is invented, and yet like living beings they too have flesh and blood, character and soul, but their lives do not follow the rules of life and death of living people. Unsuccessful ones are born to die, but successful ones can last forever. Sometimes they die in books, plays or movies, but they live again in every artistic appreciation. Art has its own mysterious laws. Because the essence of art is to create life, like human life itself, it is an ancient and eternal mystery.

Artists live through their artworks. Once their art is finished, the artist is dead – even as they are still breathing. The only way to live a long life is to be different from others and keep reinventing yourself. This harsh law forces an artist to devote all their body and mind to the task; they would happily die in this world so that they can live forever in art. No wonder they are confused in real life. But in the realm of their imaginations, they never make the slightest mistake. Strange people can create normative work. People will forgive the work, but not the artists in real life.

Real art is often not understood by the public. Prior to tomorrow's recognition, it is ridiculed today; art that is not comprehended and art that has failed is equally neglected – they are in the same situation and the feeling is identical. The artist's greatest enemy is loneliness. Artists are accompanied throughout their working lives by an audience that blows hot and cold, and a deep sense of loneliness.

That is how I think of the artist. Their problem is not a lack of worldly goods, but the inability to create a more valuable artistic and spiritual wealth. Therefore, they are natural ascetics, offering their lives to beautiful saints, while in the eyes of ordinary people, they are a pack of madmen, fools or gods. But without them, human intelligence would sink into mediocrity and life would turn into a desert – just like without mountains, the Earth is just a bald and bare sphere.

November 1987
Revised June 2020

PART ONE

上

FLOWERS GROWING IN A
DESOLATE WILDERNESS ARE
A BEAUTIFUL GIFT FROM GOD

CHAPTER 1

In his coat pocket, he was carrying a folio volume of reproduction paintings, without a cover and with a few pages missing, but he was so excited he seemed about to burst; as if he had obtained a magical tome. He pedalled hard on an old Hungarian bike, squeaking through the dark, rain-slicked streets. He liked to cycle on chilly late autumn nights such as this, after the rain had passed. The dim streetlights reflected on the wet asphalt road with a blurred light, and echoed softly the lights in the buildings between the trees, making him feel the unique tranquillity and warmth of the city he lived in. Only old cities have such intense charm.

In this era without private cars or high-rise buildings, nature still often permeated the air of old cities. The houses were old and there were few pedestrians. The pure air was full of the clean smell of wet trees, and he could not stop himself from breathing it deep into his lungs. He seemed to be passing through boundless, transparent and cool inky darkness.

When he came out, his wife Sui Yi reminded him several times to put on a scarf, but he'd still managed to forget because his head was filled with all kinds of magical images from the reproductions in his pocket, and nothing else was important. There was an icy wind blowing down his neck and onto his chest, but he didn't feel a thing. He was in a hurry to give his friend Luo Qian the same violent surprise as he had just experienced. He wanted to see Luo Qian's stunned face when he came face to face with these amazing pictures. He could imagine just what Luo Qian would look like. His tiny eyes would almost burst from their sockets!

He went into the compound where Luo Qian's house was located, rode his bike to the innermost part of the yard, hastily leaned it against the tree and locked it. Luo Qian was at home – the light was on at his window.

As usual, he could not help stopping in front of Luo Qian's house to enjoy the sight of his charming little home. He especially enjoyed its picturesqueness. His house was originally just a storage shed in the backyard of an old building dating to the 1920s to 1930s, small and simple, with only one door and one window. However, it stood well apart from the old building in front, crowded with five or six families. All alone in a corner of the backyard, it looked as if it had been forgotten by history. The roof and door were a little crooked, the paint was peeling badly off the walls, but the colour was mottled and harmonious, and several ancient trees in front of the house provided a sheltering canopy. He – that is Chu Yuntian – had once said to Luo Qian with a smile that it felt like a remote hermitage.

Luo Qian smiled. He was very satisfied. He liked this kind of life – forgotten by everyone.

His home should be more beautiful after the rain. Once he got off his bike, he didn't stop, but just rushed into the house. He took the folio volume out of his pocket and stuffed it into Luo Qian's hands without so much as a word, watching avidly for his response. Luo Qian was so occupied in turning over the leaves that he didn't look at him: he was indeed dumbstruck. With a stunned expression on his face, he asked: "Where did you get this?"

He said with a smile: "I just picked it up at a relative's house out of a pile of stuff returned to them after the Red Guards had pillaged the place." He waved his hand and said: "Let's not talk about that now. What do you think about these pictures?"

"Amazing!" Luo Qian couldn't restrain his enthusiasm. "To be honest," he said, "I've never seen these paintings before, and I don't know who the artists might be, but it must be a compilation of various people's work. Hey, Luo Fu will be here soon. He said he borrowed some great records. Let's ask him to have a look since he knows a lot about these things. Oh, he's here."

Luo Qian fell silent and the door opened. A young man burst in with a blast of cold wind and rain. He was not tall, but strong with a physique like a football player; a handsome face; thick hair with a natural curl; his deep-set eyes sparkled with vitality. He said with vigour: "Great, Yuntian's here! Did Luo Qian invite you to listen to music? Today I've really got something for you to listen to – this is the music of paradise!" With that, he threw aside his coat and pulled out a large, flat paper bag.

Luo Qian said: "There's no need to be in such a hurry. We've got something absolutely marvellous for you to look at!" He handed Luo Fu the volume of reproductions he was holding. But he didn't pass it across casually; instead, it was like he was giving Luo Fu some great treasure – something sacred and special.

Luo Fu took it in his hand and cried out in surprise: "This is – oh, it's Matisse! Van Gogh! This is another Van Gogh, and Renoir, and this one is a Modigliani! This is – who is this? I don't know, but this one here must be Picasso!" Luo Fu was a very excitable person. "I can tell you," he said, "that all these painters are Impressionist or Abstract masters! My teacher originally had a complete set of these books, all twenty-four volumes, printed by the Japanese. I've looked at them many times, but unfortunately they were all burned when his house was ransacked by the Red Guards. Whose is this? Where did you borrow it? How many days have you got it for?"

Luo Qian and Chu Yuntian smiled without answering. The more Luo Fu asked, the less inclined they were to answer.

Luo Fu said: "If you won't tell me, I won't let you listen to my records. Luo Qian, do you dare to say you don't want to listen to this record? Do you know what music this is?"

Luo Qian adored music. In this era of spiritual famine, he couldn't bear the temptation and gave way immediately. He smiled at Chu Yuntian and said: "You tell him."

Chu Yuntian then explained: "This album belongs to the three of us and we can enjoy it indefinitely."

Luo Fu was so excited that he threw open his arms and hugged Chu Yuntian. Then he opened the paper bag he had brought, which contained two vinyl records. He first took out one and said: "This one has a Chinese label. Guess what it is? It's a Chopin Polonaise, played by Gu Shengying."

Luo Qian remarked: "Gu Shengying played very gracefully and movingly – she was a very cultivated musician. It's such a shame she killed herself. I never expected to be able to hear her play Chopin again."

Luo Fu continued: "This one has a label in a foreign language. It's not English, it's Russian, so I can't understand it. Luo Qian, you learned Russian in middle school. Do you know what this says?"

Luo Qian took the record and looked at it carefully. His surprise was no less than when he saw the album just now. He opened his mouth and couldn't speak for a moment.

"What do you mean by that?" Yuntian asked him.

"This is Tchaikovsky's First!" Luo Qian said.

"What is Tchaikovsky's First?" Yuntian asked.

Obviously, Yuntian knew an awful lot less about music than either Luo Qian or Luo Fu. "Tchaikovsky's First Piano Concerto!" Luo Fu said. "His best concerto! It's as good as the collection of paintings you brought. I heard it played once before the Cultural Revolution and I was trembling all over with excitement. I always thought I'd never hear it again in my lifetime. Oh! Now I am going to hear it again today." His eyes lit up, and he went on: "I get it! I told Yannian yesterday that I missed Tchaikovsky so much because I'd never hear his music again. He took these two records out from under a cabinet and said he would lend them to me. I saw that one was Chopin and the other was something Russian which I couldn't read. I asked him if it was Tchaikovsky. He said you'll know as soon as you hear it. I guessed it would be him, but I didn't expect this piece! What a great guy Yannian is! Hey, what are we standing around here for? Let's listen to it!"

Chu Yuntian had two quite different homes. One was shared with his wife, Sui Yi: a wonderful world which belonged to them alone. The other was his friend Luo Qian's small and humble hermitage, which was the palace of his spirit. He loved this cramped, poor little house, in which everything came easily to hand without having been deliberately placed there. Freedom and relaxation were to be found here, mixed with a faint smell of oil paint and turpentine. Paintings large and small were hanging on the wall, higgledy-piggledy, placed without rhyme or reason. These oil paintings, watercolours and charcoal drawings were all by Luo Qian himself. He never hung other people's works in his house; he lived in a world of his own making. In fact, even the bed, table and sofa here had been made by him. But he didn't want to make these things exquisite; he just nailed some thick planks together horizontally and vertically, topped off with some calico cushions stuffed with rice straw or cotton bolls, with a couple of brightly coloured old blankets thrown on top, and there he sat comfortably, as if leaning on an earth slope or haystack. On the table, there were several chunky but attractive bits of pottery, enamel water cups, eating plates, as well as miscellaneous books and sheets of paper. In the centre, there was an empty wine jug with olive-green glaze, which he used as a vase. This was the most exquisite piece in the house. The flowers in the jug were arranged by Luo Qian; whenever he saw some pretty wildflowers or leaves on one of his walks, he would pick them and put them there. Sometimes it contained branches covered in little buds; sometimes it was autumn grasses just on the cusp of turning red. He had a remarkable eye, and the things he picked always had a special beauty. Occasionally he would place these flowers onto canvas and then they'd be hanging on the wall. He said: "Art can turn a moment into eternity."

There was another thing in his room, right there in the corner – something that looked like a small standing cabinet, covered with an old army blanket, quite inconspicuous. Under the army blanket was an old-fashioned cabinet player, which was Luo Qian's treasure and regularly served as the focus of the parties the three of them held here.

This record player was probably a relic of the era of foreign concessions decades back. It had once belonged to a friend of Luo Qian's, but no one listened to it – it was big and took up a lot of space, and since Luo Qian wanted it, his friend gave it to him. Inside the cabinet was a small box full of needles. At that time, the radio only played songs with lyrics from the quotations of Chairman Mao and model operas. With this old record player, Luo Qian and his friends came into possession of a little piece of heaven. The next thing they had to do was try their best to find some old records. No matter who laid hands on one, the trio would make an appointment here to listen to it. Listening to these banned records was risky. They would hold their breath, turn the volume down low, and go to the window from time to time to see if there was anyone outside. However, stealing forbidden fruit has always been a great pleasure, no matter what the kind.

Now, when Luo Qian carefully put 'Tchaikovsky's First' on the record player and then gently put the arm down on the record, Luo Fu and Chu Yuntian, sitting on the sofa, automatically shifted forward, craning their necks, such was their eagerness to hear this divine melody. When the music started, they were immediately awestruck, overcome by Tchaikovsky's incomparable charm and his magnificent and powerful music. Chu Yuntian, in particular, was hearing this piece for the first time. He felt a vast and brilliant torrent falling from the sky, which overwhelmed him, spinning his whole person around, and rolling it up into a grand, magical and beautiful noise that stirred his very heart.

This was a small, three-person salon.

Of course, they kept this absolutely secret. At that time, everyone lived in fear. In the wake of the Petőfi Incident in Hungary in 1956, the word 'salon' had come to be regarded as heresy. Several young poetry-lovers they knew used to hold regular meetings, only to be denounced and locked up, quite inexplicably, as a 'Petőfi-style gang'. Amongst themselves, however, they called this a 'salon' because it was their spiritual home, and they used this name to express the extraordinary pleasure this trio of artist friends felt when they got together. They enjoyed the feeling of being close friends with one another and immersed themselves in a kind of aesthetic joy. They also called themselves the 'Three Musketeers' to show that they were inseparable in spirit. Whenever they dug up a forbidden old record, reproductions of paintings or some literary masterpiece from the barren and desolate city ravaged by the Cultural Revolution, they would fire up their salon and prepare a hearty feast for their senses, something which they could mull over for many days.

Chu Yuntian's knowledge of music was limited, but he had a fine ear. He was easily touched and moved by music. Music seemed to be naturally related to his painting, in that it always evoked new pictures in his imagination. As he said to Luo Qian: "You ought to move your record player round to my house."

Luo Qian, who was single, said with a smile: "But that's my wife." Then he added: "If you had it, you wouldn't come round here any more."

Now Chu Yuntian was sitting there motionless, almost beside himself at the music. Luo Fu showed signs of uncontrollable excitement from time to time: jumping up, and at the blast of a trumpet he would wave his hands and say loudly: "Here comes the light." His eyes were shining as if he really were caught in a beam of dazzling sunshine. Luo Qian was still turning over the reproductions of paintings.

"Why aren't you listening to the music?" Luo Fu demanded.

Luo Qian's eyes were fixed on one picture in the album, as he said: "I have been listening the whole time. I prefer the second movement just now. It's like a pastoral. Just like the picture I was imagining."

"I agree," Chu Yuntian said. "The second movement is too beautiful. There is a little melancholy, a little disappointment and a little consolation."

Luo Qian looked at Chu Yuntian and said: "How right you are."

After listening to Tchaikovsky, they discussed his music and then the conversation turned to other topics. Speaking of Isaac Levitan, Chu Yuntian immediately thought of Chekhov's short story 'The Steppe'. Among the three of them, Chu Yuntian was the most interested in literature, and the most widely read. He said that the faint melancholy in *The Steppe* could also be seen in Isaac Levitan's paintings or heard in Tchaikovsky's music. So they discussed the Russian temperament. "I still prefer the French," Luo Fu said.

Luo Qian said: "We are talking about Tchaikovsky's music right now – we aren't thinking about the French."

"Those paintings you're holding are all done by French artists," Luo Fu said.

The aesthetic education of this generation was at once very specialised and quite warped. As they were growing up, Sino-Soviet relations were good, and Soviet literature and art dominated Chinese culture. In the eyes of Chinese people, Russian literature pretty much *was* world literature, and the masterpieces of Russian art were treasures for all humanity. This was particularly true for Luo Qian, who was three years older. Luo Fu was a teacher at an art college, so his range of vision was naturally wider. However, most people in those days were confined to their own country, and their world was only what they could imagine from the handful of books at their disposal.

Chu Yuntian said to Luo Fu with a smile: "Right now you'd better enjoy the melancholy of Russia. Keep the French for later. I suggest that we don't listen to Chopin today, but just concentrate on the Tchaikovsky."

Luo Fu looked at Chu Yuntian with appreciation and said: "I agree. We don't want to overcomplicate things. This way we can remember it properly and really appreciate it. Next time we'll listen to the Chopin. However, today I have to take those pictures home for a good look." Before Luo Qian could object, he hurriedly added: "You have the music, so give me the paintings. Right, Yuntian?"

"I agree," Chu Yuntian said. "You can't have both. One treasure per person." But then he said: "What about me? I've been left with nothing."

"You are a proletarian!" Luo Fu said.

Chu Yuntian gave up.

Luo Qian said: "You aren't a pure proletarian. You're thinking about Tchaikovsky."

Chu Yuntian realised he was right. There was little room for him to think of anything other than Tchaikovsky now.

The salon was over. It was already late at night, and they needed to get home. A little rain was falling outside, and the wind was stronger and colder than when they came. In those days people didn't much mind the wind and rain. Chu Yuntian and Luo Fu emerged from Luo Qian's little home quite contentedly. It really was very much like the artists in nineteenth-century Paris emerging from their salons in high spirits. With a folio of paintings in one pocket, and their minds fixed on the wonderful music they'd been listening to, they felt on top of the world. They each got on their broken bicycles and rode squeakily out of Luo Qian's old, dark and wet courtyard. Then they waved to each other and went their separate ways, disappearing happily in the cold, dank and rainy night.

CHAPTER 2

When you have lost everything, it may be that God hides a treasure right beside you: it is up to you to find it.

Chu Yuntian and Sui Yi found it. They found it not by looking, but through the exercise of their natural talents.

Seven years ago, when they were forced into homelessness by the Cultural Revolution, they managed to find sanctuary here in the attics and decided that after all, life was pretty good to them.

Having lost nearly everything that they owned, these two young people climbed up the crooked and broken steps leading to the attic of this old building, sure that they were going to experience misery from now on. There was normally a room up on the top floor of these pitch-roofed buildings, narrow and sloping, with a little window looking out on the east and the south sides. In the past, the attics of Western buildings wouldn't have had anyone living in them: they were used for storage and the windows were only there to provide a bit of ventilation. However, this attic was different; there was a square window in the ceiling forming a skylight. Even more unusually, since the whole building was constructed with wood, there were at least six fat pillars in the attics holding up the roof. They served to cut up the already small attic into even smaller pieces. There seemed to be columns everywhere; when the light shone in, their shadows fell this way and that, until it looked like you were in the middle of some enchanted forest. Chu Yuntian and

Sui Yi both grew up in the Five Avenues area of Tianjin where there were many foreign buildings. They'd seen all kinds of houses, but nothing like this. Although the attic room was small, it spoke to their imagination. Sui Yi raised her head and smiled at Chu Yuntian – half a head again taller than herself – and said: "I like it."

"Me too," Chu Yuntian said. It seemed that he had come upon a new world.

This was the best kind of feeling between them. The best feeling between husband and wife is one that they share.

At the end of the nineteenth century, when the British first opened a concession in Tianjin, they located themselves on the eastern bank of the Qiangzi Canal, but never crossed onto the other side. The Qiangzi Canal was dug by order of Prince Sengge Rinchen, the famous Imperial Commissioner during the reign of the Xianfeng Emperor. In order to protect Tianjin, he wanted to build a combined moat and wall; to build the wall he had to take the earth from somewhere, so naturally he put the canal right at the foot of the walls – this was the Qiangzi Canal. It was not very wide, and it winded this way and that, but for a while it formed the boundary between the old city of Tianjin and the foreign concession. The foreign concession was on the east side of the canal, the old city on the west. After the Boxer Rebellion at the turn of the century, the British leapt across the Qiangzi Canal without the slightest hesitation – they took a huge chunk of land on the west side of the river as a concession which they administered as they saw fit. As a result, all kinds of Western-style buildings appeared on both banks of the Qiangzi Canal. No one seemed to know who the first owner of the building Chu Yuntian now lived in could be. Some scholars of the city's architectural history thought that foreigners were the most likely inhabitants since they generally used imported corrugated iron to build roofs in this period. This kind of sheet iron was very thick and solid, and the surface would be painted – either dark blue or dark red. It was only much later that they gradually changed to locally fired tiles when they built a new house. Today, there are few such early corrugated iron peak-roofed houses – a strange reminder, rich in history, of the early days of the foreign concession.

The small building where Chu Yuntian lived faced south, overlooking the canal. There were three of them all in a row; none of these buildings was very tall, but they were identical – pitched roof, three storeys, with grey walls and red roofs, long iron-framed windows and lead rainwater pipes. They were undecorated, and somewhat primitive. In the early days of the concession, there was abundant land for building houses. Large grounds extended on all four sides of each small building, and they were separated by tall trees. Over time, the red roof had become mottled and old, and the walls damaged and darkened, but that was hidden, even obliterated, by the surrounding trees. If you stood on top of the steps of the synagogue on the other side of the canal and looked across, it seemed like an old painting that had faded, but that had only made it more poetic.

Only poets and painters can see the historical beauty of cities. Over the years, Chu Yuntian often put his easel down on the opposite bank and painted many watercolours of his own house. He had also invited Luo Qian and Luo Fu to paint it with him. Among his own paintings on the subject, his favourite was a snow scene. He had painted it from life, having scrambled over the canal amid the snowdrifts after a heavy snowfall. At that time, his hands and feet were frozen stiff, but he completely ignored it. He was fascinated by the scene in front of his eyes, and he was in a hurry to get it down on canvas: amid the white snow, three dark red steep roofs stood upright silently, surrounded by the tangled branches of black and ochre trees.

Luo Qian also liked this picture the best. He said: "Those three red roofs standing in the snow represent the three of us."

Luo Fu said: "One of these days we'll have to move in – one attic each!"

Chu Yuntian was glad to hear them say this.

Women often care more about the circumstances in which they live than men.

Sui Yi adored their strange attic room. She said that it was "naturally full of life". Why? Because of the sun. It changed as soon as the light hit it. From morning to night, the angle of the sun was ever different; hence, the lights and shadows in their room, together with the colour and atmosphere, were also constantly changing. The window was small, and the incoming sunlight was therefore concentrated into a beam. She liked to be quietly reading or doing things about the house, and all the while she would be paying attention to the silently shifting beam of light. The light moved in a set pattern without leaving the slightest trace behind, but the supporting pillars would be lit by you, darkened by me, while others would be completely in the shade. The window not only functioned as a clock, but also as a calendar. When there was a thick canopy outside the window, summer was in full flush, and cicadas were chirping away. However, when autumn came, the thick curtains of nature would be pulled a little open, so that the autumn sun could shine brighter and brighter through the window.

It is strange that this old wooden house, which must have been at least fifty or sixty years old, still exuded a strong smell of wood. However, people who live in cities like to smell natural scents.

Sui Yi was proudest of the skylight.

She deliberately put their small bed under the tiny skylight. She liked to lie lazily in bed, looking up at it. It was always magical: not only were raindrops falling gently, splashing here and there, with a few fallen leaves or a falling flower as a passing guest facing her through the window; but also when heavy snow encased the window, the winter sunshine still struggled through. Eventually, the thick snow sealing the window would melt in the middle, revealing the purest, highest and most infinite blue in the world. What if there was an eagle circling in the depths of the blue sky?

"Unfortunately, I can't draw it for you," Chu Yuntian said, as he lay beside her.

"It does not belong in painting – this should be poetry, prose or maybe music," Sui Yi said. "You can record it with your other pen." She looked at him admiringly.

She admired him, and of course he admired her too. Their admiration for one another served to bring them together and had long ago welded them into a single unit. For both, their fathers were doctors and friends. As children they had played together when their parents socialised; they lived in the same part of the city and it was a very special community; they'd gone to school together; and when they went to university Chu Yuntian had gone into the art department while Sui Yi studied medicine. Nevertheless, their common interest in literature and art had kept them in contact. Chu Yuntian had a natural talent for painting and liked writing poetry and prose. If he had studied literature, he would have been the same Chu Yuntian holding another pen. Sui Yi did not paint or write poetry, but she was a great lover of art. That is why she admired Yuntian, his natural extraordinary perception, and his artistic imagination. In her eyes, Chu Yuntian was a source of art – an inexhaustible source.

Yuntian admired her for her understanding of art. This understanding was innate, and invisible. It is a kind of intuition and sensibility, but as such it is the essence of art.

Maybe they didn't understand why when he was moved, she was moved too. She was intoxicated with emotion, and then he became so as well. More importantly, he worshipped art as his god; while she seemed to be born with great spiritual refinement. Who can understand what inexplicable things were going on in the hearts of these young people? What was it all about?

In the eyes of some, their attic room was low-ceilinged and depressing, with far too many pillars. They endlessly had to duck and dive, especially where the roof sloped: the tall Chu Yuntian regularly bumped his head there. In summer, the corrugated iron roof which had been absorbing heat all day remained hot all night. The place was like a furnace; when you couldn't sleep, the only option was to sit on the windowsill and try to get some air. In winter, with the thin exterior walls, the place was like an igloo. Every night, Chu Yuntian would be the first in bed, to warm it up before Sui Yi joined him. That always made her giggle, and she would then get embarrassed and crawl in herself. Why were they still proud of their humble home?

It was Luo Qian who really understood. In Luo Qian's eyes, Chu Yuntian and Sui Yi were made for one another. He envied Chu Yuntian's luck. It's not difficult to find a partner in life, but you can spend a lifetime trying to find an intelligent confidante. Luo Qian wondered why God gave such a good woman as Sui Yi to Chu Yuntian. Luo Qian might have been envious, or perhaps a little jealous – who knows?

. . .

The way in which this young couple talked and laughed all day was puzzling to outsiders. They had moved in after they'd been rendered homeless when the Five Avenues district was pillaged. Rumour had it that they'd previously been living in a really nice English-style bungalow over on Mu'nan Road. Now they'd been reduced to existing in this disorderly, half-ruined attic: could it really be true that they were so happy?

That was not a comfortable time – it was up to you to keep your spirits up. It was not difficult for them to do this, since it was natural and inborn. Whether Yuntian hung a great new painting on the wooden wall of the attic, or Sui Yi bought some beautiful scraps of fabric and sewed them into a gorgeous, elegant cushion or pillow-case, they would talk it over together, express their feelings and be happy for days at a time.

After graduating from art college, Chu Yuntian was assigned to the design office of the Bureau of Light Industry. He didn't enjoy the monotonous packaging design work, but he didn't care too much because his life was actually lived in their small salon surrounded by other genuine disciples of art and culture, and in the small and vibrant living space he and Sui Yi had created.

Even when little, Sui Yi was the kind of girl who read a book a day. Chu Yuntian knew that she also wrote on the quiet, but she didn't show him a word. That was quite different from him; he read aloud to her every word or sentence that he was pleased with. When she was a teenager, she told Yuntian that one day she hoped to become a second Li Qingzhao, the great Chinese woman poet. She had also once hoped to study literature at the same university as Yuntian. She appreciated the spirit that he often showed in his writings. She said his spirit jumped out like the Monkey King. However, the ideals of youth are always like a colourful soap bubble when confronted with reality, bursting at the slightest touch. By the time she graduated from high school, her two dreams had both come to nought. First of all, Yuntian decided that his interest in painting far exceeded that in literature. He also believed that he was in no hurry to become a writer. Most writers got into that in mid-career anyway, so he applied for art college. Second, she herself failed to fulfil her ambitions because she followed her father's wishes. Her father was one of the best ophthalmologists in China, and he thought that his daughter was so clever, quiet and calm. Although she did not look strong, she kept a cool head in a crisis, and that is an attribute you can't learn; that kind of thing comes from nature. Her father said that if his beloved daughter put on a white coat, she'd make an excellent ophthalmologist.

Their choice did not go as they hoped. At that time, college students had to obey the Party and accept where they were sent after graduation. Although Chu Yuntian was a talented student, his family background was not good enough: that got him assigned to the Bureau of Light Industry to design product packaging. This work had nothing to do with art; it ran counter to it. Although Sui Yi became a doctor, after her father was labelled as a 'Reactionary Academic Authority', she was reduced to the most menial activities in the hospital. That didn't bother either of them too much because they held to other standards and values in their hearts.

People who love art pursue artistry in their daily lives. People who love beauty love life more. People who really love life will certainly pay attention to even the smallest details of their daily routine. Sui Yi did not put her heart into art the way that Yuntian did, but she made their tiny attic a space for her imagination; she cared about the quality of everything they had at home. The tastefulness of a thing has nothing to do with its value. The key is its beautiful form, harmonious colours, and cultural resonances. Sui Yi and Yuntian shared the same principles:

"The enemy of beauty is not ugliness, but vulgarity."

Was their view a little harsh?

Luo Fu smiled and said to them: "You are a little self-indulgent."

Luo Qian said: "When you have nothing, you might as well be self-indulgent."

Yuntian said: "We don't suffer because of this. If anything, it makes us happier."

When together they pushed their broken bicycles out of the front door to that red-roofed building, they really made an enchanting young couple. Yuntian was tall, with long straight legs, long soft hair – a little messy and untidy – and a pair of eyes with a slightly melancholic expression. Beside him, Sui Yi was slim and light. Since childhood, she liked to cut her hair short, and she was dressed in blue woollen trousers (washed so many times that the dye was wearing thin), white socks and black shoes. She was not outstandingly beautiful, but she had a kind of elegant good looks, with a broad forehead, thin eyebrows above slanted eyes and a slightly upturned chin. She seldom said much and didn't smile easily, but whenever she looked at Yuntian, she would unconsciously give a gentle smile.

CHAPTER 3

Three days later, it was the evening that the trio had agreed to hold a 'salon concert'. Yuntian arrived and he had brought Sui Yi. Sui Yi seldom participated in their salon, but she couldn't miss what might be a once-in-a-lifetime opportunity to hear Chopin. Where could anyone go to listen to Chopin at that time? Yuntian had whispered to her mysteriously that this was heavenly music, which she might not hear again for many years.

As soon as they entered Luo Qian's little house, the upper corners of their host's small eyes twitched excitedly. Obviously, this was not because of Yuntian, but because of Sui Yi's sudden arrival. A long, deep red scarf hung over her coat, which set off her beautiful, quiet face perfectly. Indeed, as soon as Sui Yi appeared, she gave a different feeling to the occasion.

To Yuntian's surprise, Luo Qian's home seemed to have been transformed in the space of just three days – what could have changed? He looked again; the paintings that had previously been hanging on the wall had gone, and most of them had been replaced by new works. There was also a strong smell of oil paint permeating the atmosphere! The smell was exciting and made him want to paint something himself.

Without being quite aware of what they were doing, Yuntian and Sui Yi went over to inspect these new paintings. As soon as Yuntian's gaze fell on these pictures, he felt their fresh and powerful impact. Luo Qian's paintings did not normally have this kind of punch. He said that he was not interested in making his paintings impactful because that was something for other people, and he painted for himself. Not that he was a pure realist; he said that the academic school could not draw the line between realism and representational art, and that representational art was just a plagiarism of life. In other people's eyes, everything in his paintings was a distortion of reality. As Yuntian understood it, he would not represent the forms he saw with his eyes, but reflected the forms found in his heart. His paintings had a strong subjectivism. As for why his paintings were always a little distorted, the structure was not harmonious, the tone was cold and dark, and there was an impression of chilliness, which Yuntian could not explain. However, paintings that do not require interpretation are meaningless. Moreover, Yuntian liked his out-of-whack, obscure beauty, which reminded him of Dostoevsky. But why were these new paintings so different? Where did he get such a strong feeling and passion from? Were his paintings going to change? Why?

Sui Yi asked Luo Qian straight out: "Did the picture album that Yuntian gave you have this effect?"

This revealed Luo Qian's secret at one stroke. He asked Sui Yi with surprise: "How did you know that?"

Sui Yi didn't answer; instead, she smiled and said: "You don't get to see enough picture books. That's why it had such an impact on you! You wouldn't normally be so easily influenced by other people."

What she said was just her personal opinion, but was there a hint of criticism here?

Luo Qian didn't say anything more. His eyes showed a sincere appreciation of Sui Yi's understanding. But his gaze made Chu Yuntian feel a little uncomfortable. Quickly, they'd all deliberately changed the subject and were discussing the album of reproductions. Since right at that moment the pictures were in Luo Fu's possession, what they talked about was which one had made the greatest impression on them. Sui Yi's mother taught English at the foreign language college, so she had learned English since childhood. She had read the text carefully, meaning she could supply the title and name of the artist of most of the pictures. Chu Yuntian was most impressed by Monet's landscapes, while Luo Qian admired the paintings by Modigliani and Munch, especially Munch's 'The Scream' and 'Death in the Sickroom'. Sui Yi told Luo Qian that this latter painting was Munch's greatest masterpiece. Of course, she could not know that Luo Qian was so impressed by the two paintings because he felt a close spiritual connection to Edvard Munch.

The biggest difference between the lives of Luo Fu and Luo Qian lay in their view of time. Luo Qian was as punctual as any German. Luo Fu was always late. Chu Yuntian said with a smile: "If he were to arrive on time, he'd take it so badly."

One of the rules of their salon concert was that all three must be present and enjoy the music together. Therefore, when Luo Fu entered the room, Chu Yuntian told him: "We aren't going to forgive you easily for being so late today. Sui Yi has come specially to listen to the Chopin, and you're this late! She's been waiting almost an hour!"

Luo Fu behaved like a naughty boy. When he heard this, he jumped and spun high in the air, and said: "Let that be my apology!"

"You gave me quite a turn!" Sui Yi said.

"He used to be in the school gymnastics team," Chu Yuntian explained. "That's nothing. He should kneel."

Sui Yi waved her hands vigorously in protest, for fear that Luo Fu would bounce around the room in some other terrifying way.

Now Luo Fu deigned to explain: "I came late because several painters in the college were fighting to see your album." He took the book out of his pocket and said: "I agreed to hand it over to Luo Qian today, but I had to let my painting friends have a good look first."

Unexpectedly, Luo Qian said: "I don't want to look at it."

Luo Fu was puzzled and asked: "Why not? I've been admiring it for three days and three nights straight."

"It wouldn't be good for me to look at it again," Luo Qian said. "Give it back to Yuntian now and maybe I'll look at it later." He looked at Sui Yi as if she would understand what he meant.

Chu Yuntian noticed the direction of his glance. For a second time, Chu Yuntian felt a little unhappy. It was natural that he was not pleased. No one is happy when other men treat their wives as special confidantes. However, he absolutely agreed with Luo Qian's idea that he should keep a distance from this marvellous album. In art, once conquered by others, you lose yourself.

This is also a kind of artistic persistence.

When they were immersed in the gorgeous and violent music of a Chopin Polonaise, these young and sensitive hearts were melted. On other occasions, after listening to the music, they would enthusiastically express their feelings and emotional response. But this time it was different. Luo Qian hung his head and didn't speak. No matter what they said to him, he just shook his head and didn't say a word; this went on for a long time. Yuntian suddenly noticed a few drops of water on his trouser legs, just beneath his head. Had he been crying? No one had ever seen Luo Qian cry. Why? Was this about the tragedy of Gu Shengying, the talented pianist who played Chopin in this recording, who ended up gassing herself? Surely not. There were too many instances at that time of such things. Chu Yuntian knew that it was no good asking him. He was a self-contained person. The best thing would be for everyone to leave now without disturbing him. Some things have to be digested slowly.

When they had whispered goodbye to him and were ready to leave, Luo Qian said: "Take the record with you and return it." That was a message for Luo Fu. This gave Yuntian the impression that leaving the record there would trouble and burden him. No one asked why. Luo Fu took the record as instructed.

So, everyone quietly departed, closed the door and left Luo Qian alone with the questions he'd aroused in this old and broken-down hut.

Although Chu Yuntian and Luo Qian were good friends, Luo Qian knew everything about Yuntian, while Yuntian knew little about Luo Qian. The reason might have been that Chu Yuntian was not cagey, and he and Sui Yi did not keep secrets from each other. He was also an expansive personality and liked to tell other people what he had in mind. Luo Qian, by contrast, was silent and defensive by nature. Did he keep his mouth shut because he was too defensive, or did he appear defensive because he was silent by nature? Anyway, no one knew anything about his family, parents, experiences or his views on Luo Fu and marriage. He came from Hebei Province and had a slight Cangzhou accent, but no one could tell more than that. He kept himself to himself so resolutely that people even wondered if he'd been in trouble and had to live in near hiding. Chu Yuntian was sociable and had many friends. Luo Qian seemed to have only two friends: Yuntian and Luo Fu. And even Luo Fu had first been introduced to him by Chu Yuntian. Chu Yuntian originally met Luo Qian by chance in a paint shop. After knowing each other for over a year, they gradually became close friends. According to the clerk in the shop, he worked in a furniture factory, but they had no idea what he did for them. Chu Yuntian had once made the mistake of asking him if he did woodwork. Although he didn't deny it, he seemed very bored, which made Yuntian feel that he didn't like anyone else knowing his private affairs. He was a man who only talked about art, and how many people in that era was that true of?

Luo Qian was not short, but his back had become slightly hunched – possibly it was because he worked all day every day bent over. He had a broad face and big hands. He liked to stand with his legs apart and sit with his legs crossed. His face was perfectly ordinary – there was nothing unusual about it, but it was also completely lacking in any sign of spark. Only his small eyes with their slight upward twist at the corners could be regarded as a feature. He looked like an ordinary workman, but his paintings showed no mean ability.

His unique personality and atmosphere, the softness and calmness of his brushstrokes, the strangeness of his vision, the unexpected colour, especially the coldness and depth of expression… these were things that Chu Yuntian did not find in other pictures painted at that time. Of course, his works were excluded by the mainstream art movement. Therefore, Yuntian was very curious about the origin of his artistic vision; it was not as if he'd just dropped from the sky after all. Once when they were chatting, Luo Qian realised what Yuntian was up to with his careful leading questions and prevarications, and just said: "A person's origins are right there in his art."

Then he retreated back into silence.

Since their personalities were so different, and they had so many points where they simply did not agree, why were they always together? If they hadn't met for a few days, Chu Yuntian would run over to see Luo Qian, or Luo Qian would climb up to Chu Yuntian's attic via the rickety, creaking wooden steps. At that time, there was no telephone. In addition to writing letters, people went round to each other's houses to find them. This was the most primitive and simple method of interpersonal communication, unchanged for two thousand years.

Their relationship was unconfrontational, and they rarely did anything much together. They just looked at new pictures and chatted with each other. Of course, most of the conversation came from Yuntian.

When chatting, Luo Qian always narrowed his small eyes in appreciation of his tall friend's emotional expression of his feelings about art, nature, life, a person, a book he had just read and its author. In Yuntian's outpourings, there were always unique insights and great emotional depths. He would explain things in a picturesque way, detailed and lively, very literary. Luo Qian once said to Yuntian: "The fact is that you'd be better as a writer. Of course, being a writer is much more dangerous than being a painter."

Luo Qian's words did not negate his painting ability. No one can foresee the future. However, Luo Qian could appreciate the manifold talents of this friend younger than himself. He saw the genius glowing faintly in this young man who had yet to achieve anything at all. Probably this was the reason Luo Qian, who was a loner by nature, had made friends with Chu Yuntian. However, it is quite possible that neither of them was aware of this.

Chu Yuntian was very happy to have a friend with whom he could talk about art. In a world where art had been almost entirely swept away, where else could he find such spiritual communion, where else could he release his inner energies?

Neither Chu Yuntian nor Luo Qian smoked or drank, nor did they have any regular hobbies. Luo Qian's only vices were jasmine tea and Fuling pickled mustard. These were his only worldly pleasures. Whenever Chu Yuntian came to visit, he would happily brew up a pot of fragrant jasmine tea, one cup for each of them, poured into whatever came to hand. Yuntian usually used a white glass cup of the cheapest kind. If Luo Fu joined them, he got out an enamel cup covered in chips and cracks. Luo Qian himself used a wonky pottery bowl. He really liked this pottery bowl with its thick glaze. He said that with repeated use, a seasoned pottery bowl would make the tea taste even better. There was a plate in between them, with a torn packet of pickled mustard on it. These things helped along their spiritual feast.

In fact, as painters, the Three Musketeers had quite different styles. Their paintings had nothing to do with each other. Luo Qian only painted oils, and they were slightly abstract. Luo Fu painted academic oils. Chu Yuntian started out in traditional Chinese ink painting, working in the highly technical Song style, and he only painted landscapes. Later, he got into watercolour and gouache landscapes. His greatest interest was in experimenting with coloured inks on highly absorbent rice paper, to find a richer and fresher means of expression. Although their artistic sights were set wide, they were struggling in very different worlds. Each was set on his own path and had nothing to do with the others. The three of them could be compared to a pianist, a *guqin* player and a vocal soloist. They were communicating in a higher aesthetic realm. Their discussions with colleagues were earthly, but this friendship was heavenly. The feeling of true connection made them unimaginably happy during their time together.

CHAPTER 4

At the beginning of the twentieth century, when the British ambitiously crossed the Qiangzi Canal to open up their 'expanded concession', the French built a Roman Catholic church in Xikai district, west of the concession. At that time, this area was not under the jurisdiction of the concession; it was a wilderness. The clumps of reeds, grass and stands of trees stretched as far as the eye could see across a vast plain, right to the horizon. A network of ponds, large and small, reflected the bright skylight here and there, like mirrors scattered across the earth. At this time, the church towered above it like a giant – it was quite shocking. In particular, the strange, alien and majestic Romanesque architecture, the cross piercing the sky above the high dome, and the great red-and-white walls exuded an insufferable arrogance which made the residents of Tianjin who had lived in the city for a long time feel a faint sense of uneasiness, an ominous sensation.

This ominous feeling was later fulfilled. According to those who lived around the church, children's cries and screams could often be heard in the middle of the night. Ever since the Wanghailou Church was burned to the ground in 1870, following shocking rumours of the torture of Chinese children, which horrified both China and the West, people speculated about and feared the tricks foreigners played in this mysterious church. They became convinced that the crying coming from the church in the middle of the night was because it was haunted by the ghosts of the children who had been cruelly killed there. These strange and terrible legends were in constant circulation. Therefore, during the Republic of China, the German priest who was in charge of this church was accused of being a bloodthirsty demon who slaughtered children, skinned them and cut out their livers, all because of his hawk-like nose, sharp eyes and ferocious demeanour. Therefore, a riot occurred, during which a priest was beaten to a bloody pulp, and one eye ended up rolling down the street. This caused a very troublesome dispute between China and the Western powers.

However, all this had come to an end some years previously.

During the Cultural Revolution, the heroic young students of the nearby No. 21 Middle School broke in and ransacked the church, destroying the altars, statues, paintings, stained-glass windows and all decoration in the church, and then they threw out all the clergy. Although they were unable to demolish the entire church, they climbed up the high, steep dome and removed the three huge and heavy crosses.

Now, the church had been locked and empty for many years. With no one there, it seemed on the verge of ruin, as if one day it would simply collapse in on itself.

It had snowed heavily the night before. The three steamed-bun-shaped, copper-covered domes were white on top and green on the bottom, which made a charming colour combination with the red and yellow bricks in the old walls below. Chu Yuntian thought it looked really beautiful.

Tianjin had nine foreign concessions, and the architectural style of churches in each was quite different; this was something rarely seen in other cities.

Suddenly something slapped him on the back. He was startled. Looking back, Luo Fu was standing in the snow not far away and smiled at him. He had just thrown a snowball at him. The white snow on the ground set the young man off quite clearly. He had thick black hair, a healthy flush in his face, and he was wearing a green military coat. Running over, he said: "Wouldn't this make a great sketch?"

"Wouldn't that be a lot of trouble?" Chu Yuntian asked. "If you really want to paint it, there is no need to do it from life."

"How right you are."

Luo Fu and Yuntian were like brothers. They were fellow students at the same school in middle school, although they had been in different years. Chu Yuntian was two years older than Luo Fu, so he considered Yuntian his older brother, and naturally that made Sui Yi his sister-in-law. Actually, they'd tracked one another through the education system, since Luo Fu had followed Yuntian all the way from middle school into art college. Luo Fu admired Yuntian's talent, intelligence and vision. Yuntian had read a lot of classic and modern literature, both from China and abroad. Luo Fu didn't like reading. He was the kind of young person who only looked at the pictures in picture books, and not at the words. Of course, he was also outstandingly talented as a painter, which is what Yuntian liked about him.

They also came from quite different family backgrounds. Yuntian grew up in the old British concession, later known as the Five Avenues district. His father was one of the best cardiologists in China, as a result of which he lived in some splendour.

Luo Fu was a different story. He lived in a low, dilapidated bungalow behind the Xikai Church. This bungalow had been built by incomers to the city way back when, at a time when there was no urban planning. The first people to settle here all just bought a piece of land, built a two- or three-room house and encircled it with a small yard. There was only one common 'rule' for these families, that is, their properties did not abut each other; in other words, a three-foot wide space was set aside between each property for fire prevention, and later these were gradually turned into alleyways. The close-packed houses and their concomitant network of interwoven alleyways became characteristic of this primitive community. Due to the history of fierce conflicts over religion in Tianjin, many Christians chose to live here in order to gain the protection of the church. Over the years, the residents of these communities moved in and out, and there was a constant influx of new inhabitants, but at least half continued to be old Christians. Luo Fu's father was a devout believer, but Luo Fu himself was not religious. His gods were Michelangelo and Picasso.

Supposedly Luo Fu's father was not his biological father, but his uncle. His biological father had three sons, but since his uncle had no children, his father gave him up for adoption by his uncle. Judging from his appearance, he was a quite different person from his adoptive father; it was impossible to find any similarity at all. He was as strong as a young leopard, while his fat adoptive father was like a lazy bear. His adoptive father worked as an accountant in a grocery store, and most accountants are cautious in their words and deeds. When he came back from work every day, after eating dinner and tidying the house, he would make a cup of tea, sit down on a heavy bench in the yard, pick up his thick, black leather-bound copy of the *Ocean of Words* encyclopaedia, and bury himself in reading. Luo Fu said that his adoptive father read the *Ocean of Words* very diligently. He never skipped an item. He made sure to read every line and every word. If he didn't recognise a character, he would look it up in the dictionary. Luo Fu smiled at Yuntian and said: "My father hasn't read as many books as you, but he knows a lot more words." But most of the entries in the *Ocean of Words* have nothing to do with each other, so what's the point of reading it? To study? What kind of knowledge could you possibly gain from it? How could he get anything out of this vast sea of knowledge, each individual item as the scattered grains of sand on a beach, dry and savourless – and yet he read with such concentration? Luo Fu said that he had read the *Ocean of Words* for twenty years and had already read it from beginning to end. Having got to the end, he'd started all over again, and now he had read more than half of it for a second time. The only change in these twenty years was that he now used a magnifying glass. As he aged, the tiny characters in the *Ocean of Words* got harder and harder to make out.

How could such a passionate and dedicated artist as Luo Fu emerge from such a timid and restrained household? All you can say is that artistic talent is not a matter of heredity. Each artist is a unique gift from heaven.

Who gave him such rampant enthusiasm, hungry artistic desire and vast aesthetic curiosity? Chu Yuntian also liked the young man's simple and honest nature. Maybe Yuntian had something of the same quality, so he was easily moved by Luo Fu. Furthermore, Yuntian appreciated the strong and rough liveliness of Luo Fu's paintings. When Luo Fu put brush to canvas, this is what happened: it wasn't something he'd learned to do. His temperament was the opposite of Luo Qian's. In Luo Qian's paintings, the inner qualities were present, invisible, underneath each stroke and they quietly infected you. He did nothing to excite you; he maintained his own meditations and silence. Luo Fu was not in the least like that. His brushstrokes seemed to be brought into being as an expression of his strong, massive lifeforce. His colour was also brought into being in order to burn with his passion. It was all unintentional.

The bigger difference between him and Luo Qian was that Luo Qian seemed to have chosen his own way; although this way was very narrow and winding, with only darkness ahead, he still stubbornly persisted on his path. By contrast, Luo Fu often seemed to be standing at a crossroads, with avenues extending in all directions. He was equally interested in the scenery on every road, and no one could be sure which route he would eventually choose.

Yuntian was delighted to have two such talented and loveable friends.

Since it was the weekend, Chu Yuntian had made an appointment with Luo Fu to visit Yannian. He had never met Yannian before, but he had a very strong impression of him from Luo Fu's description of a genius pianist. But when he followed Luo Fu into one of the old buildings at the north end of Shanxi Road and climbed up the stairs, his mood began to change. At that time, there were few renovated buildings in the city of Tianjin. There were loads of old buildings throughout the city, crammed with residents. Cooking stoves cluttered the stairwell on each floor, and most of the steps were piled with all kinds of useless junk that the inhabitants were unwilling to throw away. You had to thread your way through the mess when going up and down the stairs. The walls and ceiling were blackened by coal smoke from the daily stove use; wires festooned the place like cobwebs, terminating here and there in a tangle, which nobody was prepared to deal with. At that time, lots of families lived in ramshackle old buildings just like this.

On opening the door, Yannian's appearance amazed Yuntian. Was he a foreigner? Although he wore ordinary Chinese clothing, he had deep-set eyes, a high nose and thick eyebrows – he clearly looked like a foreigner. His tightly curled hair was much more strikingly alien than Luo Fu's natural curls. In a friendly way, he reached out to shake hands with Yuntian, then he took the opportunity to say: "Luo Fu has often mentioned you. We've nicknamed you 'Longfellow' – I do hope that you don't mind…"

Yuntian knew that Longfellow was a nineteenth-century American poet, but he didn't understand why Yannian called him that. Had Luo Fu told him he liked writing poetry? He had no idea. Anyway, the name sounded good, so he smiled.

Yannian shook hands very forcefully. Yuntian did not think he was exerting any special force, but his hands were just naturally very powerful. Was that true of all piano players? Yuntian also noticed that the way he spoke, his mannerisms and expressions, his way of holding himself, all seemed foreign. They followed him into the room.

The building Yannian lived in had huge rooms with high ceilings. The rooms on the second floor would normally have been used as bedrooms by the original owners. A sliding door separated the inner and outer rooms, and this was open. His room was very dilapidated, and the furniture was practically falling to pieces. The wardrobe had lost its door; it looked like a leftover from the concession era. There was a bed in the middle of each of the two rooms. He told Yuntian and Luo Fu to go and sit in the other room; clearly, he was living there as in a bedsit. A large picture window dominated the other room, but the glass was filthy, and the curtains wide. It would be impossible to draw them again, since they hung in rags, coated in dust. Everything in the room was thrown into relief by the blaze of light coming in. Suddenly, Yuntian realised that someone was lying there in the old-fashioned, iron-framed bed in the middle of the other room.

"That's my mother. She is ill. She has been bedridden for many years," Yannian explained. "Don't mind her. We can talk, and she'll call me if she needs anything."

They chatted together in low voices. Chu Yuntian was left with two deep impressions of where he lived. First, it was bitterly cold that midwinter, so why didn't they have the heating on? How could it be so cold? Second, there was no piano in his room. How can a pianist manage without a piano?

Yannian was a very clever guy; Chu Yuntian didn't have to say a word; he'd already worked out what questions he wanted to ask. He smiled and said: "I'll play the piano for you, Longfellow." Then he turned the subject: "Do you know why I nicknamed you 'Longfellow'? It was because Luo Fu showed me a poem of yours – 'Spring Can't Wait'. I remember a couple of lines…"

He stood up and recited slowly:

Although spring is bound to come,
You can't wait any longer, but still it delays;
Don't stay silent towards it,
Shout out, Spring – come here!

He really had learned some lines of Yuntian's poem off by heart. He seemed very excited when reciting these words, and his mouth trembled, which moved Yuntian. "You reminded me right away of the great American poet Longfellow," Yannian said. "You're great!" He couldn't control his excitement and suddenly hugged Yuntian tightly. At that time, people were not used to being hugged, and persons of the same sex never hugged each other. Yuntian felt a little embarrassed.

But Yannian was not rendered awkward in the least; he remained relaxed and open. Was this a necessary part of being a pianist? Chu Yuntian was also keenly aware of how when he spoke, his hands kept moving; his mouth was expressive, and his hands likewise. He liked to interlace his fingers and kept massaging the joints of his hands. His hands were not big, but his fingers were strong, tough, flexible and powerful. Sometimes his hands seemed to be more powerful than his body and more subtle than his feelings…

Just then, Yannian's mother said something in a very weak voice. She seemed to be calling a foreign name, but he couldn't make it out. "Wait a minute," Yannian said. "Mother wants a drink of water."

They got up and said goodbye, for fear of being in the way. At the door, Yannian hugged Chu Yuntian again and said: "You're exactly as Luo Fu described you. I like you too." Then he suddenly remarked: "Are you free this afternoon? I'll invite you to hear me play the piano."

Chu Yuntian was overjoyed.

"We're still in the basement on Sichuan Road," Yannian told Luo Fu. "Four o'clock sharp." Then he said lightly: "You can also bring along that other friend of yours – Luo Qian. But don't bring anyone else."

When Chu Yuntian walked out of that ruined building, he felt completely different from when he had entered. He was astounded and filled with interest and curiosity about this pianist, who seemed like a character in a nineteenth-century European novel.

At four o'clock, when Chu Yuntian and Luo Qian arrived at the corner of Sichuan Road, they caught sight of Yannian standing under a tree by the side of the road. They walked over and Chu Yuntian introduced Luo Qian to him. In fact, he knew nothing at all about the pianist's life or career. Luo Fu hadn't arrived yet. Chu Yuntian said: "Being late is just part of any date with him."

Yannian smiled. He said he was used to it and didn't mind too much. Then he added: "He's not half a beat slow, he's two beats slow." Then he suggested they could go on ahead to where he kept his piano. Luo Fu had been there before and if he was late, he could make his own way over. Yannian led them into an old red-brick building. Due to years of disrepair, the waterproofing in the foundations had cracked, the damp walls turning crimson, and the base of each wall going black with mould. The ground in the yard was very uneven, and water had pooled here and there, surrounded by clumps of weeds. When they entered the building, instead of going up the stairs, he went around the back of the flight of stairs, opened a heavy small door, and descended a few steps into a dark, wet and cold basement. Yannian groped to turn on the light, and there in the empty room stood a battered old concert grand piano. One broken leg was supported by a few bricks, the lid was missing and the exposed keys were as battered as the teeth of an old horse. What was this place? Was he going to play on this beaten-up piano? Why was the piano here, and what did he have to do with the people who lived here in this ruined building?

Just then Luo Fu arrived. However, he was not alone since he was accompanied by a very young girl. The painters present were sensitive to visual impressions and saw at a glance that the girl was very beautiful. Yannian was startled because he agreed with Luo Fu that he should not bring anyone except Luo Qian.

Luo Fu was very clever. He immediately introduced the girl to everyone and said that she was a second-year student at his college. Her name was Tian Yufei. She was a self-confident girl and took the initiative, saying: "I'm glad to see everyone I most want to meet today!" She spoke sincerely and smiled brightly, giving off a feeling of friendliness and happiness. She was twenty at most. She said to Chu Yuntian, standing tall and relaxed in front of her: "My teacher said that listening to you is like watching a movie." As soon as she said this, everyone burst out laughing.

Chu Yuntian felt very cheerful. He glanced at her. Her handsome face was a little vague in outline. Was this because the lines of her facial features were all undefined and soft, or was it because her young face was suffused by a youthful blush? Her eyes seemed to be somewhat out of focus, which gave her an unusual natural attractiveness.

It was time for his attention to be given to the pianist. Yannian took out a glass jar from under his arm. He handed it to Luo Fu and said: "You'd better go upstairs and find Mr Yu who lives over on the left and ask him to fill this with hot water. I need to warm my hands before I play. It's too cold and my hands are a little stiff." Luo Fu took the glass jar and ran off, to return quickly with the hot water.

Yannian held the hot water bottle with both hands and said: "Today I'll only play three short songs for you. First, I'll play my own selection, and then you can choose something."

Everyone agreed to that. Yannian put the hot water bottle down on the piano, and without any formalities he began to play. Bright, pleasing and beautiful music flowed out from the broken piano, like a clear spring pouring out of a stony canyon. The clean waters seemed to be bringing spring to the mountains, which abruptly turned green; wildflowers covered the ground, white clouds drifted overhead and the sunlight shone. He was sure this melody was familiar. Suddenly, the title leapt into Yuntian's memory: Tekla Badarzewska-Baranowska's 'A Maiden's Prayer'! This is a piece he'd listened to many years earlier but had not heard played for a very long time. He wished Sui Yi was there so that they could appreciate it together. All those years earlier, Sui Yi and he had listened to this music together. If Sui Yi heard it now, it would make her heart leap.

After playing this song, Yannian didn't stop. He immediately segued into another piece, quite different in rhythm and style, which brought them into another realm: thousands of troops, swords shining, fierce and strong, moving as fast as the wind. Music is the most magical of arts. It can change the atmosphere of the whole space around you and your state of mind in an instant. When it is soft, the atmosphere becomes as gentle as drizzle and a spring breeze, and your heart is filled with love; when it is fierce, your environs become violent, and it incites the wildness hidden in your heart. As he played, Yannian was clearly transformed by the spirit of this music. His flying arms and twisted body, his curly hair tossed as by a whirlwind, his hands speeding up and down the keys like two insane birds: it seemed as though he was going to destroy the piano. At the same time, it made his audience wonder how he could produce such crystalline, bright, pure and amazing music from this battered instrument.

The sound resonated like the roar of the sea.

The piano's notes were like foam tossed into the sky by the waves.

The changing melody brought one picture after another into their minds.

They applauded to express their gratitude and almost overwhelming admiration. Yannian stood up, put one hand on the broken piano and the other on his chest, bowed and thanked them, like a curtain call at the end of a concert. He did it very formally so that everyone had a sense of how sacred music was to him. Then he asked the audience to choose another piece of music. Yuntian called on Luo Qian to select something. "You just played Brahms's Hungarian Dance Number Five," Luo Qian said. "I prefer the first."

Yannian was surprised. "Oh, you know about music!" Then he turned to sit down on the stool and launched into an elegant, deep and profoundly melancholic piece. Although Yuntian was hearing this piano classic for the first time, he was profoundly moved. This 'Hungarian Dance No. 1' was indeed more beautiful, and intensely moving than 'No. 5'.

When Yannian had finished today's performance, a girl named Tian Yufei walked over to him and handed him something, which looked from a distance about the size of a tube of toothpaste. Tian Yufei said: "This is a present from my teacher. A little thank you from everyone."

Yannian was surprised. He opened the wrapping paper and exclaimed happily: "Oh, it's chocolate! My favourite!" He opened his mouth and ate a piece. The way he ate was a little peculiar – he seemed terribly hungry. He wolfed down a huge chunk of chocolate and quickly swallowed it. Then Yannian looked even more excited and came over to hug each of them.

After the concert, they walked out of the old building, their minds filled with great music classics. The drier and more barren the land is, the more every single raindrop has a magical feeling that seeps into the heart of the earth. Of course, they also felt a profound admiration for this pianist of genius.

On reaching the crossroads, they all set off in a different direction. Luo Qian and Yannian were going the same way, heading south across the bridge. Yuntian turned west with Luo Fu and Tian Yufei, since they were bound for the Qiangzi Canal. This allowed Yuntian to learn something of Yannian from Luo Fu. It transpired that Yannian looked foreign because he was part Russian. Apparently, his father was a White Russian who'd fled to Tianjin following the February Revolution, and his mother was Chinese. Originally, he lived on Xuzhou Road, just near the Kiessling Restaurant, which was an area with a big community of White Russians and Jews. Later on, his father died, and he and his mother moved to Shanxi Road. His mother had been bedridden for many years, and the two of them didn't have any other family.

Everyone in the city's musical circles knew that Yannian played the piano very well, but he looked too obviously foreign. They were suspicious of who he might be and what trouble he might get them into, so no one dared to invite him to perform, and the local conservatoires did not dare to hire him as a music teacher. He was reduced to working as a private piano tutor for various families in the neighbourhood. During the Cultural Revolution, very few people wanted to learn to play, and he'd had nearly no work. They'd sold pretty much everything they owned, and things got so bad that there were times when he'd been reduced to one meal a day, enduring near starvation, which is why he'd behaved so oddly on being given a bar of chocolate.

Luo Fu explained that Yannian had been taught to play the piano by his mother, who had been a primary school music teacher. His family had once owned a piano, but it was smashed to pieces during the Cultural Revolution. He'd spent years looking for a replacement. This building was returned when the government handed back confiscated property. At one time, he had taught members of the family to play, so they allowed him to practise there twice a week. He was afraid he would lose the skill held in his hands.

Luo Fu said he knew these things because he and Yannian had been classmates in primary school. At that time, Yannian was often beaten up by his classmates as a 'foreign devil' because he looked so different. Luo Fu often came forward to rescue him, so they had been good friends since childhood and remained in contact ever since.

While they were talking, Tian Yufei walked on the other side of Luo Fu, keeping her head down in silence; she didn't ask any questions. At a fork in the road, when they were about to go their separate ways, she still hung her head. "Aren't you going to say goodbye to Mr Chu?" Luo Fu asked. "Don't you want to see his paintings and listen to his stories?"

Tian Yufei raised her head. Chu Yuntian found that the girl's eyes were red, and teardrops were sparkling on her long eyelashes. It turned out that listening to Yannian's story just now had made her feel sympathetic, sad and tearful. Her kindness touched Chu Yuntian. After they said goodbye, Chu Yuntian turned his head twice to look at her vanishing back.

CHAPTER 5

Chu Yuntian spread a piece of white Xuan paper on his temporary painting table, weighing it down with a piece of bluestone at each corner. He didn't have the proper kind of weights, so he used four stones he'd picked up during his sketching trip to Panshan in Jixian County the year before last – they were more natural. As long as the paper was spread out flat, he could be the creator of the new world to come.

He first dipped his sheep's-hair brush into clean water and then into light ink and dashed it across the top of the paper with strokes full of vitality, so that a vast sky filled with roiling clouds soon appeared. Long, dark clouds swam like dragons, racing across the sky with wind and rain. He didn't forget to leave a blank space in among the thick and light ink. This space was the last piece of sky that had not been swallowed up by dark clouds, shining and bright. He enjoyed the magic conjunction of ink on Xuan paper and was fascinated by the fragrance of the wet paper. This scent was far better than any wine. Afterwards, he took out from his brush holder a long, narrow-tipped brush, spread out the filaments, rolled them through the pool of the ink and then made a series of short, sweeping movements upward from the bottom edge of the paper. A clump of reeds swaying in the wind was thereby created, filled with great vitality and power, and even he was conscious of their forcefulness.

He cried out unconsciously: "Ah!"

There was no one present so no one answered. Only a beam of sunlight from the small window caught at some floating motes of dust.

Now he changed a long, thick-stemmed brush, dipped it in thicker ink and drew several long stems and leaves in front of the stand of reeds. Without him even being aware of it, the skills accumulated from studying Song-style painting in his early years showed when he used his brush; he felt as if strength was being drawn from his whole body and transmitted to the tip of the brush through his wrist. Like an awl drawing in the sand, the force went right through to the back of the paper. He also felt the existence of something that seemed to have been suppressed in the bottom of his heart for a long time was finally being set free... it made him infinitely happy! So he couldn't stop himself from drawing a lone goose in the blank space left for the sky, which was the only bright place in the whole picture. The lone goose flew there, solitary and free. He couldn't help but recite two lines of Lermontov's 'The Sail' to himself:

Why sail so far away?
Why leave so much behind?

"The birds in your paintings are all self-portraits." This was something Sui Yi had told him.

Sui Yi never regarded his landscape or scenery paintings as just simple landscapes or scenery. She regarded them as an insight into his true feelings.

Today, the little attic room belonged to Chu Yuntian alone. Since it was the weekend, Sui Yi would be on duty in the hospital all day. She knew what he planned to do that day, so first thing in the morning she'd prepared meals for him and put them ready. That was everything he needed! Today he would be his own master and the king of this tiny wood-framed room. He was full of energy and passion from the moment he woke up. He opened the window and let the morning wind outside the glass blow in and fill his world. Of course, from time to time the shadows of birds would also flit through the room.

At the beginning of April, it is already spring. All the trees outside the window were gradually putting out vibrant new leaves, which grew bigger day by day. Green leaves are another kind of spring flower. The squeaking of newly hatched sparrows could already be heard. Because his small building was exposed and set back, the roof had become the safest place for sparrows to build their nests. There were nests on the southern and eastern sides of the roof. Just like Chu Yuntian and Sui Yi, these sparrows regarded the roof space of that small building as a safe haven. Because of this, as soon as it got light, the waking birds could be heard moving about in their nest up above. They never disturbed them; indeed, they felt similarly blessed.

The breezes of an early morning in April are still a little cool, but they were particularly refreshing for Yuntian and made him feel bright and clear-headed, sensitive to the slightest impression, and his mind was overflowing with inspiration. At that time, Xuan paper was white and delicate, and as pliable as a woman's skin. The touch of a brush would arouse myriad sensations, and what were his long and short brushes if not extensions for his fingers? And were his fingers not in direct conjunction with his heart? Were his paintings merely an expression of skill and training, or did they contain a more spiritual inner dimension?

Thus, the ink, water and colour laid out on the table were no longer the tools of his trade, but instead his emotions, moods, feelings and language. The ink washes on the wet rendering were clearly his indulgent emotion, and every line was the track of his mood. In the tonal variation between thick and light ink, you could see an expression of his artistic language. However, once he expressed it casually, frantically and confidently, he entered the highest realm of painting. This realm is both absolutely selfish and yet selfless.

Free selflessness and selfless freedom.

Yuntian spent the whole morning painting. Afterwards, having eaten lunch and taken a nap, he woke up feeling as energetic as in the morning. As usual, he removed the painting table, tied a string between two pillars in the room and hung up today's masterpiece on clips, so that Sui Yi could see it as soon as she came back from work. He was in a cheerful mood and feeling very confident because he had painted such a satisfactory picture today. He was too excited to stay in the house and wanted to go out for a walk, but he couldn't think of where to go until he was actually wheeling his bike out of the yard. He'd only thought of going round to see Luo Fu or Luo Qian. He wanted to give vent to today's pride and excess artistic emotion. He suddenly came up with an amusing idea: he would go and visit whichever of the two had more strokes in their surname. He wrote out the characters on the broken saddle with his finger. Luo Fu's surname had nine strokes, but Luo Qian's 'Luo' was one stroke fewer: eight in total. He decided to sacrifice Luo Qian and go and find Luo Fu.

He went to the Xikai Church by bike, but Luo Fu was not at home; only his adoptive father was there reading his black-bound copy of the *Ocean of Words*. He explained that Luo Fu had gone to the art college. Chu Yuntian was in a good mood that day, and it was not too far away, so he set off on his bike, pedalling in a north-westerly direction, bypassing the old city and crossing the bridge to the art college. He searched around the campus and finally located Luo Fu in the teaching building.

At that time, few people came calling. As soon as he opened the door, he saw large and small drawing boards erected everywhere in a vast room, with stools and chairs in between. Luo Fu stood at a table near the front with some youngsters around him; it was obvious at first glance that these were his students. Luo Fu liked to speak with emotion – it seemed that emotion was the driving force in his conversation. Just as he was energetically waving his hands about, he turned his head and spotted Chu Yuntian. Hailing him delightedly, he introduced Yuntian to his students. "Mr Chu is a talented student who graduated from our college ten years ago," he said. "He's a good friend of mine."

The students greeted Chu Yuntian politely. Some had probably heard of him, but now meeting him in person, they looked pleased to see him. Just then, he noticed one of them was smiling at him, looking like a beautiful flower in these drab surroundings.

That familiar, gentle, hazy, soft and beautiful face: wasn't she the girl called Tian Yufei he'd met when listening to the piano in the basement of Sichuan Road a few months ago? Somehow, as soon as he saw her, he felt that she had an unstoppable presence. Next, no matter what he was saying to Luo Fu, where he looked, what he chatted about or how he expressed his views on art, he seemed to say it to her, even for her. He didn't understand why he felt like this. Luo Fu took him over to an easel, on which was an almost-finished oil painting of a crab apple in full bloom in the shadow of a dark fir. The colours in the painting were very bold, and its brushstrokes seemed to sing, drawing out the vitality, freshness and fragrance of flowers in spring. He said to Chu Yuntian: "I sketched this here on campus these last two days. I daresay you're going to scold me for being over-influenced by your picture album. It's too much like a Van Gogh."

"And what's wrong with that?" Chu Yuntian asked. "Besides, you have your own feelings. I like the passion in your painting. In spring, everything is so vital." He joked: "It almost looks like there are bees flying among your crab-apple flowers. Van Gogh wouldn't have that."

A somewhat dull male student asked: "Why can't I see any bees?"

Tian Yufei took up the cudgels: "Mr Chu is talking about impressions."

Everyone laughed. This made Chu Yuntian cast an involuntary glance at Tian Yufei. Her remark seemed to be directed not just at the emotions evident in Luo Fu's painting, but also demonstrated her understanding of Chu Yuntian's comment. She was clearly very sensitive to nuance. When he looked at her, her pretty face and those unfocused eyes seemed unusually attractive.

He was touched by her all over again.

It was late, and Luo Fu said he would take Chu Yuntian to a small Hui-Muslim restaurant to eat mutton tripe stew. Several of his students escorted them out of the building, including Tian Yufei. Tian Yufei suddenly said to Chu Yuntian: "If you have time, I'd like you to give me some pointers on my painting."

She was Luo Fu's student, so he didn't like to promise anything. He just made vague "ah" noises, but at the same time he felt that she had taken the initiative in their relationship, and that aroused something in his heart that he'd never felt before. He didn't know what it was.

Back home, Sui Yi was waiting for him in their tiny attic room with a smile on her face. He asked her why she was so happy. Sui Yi turned around to switch on the light. The lamp was facing the picture he had completed during the day, which was then brightly illuminated. When he looked again at the painting he'd done earlier in the day, it looked wonderful! There was such strong emotion in the painting. The vitality in the brush and inkwork was quite entrancing! At this time, the high spirits he'd felt when he was painting returned to him. That evening, they both talked about the painting.

It should be said that the strange sensations Tian Yufei had aroused just now were still just a weak note on his piano keys.

CHAPTER 6

It took Chu Yuntian a whole day to finish the colour samples and design drawings for a water-cup packaging box for a factory owned by the company. In the era of the planned economy, products were bought and sold under central control, and the quality of packaging was naturally not an issue. There was no need to pursue novelty or striking design, as long as the work was up to standard. However, his most difficult task for the day was to write one of Chairman Mao's quotations in Song-style calligraphy on one side of the carton. You needed to concentrate when writing the quotations of Chairman Mao because not even the slightest mistake would be tolerated.

The whole time he had one thing at the back of his mind; as soon as he got off work he was going to go and find Luo Fu, to ask him when Tang Ni, one of Mr Xu's students from Xinhua Middle School, would arrive from Beijing. He really wanted to meet this young female printmaker, who was known as 'China's Käthe Kollwitz'. After graduating from Xinhua Middle School, Tang Ni had been admitted to the Central Academy of Fine Arts in Beijing to study printmaking. Afterwards, she'd been assigned to the Beijing Publishing House as an art editor. She was only just over thirty and was already famous in art circles in the capital – it was an impressive achievement. Painters in Beijing had high standards and it was hard to stand out.

The legendary Tang Ni was even more amazing. Although she was a woman, her temperament was bolder and more unrestrained than any man. Her paintings were very rough and wild, in a style not dissimilar from that of the German female printmaker Käthe Kollwitz. It was said that she spent every day in the studio, with the most terrible habits – sometimes she didn't eat all day, but simply carried half an apple or steamed bun in her pocket, and whenever she felt hungry, she'd pull it out and take a bite. Someone who valued art over her very life was worth getting to know.

He tidied up the things on the table, picked up his backpack and went downstairs, on his way out of the design institute. It was the time of day when people generally got off work, so there was a big crowd in the streets in front of the institute and lots of cars. Just as he was about to get on the bus, he saw a woman standing under a telegraph pole by the side of the road, slender and beautiful, smiling at him – he almost felt as if he were in a dream. He immediately realised that it was Tian Yufei. She was dressed simply but brightly. The sky-blue coat set off her pretty, slightly pink face. She stood there like a pear blossom tree just drenched by fine rain. Why was she standing here? Obviously, she was waiting for him.

He wheeled his bike over and asked her what she was doing.

She smiled and said: "I'm waiting for you. Didn't you promise to give me some advice on my painting the other day at the college?"

"Oh, did I say that?" Chu Yuntian said.

"Of course. You said 'OK, OK.'" She changed his casual "ah" that day into "OK". Chu Yuntian could hardly argue, so he looked at her. As soon as he looked into her eyes, he didn't know what to do.

Tian Yufei said: "Just come to my house for a quick look. When I heard today that you'd be working here and found out that you'd be so close to my house – just three streets away – I started singing at the top of my voice. Maybe you heard me…" Having finished saying this, she laughed.

In a complete daze, Chu Yuntian found himself dragged to her house.

She lived on a quiet little road running alongside the Hai River. Although it was part of a larger complex, her family lived right by the gate, with a small black lock on a plain wooden door. She undid the lock and opened the door, revealing a very spacious room. At that time, nobody lived in luxury, but her home was neat, clean and well-appointed, and they seemed to live in some style. She said that she only shared the place with her mother, who worked in an embroidery factory. Although there was nothing very fine in the room, the furnishings were appropriate and harmonious, showing the owners' care. There were two beds and two tables in the room; one was a dining table, and the other a long narrow table stacked with painting tools and books. It seemed that it was Yufei's desk-cum-painting table. When she entered her home, she became a little awkward; she invited Chu Yuntian to sit down, poured him a glass of water and blamed herself for not being ready for his arrival. Chu Yuntian said: "You don't have to go to all this trouble. Just let me look at your paintings."

Tian Yufei took out a stack of paintings from the portfolio under the long table and showed them to Chu Yuntian one by one. Most of them were student sketching exercises: watercolour, gouache and traditional Chinese painting. She seemed to show some talent in her brushwork, but what made Yuntian really sit up was the understanding and perceptiveness of her comments. This understanding, and how she expressed it, underpinned their conversation. She was very expressive. Art and perceptiveness both come from the heart. If perceptiveness is linked to communicativeness, that is a source of pleasure. During the conversation, Chu Yuntian looked attentively at her. When a woman's beauty is impossible to quantify, impossible to describe, that is real beauty. When her delicate petal-like skin, eyelashes so long that they seemed artificial, tip-tilted nose and dreamy eyes were close to him, he was a little afraid. Was he afraid of her or of himself? He said: "I've got to go. I've seen your paintings and I've given you my opinion." He seemed to be trying to escape.

Unexpectedly, she suddenly put her small hands boldly against his chest and said: "You can't go. I love to hear you talk. I want to hear some more."

She looked irresistibly appealing.

He felt his face burning. He was a little afraid of her, and at the same time he was afraid of himself. He tried to calm himself and said something to distance himself from her. However, in the end she didn't let him go until he promised her that he would come again.

Chu Yuntian was cycling down the road. The more he thought about the situation just now, the more confused he became. He and Sui Yi had played together since childhood, and until the Cultural Revolution began they were like brother and sister to one another. They had apparently never experienced first love. They had never been through sudden storms with lightning and thunder, whipped by the wind, nor had they experienced the clear changes of the seasons; for them, it had always been a brilliant summer. He was a little scared at this kind of feeling which was so ambiguous and at the same time something he'd never felt before. Of course, this was a sweet fear, a temptation to avoid, an expectation to refute... Musing in this way, he took the wrong road several times on his way home and almost managed to return to his own office.

The next night, Luo Qian came to his house. They had agreed to go to Mr Xu's home to meet Tang Ni. Sui Yi joined them. To begin with, she didn't want to go, but Luo Qian insisted on dragging her along with them. He criticised Chu Yuntian for being out all day and "abandoning" Sui Yi in that attic room. Sui Yi said that she was perfectly happy spending time at home alone. She liked the peace and quiet; and Yuntian had just borrowed two novels from his friends, one of which was Jane Austen's *Pride and Prejudice*. She had heard people say all kinds of good things about this book for a long time, and she was desperate to read it. "I don't see why this has to interfere with your reading," Luo Qian said. "If you get to meet some really talented people, that expands your horizons."

    Sui Yi smiled and said: "True enough." Then she agreed to join them.

・ ・ ・

When they walked into Mr Xu's house together, his large living room was crammed full of people. All of them had been his pupils at one time or another.

Although Mr Xu was only an art teacher at a middle school, art classes weren't part of the core curriculum. However, strange to relate, his pupils seemed to get accepted into the best art colleges in Beijing every single year. The Ministry of Education even sent officials to Tianjin to learn about this unusual art teacher hidden away in an obscure middle school and see what special techniques he had developed to teach children with artistic potential. His answer was puzzling: "I let them follow their bent." When they inquired further in the art world, most people had no idea of his existence. A handful who had seen his paintings said that they showed fine taste but contained too many Impressionistic elements. Since this was not currently fashionable, nobody paid much attention to him. He never sent his work to exhibitions, and he was not even a member of the Artists Association. However, over the course of some twenty or thirty years, a number of his students had shown their mettle and become famous in artistic circles. Nevertheless, he remained as free as a bird, flying leisurely among the mountains, rivers and clouds. Interestingly, although the Cultural Revolution swept away so many big and small luminaries in the realm of painting, he escaped censure. This was because he had never been a figure there. He had spent his entire life in the wilderness and was still there now. Originally no one regarded him as a painter, but now he had become the idol of a group of young art aficionados.

There are always people in this world who love art. When a big tree is cut down, weeds and wildflowers grow everywhere. Famous and beneficial achievements are abandoned, but real non-utilitarian art breeds freely. Among the people gathered in this house right now, not one was a famous painter, but each of them worshipped art as they would a god.

Mr Xu sat in an armchair as usual, smoking his pipe and stroking his shiny bald head from time to time, and looking smilingly at these delightful young people who loved art so much. As the host, no matter who came in, he wouldn't stand up to meet them, and he wouldn't escort anyone to the door on their way out. Instead, he would just raise his hand in a wave in response to people coming and going.

Chu Yuntian and the others came in and greeted Mr Xu first. Everyone said hello; there were some people he knew and some he did not. They caught sight of the talented Tang Ni. She had dark skin, short hair and stiff movements, which made her appear a little masculine. Fortunately, she was not in the least pretentious; when she met them and shook hands, they each gave their names. This time, Luo Fu had managed to arrive ahead of them. Chu Yuntian saw a woman standing beside Luo Fu – Tian Yufei. Seeing Tian Yufei now was different from the previous two occasions. When Luo Fu spotted them, he introduced Tian Yufei to Sui Yi as his student. Sui Yi looked carefully at her and said: "You look so pretty, like that girl painted by Ingres."

Tian Yufei's face turned red. Luo Fu said: "The girl painted by Ingres didn't have any clothes on."

Tian Yufei was even more embarrassed and hid her face with both hands. Sui Yi gave Luo Fu a little smack and said: "Don't talk nonsense. She's your student, but you don't seem to speak professionally about her! I was just thinking about the beauty of Ingres' model – there's a real resemblance!"

In order to move away from this topic as quickly as possible, Tian Yufei took the initiative to say hello to Luo Qian and Chu Yuntian. Sui Yi then discovered that they had met before.

There were some chairs and stools of different sizes placed around the room. Mr Xu asked everyone to sit down and talk. A man in his thirties was sitting in a high-backed, old-fashioned chair in the corner; and Mr Xu said this was his former student, Yue Peng. But Yue Peng didn't have a smile on his face, and he didn't get up. He sat there and waved his hands and said: "Sit, sit." Chu Yuntian felt a little irritated.

Mr Xu knew exactly how to open today's session, so he asked Tang Ni to show her pictures to everyone. When she took out four or five black-and-white prints from a green canvas portfolio and put them on the front desk one by one, the room was immediately shrouded by an atmosphere of shock. For a moment, no one spoke. Some of the guests stood up and walked over, bending their backs to look more closely. Luo Fu stood opposite these prints, as motionless as if he had been frozen in place. Only Yue Peng stayed sitting in that high-backed chair, crossing his legs. He didn't look at the pictures; he didn't seem to think that they were worth looking at.

Everyone had now seen the prints, but no one made a sound. Was this because these pictures were so unique and shocking that it was difficult to express an opinion, or because there were afraid to open their mouths and say something wrong… something not sufficiently elevated?

Most surprisingly, Tang Ni was the first to speak. She wasn't talking about herself, but about Chu Yuntian. Chu Yuntian had never met her before, so he wasn't expecting her to talk about him and his paintings. He said to Tang Ni: "You haven't seen any of my paintings. What can you say?"

"You have a friend called Fang Haitao, don't you?" Tang Ni replied. "He's employed by the National Palace Museum in their reproductions division – he studied under Feng Zhonglian. Last year or the year before last, you gave him two paintings, didn't you? Since then, some of us have come to know that there is a good painter of ink landscapes in Tianjin – they were really great!"

To be called 'great' like that made Chu Yuntian feel a little embarrassed. He said quickly: "In that case, I'd like to hear your opinion."

Chu Yuntian's words were obviously sincere, and so Tang Ni became even more forthright. She said: "I just wanted to say that you have strong traditional technical skills, but your ink paintings are not at all traditional. Your painting is more like a kind of prose. I can see that you have a great love of literature, your ink painting has a kind of lyricism, and the underlying artistic conception is strong. I guess I have already praised you to the hilt, so this is where I turn round and stab you… there is a problem with the structuring of your paintings." As soon as her head turned, her short hair stood out like spikes on both sides of her face. Her eyes fixed on Chu Yuntian and she said: "You lack a profound internal conceptualisation of the overall structure, so your painting lacks sufficient strength. It'll be difficult for you to produce big paintings." Her words were indeed critical.

Chu Yuntian was hoping to hear more detailed opinions, something he could learn from. Therefore, he asked: "Structure? Can you be more specific? What structure?"

Tang Ni's next words were more straightforward. "Don't you understand? It's fine for you to be unstructured, but the overall composition – the body and drawing – seems to be something that you completely disregard. It is like in your paintings you regard presence and absence as a matter of opinion." Her concluding comments were hard for Chu Yuntian to accept.

Few people had ever criticised him so ruthlessly in public.

Chu Yuntian didn't speak. He was afraid that if he didn't say something apposite, it would turn into a row. Unexpectedly, Tian Yufei interceded: "I think Mr Chu's paintings are quite different from yours. He doesn't pursue visual impact, but inner expression. You can't demand that everyone else fit in with your own artistic views."

The young girl's words surprised everyone present. Of course, they were surprised by different things. Some thought she showed great discrimination, while others felt that her words had clarified the essence of their respective arts. Chu Yuntian felt that Tian Yufei had decided these comments were unfair; she showed a kind of chivalrous courage which moved him. However, Luo Fu was annoyed at her for butting in and showing off in that kind of company, so he glared at her and told her to shut up. At this point, Tang Ni said to Yufei: "You're right. All too often I do demand that everyone else fit in with my own artistic views. If other people listen to my opinion, they may lose themselves." She was just as straightforward towards herself as to everyone else. As a result, Chu Yuntian ignored the slight feeling of unhappiness caused by her bluntness just now.

Then Tang Ni asked Chu Yuntian: "Tell me, what do you think of my pictures?"

"They are quite masculine," Chu Yuntian said.

"That is not a proper judgement of my art. That's gender discrimination." Tang Ni's comment made everyone laugh. She said to Yuntian: "You mustn't think that you can't criticise me just because I criticised your painting. Your criticism should only express your views on art. It should not be anything about me. Just like how I criticised you just now – if you don't like it, you can just chuck it in the nearest bin."

Her frank and insightful words relieved Chu Yuntian, and he suddenly felt quite happy. So he told her what he wanted to say: "The bold, massive qualities and wildness of your pictures are innate – they are your essence. But you also need something exquisite. Qi Baishi, Bada Shanren and Picasso all have this quality. They seem uninhibited and unrestrained, but there will always be one or two exquisite, unexpectedly fine details that are very subtle and marvellous – quite beyond compare. I think their bolder works are brought to life by these exquisite details!"

Tang Ni became more and more excited as she heard this. She tried to interrupt Chu Yuntian several times, but she was stopped by Chu Yuntian stretching out his long hand. Chu Yuntian insisted on saying one of his most dearly held maxims: "This detail cannot be artificial or deliberate. It must be accidental, a kind of spiritual quality–"

"A gift from God!" said Tang Ni, finally managing to get a word in edgeways. She thought about this for a moment and continued: "But that's very rare. In a hundred paintings, you might only see it once."

"Yes! That's why even the greatest artist will only produce a pitifully few masterpieces in his lifetime," Chu Yuntian said.

All at once they felt as if the room were full of light, as if they had opened the door to an artistic paradise. They asked Mr Xu to say something. Mr Xu said: "You all understand, so I don't have to say anything more." His expression showed that he agreed with and liked these young people. In fact, this was precisely how he'd always taught his students and why he'd left no trace behind.

Even though there was still much to discuss, it was already very late. Everyone emerged from Mr Xu's house to say goodbye to each other, and then they went their separate ways. Yuntian and Tang Ni gave each other a high five and said happily: "Bye, and we'll talk again soon!"

When Luo Fu and Yufei peeled off from Yuntian and the others,

Sui Yi said to Yufei: "Come to my house with your teacher when you have the time."

Luo Fu said: "She'll just ask Yuntian for pointers about her paintings."

Yufei only smiled. When she looked at Yuntian, she didn't give him any meaningful glances, but she'd clearly hidden the fact that she'd already asked him for advice. She was keeping this hidden from Luo Fu, and from Sui Yi; something known only to herself and Chu Yuntian. In this way, it became a secret between them. Why did she want to do things this way?

Secrecy is a seed. Who knows what it will look like once it sprouts? Will it be beautiful, or will it be shocking? But as it is full of desire, it will inevitably sprout!

CHAPTER 7

In the morning, the sun was shining. Luo Fu came out of the house on his rickety old bicycle and rode along happily, his loose curls flying. He moved through the streets and into the alleys, turning east and west, completely relaxed. Judging by how he was putting his back into it, if you'd given him a pair of wings he would fly. The roads in this part of town were all wriggling, narrow alleyways, with cracks and potholes everywhere. In some places the ground had buckled, and in others it had collapsed into sheer cliff-like ridges. But the people who grew up in such places wouldn't trip even if they walked around with their eyes closed. He hummed, shifted his bottom about on the saddle, raised his eyes from time to time and looked at the towering copper-green dome of the old Xikai Church through the gaps between the dark, ruined buildings. A group of white birds rose and fell high above him, which reminded him of some childhood memory. Nowhere else in this city could he enjoy the kind of quiet beauty possessed by this abandoned old church near his home.

He had made an appointment with Luo Qian and Chu Yuntian to come to the college for a chat.

Since meeting the talented female artist Tang Ni at Mr Xu's house that day, the three of them hadn't had an opportunity to talk about her. They would certainly have different views on that remarkable woman. Everyone would be interested in this subject.

Around ten o'clock, the Three Musketeers gathered at the art college. This college had once been a very famous school. Various fine old buildings were situated at the front and back of the campus. This time Luo Fu led them into a square dark grey brick building. There were two rows of such buildings, one in front of the other, four buildings in each row, each only two floors high. The corridors were wide, and the rooms were filled with light. They had originally been used for classrooms, but now they mostly sat empty. There were no rows of tables and chairs here, which made the room seem even more open and high. Six or seven empty wooden boxes stood in the middle of the room, which were perfect for sitting on while they chatted. On one side of the room was a row of huge windows, and the heavy shadow of the trees outside was thrown cold and dark across the floor inside. Sometimes a slight breeze would quietly blow a silent, imperceptible breath of fresh air through the tree leaves into the room. That brought an indefinable sense of comfort, which could arouse people's interest in painting.

"I would want to learn from anyone who had a studio like this," Chu Yuntian said.

"Well, that's easy enough! This is the studio I've just dragged out of my bosses," Luo Fu said complacently.

"You might as well go ahead and crown yourself emperor!" Luo Qian could not restrain his envy.

"Then you'll be guilty of lèse-majesté," Luo Fu told Luo Qian.

"What do you mean by lèse-majesté? We've got rid of all the emperors..." Yuntian teased him with a cheerful smile. Then he asked: "How *did* you get such a big studio?"

Luo Fu smiled without answering.

As usual, among the Three Musketeers, only Luo Fu was truly happy in his career. Chu Yuntian had not managed to make his art pay; his work was merely art-adjacent in that he was a designer of mock-ups and packaging for commercial products. Painting was only a hobby for him. Luo Qian's situation was different again. His paintings were not accepted by the mainstream or admired by ordinary people. He didn't ask for recognition from anyone. He just painted for himself – an oddball. He didn't care whether anyone else liked it or not. But Luo Fu understood art. Although he was a professional, teaching students in art colleges and working in the mainstream, in the eyes of ordinary folk he was a proper painter. But in Luo Fu's heart, Luo Qian and Yuntian – his two friends who were unknown and out of step with the rest of society – had a very special place. They stood like two giant trees above a wasteland. They were lonely there, ignored by others, but Luo Fu knew their true qualities and their real value.

In that era, when family background was all-important, Luo Fu's poor background gave him an advantage over Chu Yuntian. Everything before him was clear, and he faced no obstacles. In addition, he was genuinely talented, and his technique was first-class. His realistic paintings were also in the artistic language advocated at that time. After most of the painters of an older generation had been swept away by the Cultural Revolution, he naturally became the backbone of the college's teaching staff, and all the creative tasks imposed by higher-ups were given to him first. However, one of Luo Fu's loveable qualities lay in acceptance of the fact that in deep knowledge of the meaning of art, in understanding and depth of thought, he was greatly inferior to his two older friends. So today, he wanted to hear what they thought of Tang Ni, especially Luo Qian.

Luo Qian said to Luo Fu: "She has the same thing going for her as you do – your pictures are very strong. Half of this strength is inherent in you, in your life, and the other half is because you both pay attention to structure. But she is not as good as you, in that her pictures are too rigid, while your paintings are looser."

Luo Qian could always come up with an original thought or viewpoint. Chu Yuntian was immediately inspired. He said: "Luo Qian mentioned a very important problem – looseness. Only when a painting is 'loose' can everything in the painting show a natural and free state… a true-to-life state." He thought for a moment and then added: "If it is too rigid, the painting will be dead. Moreover, everything in the painting will just be on the surface, which is very limiting."

"No one else can enter your painting," Luo Qian added.

"I felt that at that time," Luo Fu said. "Why was her painting so rigid?"

"She pays too much attention to matters of technique. It's an academic problem. She thinks too much and concentrates too much on structure, knife technique, colouration and form. Her problem is being too professional, just like mine is being too unprofessional." When Luo Qian said these words, all three of them smiled.

Luo Fu said to Luo Qian: "Do you think this 'looseness' is a subjective thing?"

"This is what I want to ask, that is – objective things ought to be presented in a subjective way," Luo Qian said. "We can't be prisoners of our own personal vision."

"Chinese painting emphasises this very strongly," Chu Yuntian reminded them, "so Chinese people don't use 'painting' but 'writing' to express themselves. 'Writing' starts from the subjective, integrates the objective into the subjective and also integrates the subjective into the objective. The subjective includes emotion, feeling, aesthetics and meaning. If you look at really great Western artists, don't they also paint very loosely?"

When a new topic aroused everyone's interest, the conversation would become more and more intense. Luo Fu had already got up from the wooden box where he had been sitting to walk about as he thought, expressing his opinions or asking questions.

During this conversation, Chu Yuntian was the only one to feel a little distracted. He'd been here in the college today for more than an hour, but he still hadn't caught sight of Tian Yufei. Did she know he was coming? She was close to Luo Fu, so he would have told her that he and Luo Qian would be there. If she knew, she would surely come. This was based on his judgement of the good feeling between them. When they were chatting, he kept expecting that she was about to push the door open with a smile and instantly bring a fascinating glitter to this bright big room. But she never showed up.

After a while, the door was indeed pushed open. Yu Miao, a teacher in the oil painting division, came in. He was also one of their more important oil painters. Since everyone knew each other, there were no formal greetings. Yu Miao was very thin, grey, with sparse hair, and wore a pair of round narrow-rimmed glasses. He was not very talkative and looked a little like an old-fashioned ivory-tower-bound scholar. However, his paintings were quite the opposite to his appearance. He was good at painting portraits in the super-realist style. He was also good at incorporating fine details and strong texture, so his paintings were very lifelike. Holding a roll of paper, he went straight over to Luo Fu and said: "I've just been to the carpentry workshop to have a look. The picture frame has been put together and the canvas will shortly be stretched. The folk in Beijing have said that all the paintings for National Day gifts will be reviewed in the middle of August and the results will be out in early September. Time is very short. I've revised a few details of your sketch, so you'd better have a look."

"Since these two are here," Luo Fu said, "let's all have a look, and we can listen to their opinions."

Yu Miao was very pleased and unrolled the sketch on top of a box. He said: "This painting is on the theme of 'Up to the Mountains and Down to the Countryside'. There are a lot of figures, and the content requirements are very specific. It is difficult to draw if there is a plot. In particular, neither of us has ever been to the northwest."

Luo Qian said: "Luo Fu went to the railway station to see his cousin off to Inner Mongolia."

"How could I draw a scene like that, with so much crying and howling?" Luo Fu said with a smile. "They want us to depict educated youth accepting re-education from Mongolian herdsmen."

Luo Qian smiled. He didn't say any more and didn't look at the sketch. Obviously, he was not interested in this kind of propaganda painting. "How big is this one?" Chu Yuntian asked Luo Fu.

"Seven metres by four," Luo Fu replied. His answer surprised Chu Yuntian. Luo Fu continued: "Otherwise, they wouldn't have given me this big classroom – the terms for this painting specify that it must be a cooperative effort."

Luo Qian was bored at all this. He was about to say goodbye when the door opened and a group of male and female students came in. Some of these students knew Chu Yuntian and greeted him warmly.

Chu Yuntian immediately thought of Tian Yufei. Looking more closely, she was not among them. He felt sure that she was coming, so he carried on talking about nothing with Luo Fu and Yu Miao, trying to delay a little and wait a bit longer. But why didn't Tian Yufei appear?

Luo Qian finally announced that he was leaving.

Since last time when he went to Tian Yufei's house to look at her paintings, he thought that in the future she would be waiting for him again under the square cement electricity pole when he came off work. The scene was like a picture: a beautiful, innocent and pleasing girl against a grey city background. That's right – a small pear tree drenched by the fine rain in the middle of a noisy city.

But as time passed, this anticipated sight did not reappear. Later on, he wondered: did all this come from his excessive sensitivity… or was it a kind of narcissism or delusion? Therefore, he told himself that this was all just accidental, a misunderstanding or misjudgement, a silly personal assumption. In retrospect, from start to finish, there had been nothing going on between this girl and himself.

But he still felt a little let down.

Two days later, old Mr Zhao, who was in charge of reception, handed him a letter when he delivered newspapers to the design room in the morning. This letter was very unusual. Usually official letters came in brown paper envelopes, while private letters were sent out in white paper envelopes with several green lines filled in with the name and address of sender and recipient. But this envelope was light blue, and it was smaller than the average envelope. It was obviously homemade, and the envelope seemed to be empty since it was so thin. Apart from the name of his work unit, it just said: "Addressed to Mr Chu Yuntian." There was neither the sender's address nor signature below. There were only two additional words "See Inside", as if some secret was contained inside. The handwriting on the envelope was beautiful and fresh, which gave the letter an elegant appearance and filled him with expectation.

He opened it quickly. Sure enough, it was from her – from Yufei. On a piece of paper slightly smaller than the envelope and also light blue, were the following words: "I've not been feeling well. I've been at home. I'm sorry I didn't get to see you when you visited the college!"

There was no preamble and no signature. But he and she were both present in this little letter. It revealed her feelings, a pitiful expression of disappointment.

A few seemingly ordinary words, at this moment, contained myriad emotions. One of the voices he heard most clearly was calling on him to go and see her.

When he left the institute early to go to her house, he also felt that this note was an excuse for him to see her.

When he knocked on the door, he was surprised at the sight. She was not at all as he expected: hair dishevelled, body weak and unwell-looking. She brightened before his eyes, and her joy and excitement made her seem to glow. She wore a light pink coat, a pair of dark blue cloth trousers, with long black hair hanging down behind her shoulders, and her beautiful face was like a flower just washed clean by the rain. He could smell the fragrance of flowers. Behind her stood a number of drawing boards, each with a new painting on it. New paintings always bring forth fresh vistas and artistic emotion, which made Yufei's room light up.

Chu Yuntian asked: "Are these your new paintings?"

"I started painting after your last visit," Yufei said. "All of them are new! Let's see if I've improved after your last criticisms."

"I thought you were sick."

Yufei smiled mischievously and replied: "If I hadn't said I was sick, would you have come?"

Chu Yuntian hadn't expected anything like Yufei's new work. These paintings were obviously different from those he'd seen last time. No matter whether in terms of depth, colour composition or brushwork, where did she get such perception and conceptualisation, to achieve such a massive breakthrough in such a short time? Could it possibly be from the various tips he'd given her last time? Could she really feel it so keenly, and get it down so clearly in her pictures? Does she really have such artistic understanding and ability? Last time he looked at her exercises, he didn't think she had such rich talent and potential.

The talent she now showed made her seem even more beautiful and lovely. In Chu Yuntian's eyes, she saw something coming from his heart. Part of love is a kind of perception that does not need words.

He noticed that there were a pair of small pottery vases, beautiful and unusual in form, arranged on the first level of the cabinet. There were several vermilion strokes across the grey glaze, simple and generous. He praised them and said they must be Japanese ceramics. He told her that the Japanese had learned ceramic art from China since the Song dynasty, and now they had their own style and development.

Yufei told him that these had formed part of her mother's dowry. She said that her mother was of mixed Chinese and Japanese ancestry. She inadvertently explained the hidden reason for her unusual temperament to Chu Yuntian. He didn't understand why she told the secret of her own family background so readily.

Love makes people drop their guard and boundaries.

She looked at him. There seemed to be a flame in those bright and unique eyes.

Suddenly, she told him to stand with his back against the wall, his arms spread out horizontally, close to the wall. She said she would measure his arm span with a ruler. He did as she said but had no idea why she wanted to record his reach.

She seemed to have had an inspiration. She picked up the two small pottery vases from her mother's dowry, put them between the backs of Chu Yuntian's hands and the wall, and asked him to press them hard. "What are you doing?" he asked in alarm.

"This is to keep you still," she said. "As soon as you raise your hands, the vases will fall."

He didn't move. She came up to him and looked into his eyes. Suddenly she threw herself against his chest, raised her red, soft, wet and trembling mouth, and kissed him with all the warmth and passion of life in her heart.

He did not dare to move because he was afraid of breaking the pottery vases. Instead, he passively let her give expression to her love.

She was pressing closer and closer to him. His body felt the heat of her body. She was about to merge with him like a liquid.

CHAPTER 8

Autumn always invades the world of summer quietly, when summer is not paying attention, dissolving its omnipresent and dominant green, little by little, until even the deepest and densest verdant patches present the characteristic symbolic colour of autumn – golden yellow.

The arrival of autumn is always silent. Its first act was to turn this small, insignificant leaf yellow.

Who could have thought that this single golden leaf would gradually become a vast expanse, stretching between heaven and earth?

There are two things that people can't control: one is the natural roll of the seasons, and the other is the great events of life, love and death. The former belongs to heaven and earth, and the latter depends on existence itself. No matter how much you cherish spring or autumn, or how much you desire immortality and eternal life, you can't stop the will of God. What about love? Life is the beginning and death is the end. The greatest thing in the middle is love. Love is a desire and burning of life, and it can't be stopped. But compared with life and death, love is a little more complicated. First of all, love is random, changeable and unpredictable. Second, it occurs between two people. It doesn't necessarily mean that those concerned are moving on the same trajectory to meet in the middle. They may each make an effort, only to find themselves going in different directions. Ultimately, this can destroy love, and may even result in destroying themselves.

This little flower that had just opened between Chu Yuntian and Yufei – what would happen to it next?

Chu Yuntian had a simple nature, vast knowledge and great expressiveness, and like any other lively young man, he didn't lack friends. Of course, the most important group in his heart was the Three Musketeers. What bound them together was their common love of art.

But for Chu Yuntian, this little circle was not enough, because Luo Qian and Luo Fu had nothing to do with his other love – literature. Although the elegant and refined Sui Yi loved poetry and literature, and her critical perceptions were pretty good, she was his wife after all, and he needed a wider range of insight.

Only Su Yousheng could really talk to Chu Yuntian about literature at the same level as his conversations about art with Luo Qian and Luo Fu. He greatly admired Su Yousheng, who was a few years older than him and was more widely read than him. When the other people sat down with him, they all listened to him. At that time, most of the books in the library were locked away. If you wanted to get your hands on a really good book, you had to search with the same dedication as a sparrow looking for food after a heavy snowfall. If a good book appeared, you had to pass it around among your friends. Everyone had a strict time limit for reading, and sometimes even for a long novel, you would only get one day. Such a good book would be passed around among friends like a whirlwind, before spinning off who knows where. Among these spiritually famished young people, Chu Yuntian, with his great knowledge of literature, was naturally like a small bonfire in the cold snow. As soon as he appeared, everyone would surround him to absorb some of that warmth.

Chu Yuntian, who was good at storytelling and expressive in his renderings of tales, had become a folk hero.

He could willingly and vividly recount the plot of any book that he had read, or recreate their most amusing passages. Most of his stories came from famous works of literature that the young adults listening had never read. He didn't know where he got this ability from. He was very good at building up the atmosphere, crafting the story skilfully and deleting all the long-winded and boring sections in the original, distilling its essence. As an artist, he had the ability to tell the story distinctly, with a strong visual sense, so as to make the characters lifelike and engaging to his listeners. When he himself entered the story he was telling, he would become inspired and invent even more wonderful, moving and unexpected plot twists or details. Once, Luo Qian was there and said to him with a smile: "Did you make up the end of the story?"

"How did you know?"

"I haven't read the book," Luo Qian said. "However, I felt that this ending was the kind of ending you like – sentimental."

Chu Yuntian said: "When I saw this book, several dozen pages were missing at the back. I don't know the ending. I just made it up according to what had gone before."

"Do you think a person's end is determined at birth?" Luo Qian asked him. "Or are there many possible endings, and it's up to you to choose?"

"I think the reason why people can live at all is that they don't know how they will end up," Chu Yuntian said. "But I believe there must be personal components to a person's final ending."

"What do you mean by personal components?"

"Time, character and choice."

"Is there any accidental factor?"

"Necessary chances and chance necessities."

Luo Qian pondered these words for a moment and then said: "Literature is much deeper than painting."

Lately, Chu Yuntian had been in more contact with Su Yousheng. The main reason was that he wanted to borrow some Western literary classics from him. Su Yousheng was a man of deep cultivation and fine character. Chu Yuntian called him 'Old Su' because he was several years older than himself. Old Su was thin and strong, with a large, talkative mouth. He liked to speak at the top of his voice and laugh loudly, and all the while he would be smoking fiercely. Chu Yuntian had hardly ever seen him without a cigarette between his fingers. Old Su also smoked as he walked. Only real nicotine fiends want to smoke as they walk. When Yuntian had just been thrown out of his home to live in that red-roofed attic, the original inhabitants of the house were also forced out, and for the longest time all the rooms on both floors were empty. Every time Old Su came to visit, Yuntian and Old Su would go down to one of the empty rooms on the second floor with two stools, a thermos and two cups. They often talked all afternoon until it got dark. They couldn't continue their talk after dark because there was no electricity on the second floor. Literature was their only topic of conversation.

Old Su had graduated from the Central Academy of Drama; he was very talented and well-educated, with a surprisingly good memory. He boasted that his achievements were quite comparable to those of Wang Anshi with his photographic memory as described in Feng Menglong's short story *Wang Anshi Thrice Corners Su Dongpo*. Unfortunately, since his father was in Taiwan (and had been an officer in the Kuomintang Army), it was impossible for him to get a decent job and he'd been demoted to a small troupe in Tianjin – the Yu Opera Troupe – as a writer. In the 1970s, naturally, there were no plays to write and nothing to do. He was innately cheerful and optimistic, quite carefree, and he ignored everything that life threw at him, as if all he ever wanted to do was read books, smoke cigarettes and chat. They would talk up hill and down dale, from Pu Songling's *Strange Stories* to O. Henry, from Stanislavski's *An Actor Prepares* to Mei Lanfang, from the Peking opera *Xu Ce Runs the City Wall* to the remarkable use of blank space in Chinese painting. They would talk about past and present, and every topic under the sun… They would chat from the moment that the sun first came peeping through the window until it sank over in the west and the empty room was filled with shadows, and Old Su's cigarette end lit the darkness – and then their conversation would draw to a close. At this time, Sui Yi would bring down two large bowls of soup noodles topped with slices of fatty meat and leafy vegetables, and they would use a square stool as a table. When he got paid at the beginning of the month, he would add a bottle of beer and a packet of fragrant five-spice peanuts. This was a very happy day for them, a day of great fun and enjoyment.

Old Su manifested his close friendship with Yuntian by lending him books. He never lent books to anyone else – only to Yuntian.

His rules for borrowing books were always very strict – strict to the point of brutality, in fact. He would lay down in advance how many days he would lend it for, and then when the time was up you had to hand it back; if you didn't get it back in time, he wouldn't lend again. The peculiar thing was that the house where Old Su lived over on Zhenshi Street in the west part of the city contained only a few sticks of furniture and no bookshelves. But should Yuntian want to read a famous title, Old Su would give it to him. He had a collection of at least a couple of thousand books, but where did he keep them? Yuntian knew this was a question he was not allowed to ask. At that time, these books were part of the 'Four Olds' and hence forbidden. There were very few who would lend you books so generously.

Today, Yuntian wanted to borrow Tagore's *Stray Birds* from him.
Old Su said: "Haven't you already read this book? Didn't you even learn some sentences off by heart?"
"The feeling will be different when I reread it," Yuntian declared.
Two days later, Old Su sent him the book wrapped in newspaper. Yuntian was very happy, but this was not because he wanted to read it. He intended to recommend it to Yufei.

Ever since that day – and what kind of day was it? Anyway, it was a kind of day he had never experienced before – Yufei had become an 'infinitely gentle presence'. For the first time in his life, he had a secret. A sweet, happy, unexpected secret that he could not possibly discuss with anyone else. Because the secret incorporated that magical and bold kiss, it had all the joy of stealing forbidden fruit.
Everything happened too quickly. From the impossible, it had become a reality before he had even realised that it was even a possibility. Until now, he didn't have time to think about it, let alone judge whether his behaviour was right or wrong. He just carried on as if sleepwalking, carrying this infinite pleasure with him. Who was he walking with? With her? Where was she going? She was not God; she was the spirit of love. No one could say whether the spirit of love was right or wrong and where it would lead him.

He just wanted to keep in contact with her, to meet her and then meet her again. When he found out that Yufei liked poetry and prose, he had an excuse to get in touch with her. Last time he had lent her a copy of Kahlil Gibran's *The Prophet*, which was a prose poem he owned and particularly liked. Yufei read it and admired it very much. When returning the book to him, she put a piece of paper in it and wrote a sentence according to Gibran's sentence pattern:

I am a gust of wind. How can you find me?

This sentence seemed to embody her mischievous, smiling countenance.

Accordingly, he lent her Tagore's *Stray Birds*, which were prose poems, just like *The Prophet*. When he gave her the book, he also slipped a piece of paper inside and replied to her in the same sentence pattern:

The willows quiver gently. I know where the wind is hiding.

They both liked to make life poetic like this. It brought them great spiritual solace.

Although they were eating forbidden fruit, and both wanted to continue to do so and to make it even more romantic, neither of them was under any illusion, and they were not driven by pure lust. It was because they were both disciples of art, they regarded each other as they would an image in the painting and they pursued their mutual poetic and romantic assumptions, only to have the impulse of love gradually become involved. Chu Yuntian thought of a sentence in Roman Roland's *Jean-Christophe*:

This was not selfish lust, but a precious friendship in which the body should also participate.

Moreover, they were far from crossing this final line.

He couldn't always go to her house by the river; he was afraid of meeting her mother and he also did not want Luo Fu to know. Yufei was his favourite student. If Luo Fu knew about their relationship, the consequences would be unimaginable. It was also impossible that she should always be waiting for him in the busy street near his office, for by the same token she might bump into some acquaintance. The only way to communicate was by letter and the occasional phone call. However, at that time, people did not have private phones, and she had no fixed landline. In this way, it was very difficult for them to meet up with each other. They missed each other so much that they became fidgety.

Once a woman falls in love, she is much cleverer than a man. Later, she came up with a system: she would send the very quiet child of one of her neighbours directly to the institute to find him, on the pretext of picking up or returning a book. If she was missing him intensely, she would write a note, putting it in the book she was returning, and ask him to meet her in some very distant and quiet place. But once, when she was almost beyond the city limits, she heard a man calling her. She turned around and saw that it was a classmate. She quickly thought of some excuse and sent the classmate away. Afterwards, she became even more afraid. Fortunately, Chu Yuntian hadn't yet arrived at the time, but what if the student had bumped into him? He knew Chu Yuntian. In such a big city, there was nowhere for them to hide.

Once, they agreed to meet outside the Xiying Gate because they were desperate for each other's kiss. They got into the gap between several large trucks parked there. As soon as they kissed, a noise came from the truck, which scared them so much that they leapt out and ran away, like two escaping thieves. After running straight across a number of streets, Yufei was still so terrified that she was hardly able to breathe. They never knew which truck it was or what had made that noise.

One weekend, at around 4 pm, Yuntian and Sui Yi were at home, and Yuntian was sorting out his paintings. Sui Yi was inserting the many beautiful fallen leaves she had picked up from the yard into the mirror frame. She was very interested in how to arrange these differently shaped leaves in attractive combinations. At this time, she heard the stairs start to creak, indicating the arrival of a visitor. Sui Yi ran out of the room to have a look. Yuntian was surprised and happy to hear Sui Yi say: "Oh, I wasn't expecting you. I didn't expect that. Please come in, but the place is in chaos!"

By the time Chu Yuntian had got to his feet, the guests had already entered the room. He didn't expect to see Luo Fu and Tian Yufei! Why did they suddenly want to visit him?

As soon as Luo Fu entered the attic, and before he'd even said hello, he shouted: "Look, Yufei! This is Chu Yuntian's castle! Isn't it great!"

Yufei put her hands together in front of her chest, as if she was really entering a castle of the kind described in books. She exclaimed: "It's so beautiful and amazing. I've never seen such a place! It's like a cabin in a fairy tale." Then she said that she adored these columns, the sloping roof, small windows, skylight, wooden walls and every aspect of layout and decoration. Until Sui Yi asked her to sit down, she didn't stop praising and admiring the place.

"Yufei has been pestering me for days," Luo Fu said, "asking me to take her to visit you. I've been working away at that huge painting for ages and couldn't leave it. Fortunately, Yu Miao is going to be putting in the details today, so I'm free and I brought her round."

Yufei said with a smile: "My teacher has always said that Mr Chu is better than him. He's told me that I should 'learn from others'." She spoke quite naturally.

Luo Fu asked Chu Yuntian to show her his pictures. Yuntian's paintings always had a liveliness and beauty that struck the observer at first glance. When he put some of his paintings out on the table, chair and cabinet, the atmosphere of the whole room changed. The storms, clouds, torrents, hurricanes, haze, wilderness and dazzling sunsets rendered the people in the room speechless, including Yuntian and Sui Yi themselves.

"Mr Chu, can I study painting with you?" Yufei said sincerely. Her eyes were filled with emotion.

Chu Yuntian didn't know how to respond.

Yufei turned her head and said: "Ms Sui, can I study painting with Mr Chu?" Seeing that Chu Yuntian didn't say anything, she turned to Sui Yi for help.

"Of course! I'll agree on his behalf. Come round as often as you like," Sui Yi said simply and cheerfully. Then she took Yufei's hand

and said to Luo Fu: "Last time, when I met her at Mr Xu's house for the first time, I liked her very much. She seems so bright and straightforward." She spoke warmly, and turned her head to Yufei to say: "The key is whether Mr Luo agrees to let you study with someone else."

Luo Fu said with a smile: "If you like the idea, how would I dare to oppose it?"

Everyone laughed. Chu Yuntian was especially happy. Now, there would be no obstacles to seeing Yufei again.

But was this a blessing or a curse?

CHAPTER 9

Every time Yufei came, climbing up the squeaky wooden stairs leading to the top floor of Yuntian's home, she felt like she was ascending into heaven. Was this because she liked the unique beauty there? Was it because it felt like a kind of otherworldly haven? Or was it because she liked the fresh air that filled the space, towering high into the numerous branches?

She loved the romantic notions she had about it.

Here, there was nothing vulgar, no affectation or flaunting, and no coarseness of spirit. Neat, poor, elegant and meticulous, even the groups of objects on the cabinet were placed together in moderation and harmony like the subjects of a painter's sketch. She remembered he had once slipped a note to her in a book: "The essence of all art is to make beauty conquer everywhere."

It was the owner of this attic who made it so romantic.

Isn't beauty the essence of romance?

Here, she would chat with Yuntian, and sometimes Sui Yi would join in. Together, they discussed painting, books, poems and the meaning of life, a long-unsolved problem. Women tend to like emotional topics, while men prefer rationality. Every conversation always ended with Yuntian's incisive analysis. Yufei gained rational analysis and exploration, and Yuntian gained the intelligent, rich and fresh perceptions of the two women.

Yuntian not only talked to her about the painting but also painted for her to watch. The unpredictable changes of ink when it came into contact with the remarkable qualities of Xuan paper surprised and amazed her. She vowed to learn these skills. At that time, everything seemed natural and beautiful. As the days passed, she came more often. Sui Yi called on her for help when she was doing the housework. Sometimes they went shopping together, and when they came back, Yufei would be carrying the small bag or basket. She was like a smart, clever and beautiful little sister around Sui Yi. They were always talking and laughing as they came upstairs.

They all liked this atmosphere. Yufei sometimes brought along a small bag of Beijing preserves – sour plum or green Chinese olives – which were Sui Yi's favourites. She seemed closer to Sui Yi than to Yuntian. But when Sui Yi went out to work or hadn't come back yet, the situation was different. She couldn't help leaning her fluffy head on his shoulder. When Yuntian's passions surged, he would take her in his arms. They did go some way towards having an affair, but not too far. Maybe they didn't have the courage to cross that line, or maybe they were still constrained by morality. Or perhaps they just hadn't reached that point yet.

As relationships develop, those involved may not notice, but onlookers will often spot inconsistencies. Sui Yi was the first to realise that something else was going on.

Recently, Yufei had been coming to their house every second or third evening. She seemed to have become a member of the family, and she came as if it was natural to do so. Sometimes, she stayed very late, and when she left, she showed some hesitation. Why should she be so reluctant to leave? Once, when Sui Yi had her stay for dinner, she bit into a piece of chicken and ate half of it. She said it was delicious, and put the uneaten half into Yuntian's bowl. She said she wanted to "honour her teacher", but what kind of relationship did they have that she could give an uneaten bite of food to him? This little detail seemed to indicate that big changes had taken place behind the scenes.

Sui Yi had grown up in a family of intellectuals of great refinement. She was simple and kind, and unprepared to defend herself – she was also not in the least competitive. Her relationship with Yuntian had never been tainted by suspicion; they had grown up together in a natural, sunny way. She had never imagined that there would be any threat to their life together. When she began to anticipate trouble looming, she didn't know how to find out how far it had gone, nor did she have a clue how to deal with it. For example, when she came back from work, she saw Yufei's bike parked in the yard and knew that she was upstairs with Yuntian. What would they have been getting up to together? If it had been another woman encountering this kind of thing, she might have sneaked up and suddenly appeared to catch them out. But Sui Yi was incapable of that kind of thing. Didn't she think of it? No, no, she was afraid that she might see too much; she was afraid of turning suspicion into fact. She couldn't bear the consequences. Therefore, whenever she encountered this situation, she deliberately made lots of noise climbing the stairs.

Was this fear, avoidance, weakness or an expression of her natural generosity and kindliness, as well as a sort of dignity and pride due to her family background?

Thus, she found herself trapped in the pain of suspecting others and distrusting the people she had always loved. Who could share this agony with her? This wasn't the kind of thing she could tell anyone; even when she went to see her own mother, she couldn't speak of it. This was something that she had to bear alone.

For a long time, she waited in silence. Suffering like this, she inevitably became depressed and unintentionally revealed her sadness. Could Yuntian remain oblivious?

Once, Sui Yi went to Shanghai with a couple of other doctors for a professional colloquium. After dinner that day, Yuntian was at home alone, and Yufei turned up. She and Yuntian set aside this time to enjoy their intimacy. However, just as their passion was at its height, they heard the sound of someone climbing the stairs. The steps were light, but the stairs were very old, so they rang as soon as someone stepped on them, and this sound was particularly clear at night.

They were startled and Yuntian made haste to release her. He saw that it was a man ascending the stairs: Luo Qian. He stood at the door and asked: "Why are you here?"

"Oh, nothing much. I came round to have a chat," Luo Qian said. He stood on the stairs and raised his head. He noticed that Yuntian's hair was all messy and asked: "Did I get you out of bed this early?"

"I've been feeling a little tired today. I guess I must have dozed off," Yuntian said. He kept standing at the door, as if to prevent anyone from entering. He wanted to keep Yufei out of it; but there was nowhere in the attic that she could possibly hide.

Luo Qian looked at him and felt that something strange was going on. Regardless of whether he was tired or not, Yuntian ought to have invited his visitor in and let him have a seat. It was very peculiar that he didn't invite him in, unless there was some secret in his room. Luo Qian gave in and said: "Well, I'll guess I'll just go home. Go back to sleep." Then he turned and went downstairs.

Yuntian was caught off-guard by his sudden arrival and didn't even go to see him off. He just said: "I'll see you around in a day or two."

Chu Yuntian turned back into the room and judged that he'd been too nervous just now. He recalled everything that had happened after Luo Qian's arrival, and he felt that he'd been flustered and rude – he must have given the game away. Yes, he should have let his visitor come in. But in the circumstances, how could he?

They had thought that this was a heaven-sent opportunity, but now they had lost all interest. Yufei asked him what had happened. He didn't want to explain, so he asked Yufei to leave, just in case Luo Qian came back again.

When he calmed down, he thought the matter through carefully and decided that this was no accident. Why hadn't Luo Qian asked whether Sui Yi was at home? Before she left, had Sui Yi asked Luo Qian to come round to the house and investigate? Sui Yi always relied on Yuntian to deal with any difficulty, but now it was she herself who had created the problem. All by herself, who would she ask for help? It could only be Luo Qian. Their old friend was steady and reliable, and had a close relationship with both of them. The more he thought about it, the more confident he felt that he had guessed right – and how the mighty were fallen! The most important thing for him to do tomorrow was to inform Yufei that she shouldn't come back as long as Sui Yi was away.

After Sui Yi came back, for the first few days, everything was as usual. At that time, going anywhere on business was like travelling abroad would be nowadays. After her trip to the south, she was feeling a lot more relaxed. She'd brought her mother some pear syrup candy and Shanghai muffins, which were her favourites. She'd bought her sister-in-law Ya'nan a pair of comfortable loafers, which the whole family admired. She and Yuntian had a lot more to talk about together than had been the case before she left; and she enjoyed telling him about the things she'd seen and done on her visit. Chu Yuntian secretly laughed at his fears. He had just been paranoid, frightening himself over nothing. But still he secretly told Yufei to come by less often. In its own way, this was very effective; Yufei did visit every so often, and she'd chat and laugh with Sui Yi completely naturally. This meant that Yuntian was able to relax from earlier tensions.

One day, when Yuntian looked at Sui Yi and Yufei sitting there talking, he had a startling thought. He realised that these two beautiful, talented women had both kissed him. He was secretly proud of this fact, to the point where he even felt a sense of achievement.

Heaven is watching everything you do. He would have to take the consequences of his 'evil' thoughts.

One day, Yufei came past with a bag of small golden oranges. She explained that they were sweet oranges brought by her mother's colleague from Guangxi, and she'd asked her to give them to her teachers. She put down the oranges and said she should leave. The wind outside was getting up, and it seemed like it was about to rain.

Having said this, she started running down the stairs. Shortly after she'd left, the sky outside the window darkened, and the wind blew so fiercely that the attic creaked and even shook, and this was followed by dazzling lightning and rolling thunder. Heavy rain fell in a torrent from the sky, beating against the skylight like gongs and drums, as if to break it, and this was followed by further torrential rain. A corner of the attic where the roof leaked turned into a waterspout.

Sui Yi positioned a small basin to collect the water, and exclaimed: "Goodness, it's pouring down, and Yufei wasn't wearing a raincoat. She can't have gone far. You should go after her and give her this!" She handed her waterproof to Yuntian.

Chu Yuntian grabbed hold of the waterproof and ran downstairs. Sui Yi called after him: "You ought to wear a raincoat yourself!"

He turned around, grabbed his raincoat and ran down in a few steps. He felt like a hero rescuing a maiden in distress.

That was an aspect of the matter that Sui Yi also felt keenly.

Chu Yuntian pedalled hard through the torrential rain. He fought against the heavy rain and the headwind. He kept wiping the rain off his face with his hand. The scene in front of him was like as if a river had been emptied on top of them, and he was struggling in the torrent. Suddenly, he heard a voice call him. He thought it was Sui Yi, but how could it be? He looked left and right, and saw someone waving to him in the doorway. It was Yufei! She'd taken shelter from the rain there.

It took him a lot of effort, fighting against the wind and rain, to get there. Yufei was drenched to the skin. Her thin clothes were clinging to her body, and her hair was sticking to her face. She looked a mess and was shivering with cold. He quickly put her into the raincoat he had brought and wrapped his arms around her. He'd helped her in her hour of need, and moved by this, she raised her lips and kissed him. He said with a smile: "The rain is still running down your face!"

"I like it this way..." Then she suddenly pulled him out into the heavy rain beyond the doorway, kissed him warmly and passionately, and let the rain pour down on both of them. The cold rain flowed down their cheeks and skirted their warm mouths. They felt an intense enjoyment from this crazy moment of romance! They stood still in the rain for a long time, as if they had been turned into statues.

· · ·

Soon after this prolonged drenching in the icy rain, Yuntian fell ill with a fever. Sui Yi didn't understand how he could have got so soaked given he was wearing a raincoat. When she asked him that, he didn't know how to answer. They had never lied to each other, even as children. Facing her innocent eyes, he couldn't find an explanation. This made Sui Yi suddenly understand what must have happened. Of course, she couldn't imagine how romantic and freeing it had been for him. She didn't ask again. Her suspicions had now taken concrete form.

On the fourth day that Chu Yuntian was sick, he lay in bed with a burning head. Sui Yi had asked for leave to look after him at home and was brewing up a traditional Chinese medicinal stew. There was little talk between them. One didn't want to speak and the other had nothing to say.

Then the stairs started creaking. Both Yuntian and Sui Yi could hear from the sound of the footsteps on the stairs that it was Yufei coming up. Sui Yi went out. Chu Yuntian lay in bed and could hear them talking on the stairs outside the room. From their conversation, it was quite clear that Sui Yi was no longer the same person she had been before all this.

"I've brought your raincoat back," Yufei said. "Thank you. It was quite a downpour that day, and I really needed this."

Sui Yi replied: "I'll take it." That was all she said, very stiffly.

"Mr Chu got soaked," Yufei said. "Is he OK?"

"He is ill." Just those three words, again spoken very stiffly.

Yufei was a little worried. Her voice couldn't help becoming distressed. She asked: "Is it serious? Should he go to the hospital? I'll go with you!"

"No," Sui Yi reminded her, "I'm a doctor." She was surprisingly calm and unusually unmoved. The tone of voice and the expression on her face were both indifferent. Indifference is a kind of rejection.

Chu Yuntian could feel the atmosphere outside the room. Then he heard Yufei say: "I won't disturb you. I'll be off now. Please take good care of Mr Chu. If you need anything, just let me know."

He didn't hear anything else being said, and this was followed by the sound of Yufei going downstairs. Then Sui Yi opened the door.

She hung up her raincoat, poured herself a cup of water, sat down by the window and looked outside. She wasn't admiring the scenery, she was letting herself calm down. She had never experienced such an emotional crisis before. On the surface, she was calm and silent, but she felt as if she had just been through the wars.

She couldn't carry on living like this.

From this day onwards, Yufei no longer visited. She didn't know if Yuntian was contacting her in other ways after going to work. Anyway, Yufei hadn't reappeared again. Sui Yi's life with Yuntian carried on without her, but they had also stopped talking to one another. Sui Yi didn't say anything, and Yuntian didn't dare to mention it. The more he felt unable to mention it, the more certain she was that something serious was going on between them. After all, Yufei was still living right there in the same city. Was she just escaping her vigilance, but still remaining an invisible presence in his private life?

She could not ask, and she would have been ashamed to question him. She believed that love could not be won through fighting, nor was it a prize for the victor. She had her dignity. Thus, this unspeakable secret was a terrible torture for her.

CHAPTER 10

He hadn't been to Luo Qian's house for a long time. One potential reason was because of what happened the night of Yufei's tryst with him when Sui Yi was away on a business trip. He still suspected Luo Qian. But then he thought that Luo Qian wouldn't have known about Yufei, who was one of Luo Fu's students, unless Sui Yi asked him for help. This became an inexplicable, undefinable obstacle in his relationship with Luo Qian. He sometimes really missed the little salon where he could talk about calligraphy and painting while listening to music. In that lonely era, there was nowhere else to find such a paradise where art was truly worshipped, and where spiritual hunger and suffering could be comforted.

Today, when he came home from work, he found a note at the door of the stairs. Luo Qian had left it for him, asking him to visit. He wondered if Luo Qian was going to talk openly with him about his private life. But after he arrived, Luo Qian was the same as before. If anything, he was more amicable, having not seen his friend for many days. This convinced him that all his suspicions were paranoia, and that he'd been unkind. Once this was resolved, he felt an inexpressible pleasure. For many years, the relationship between the Three Musketeers had always been like the small river bend surrounded by weeping willows opposite his house – calm and gentle, flashing in the sunlight or glittering in the moonlight. It is one of the happiest things in life to have good friends when one is young.

"I wanted to ask Luo Fu to join us, but he's in Beijing. I heard that his big painting has been on display in the art museum, and it's been highly acclaimed. There were lots of people looking for him, so he's very busy," Chu Yuntian said.

"When he finished the painting, he took me to see it," Luo Qian said. "He's very clever. Do you remember when we said to him that painting should be 'loose'? He really paid attention to this when he painted that huge canvas. It was very loose, very comfortable, atmospheric but without losing the overall momentum. If Yu Miao hadn't done the main characters in neurasthenic detail, the whole painting would feel better."

Chu Yuntian listened and thought to himself, why didn't Luo Fu invite him to see the painting? This was a little unusual. Was it because of Yufei? Did he know something? Had Sui Yi involved him, too? At this time, he was very sensitive to everything, even a little suspicious.

Luo Qian didn't know what he was thinking. He was still chatting away with him. He asked him whether he had read any great books this time or painted any pictures. He wanted him to tell him what he had learned.

Chu Yuntian was full of ideas. As soon as he heard this, he repeated the conversation about 'artistic conception' he had with Yufei a few days earlier. He was proud of his new idea. He said he could give artistic conception a modern explanation.

He said that what the ancients called artistic conception is actually what modern people call 'cultural value'.

He said that the word 'conception' referred to the spatial image in painting, and 'artistic' to its poetic qualities. Artistic conception is to put poetry into the visual image in the painting.

He also argued that artistic conception was regarded as the highest standard by Chinese painters. This standard was established by Wang Wei and Su Shi in the Tang and Song dynasties, while Western painting did not particularly emphasise artistic conception. This was because most ancient Chinese painters were literati, and hence proficient in poetry and prose. On the other hand, in Chinese history, literature reached artistic maturity long before painting, which made the influence of literature on painting so significant.

Luo Qian listened with narrowed eyes. He always admired his friend's rhetorical flourishes. In Luo Qian's eyes, there were few people like Yuntian, so rich in soul and so constantly inventive in mind. He was always blurting out all kinds of highfalutin theories, and coupled with his natural infectious eloquence, he was easily worshipped by the opposite sex. In Luo Qian's opinion, once he was moved by those women who were infatuated with him, he would inevitably get into trouble. People who are over-sentimental have a weak side, and they find it difficult to extricate themselves when they become emotionally involved. Once, Luo Qian said to him: "You mustn't let other women drag you down. You should understand that even the best of them can't hold a candle to Sui Yi."

After Yuntian had incisively and vividly expressed his opinions on the relationship between painting and literature, Luo Qian said: "I agree with your theory – it is interesting and quite logical. However, I want to remind you that Russian painting forms a unique tradition within Western painting. In other words, Russian painting is a fantastic alternative to the whole corpus of European painting. Soviet Russian painting also pursues a literary quality."

Chu Yuntian was stunned, and he started thinking. Luo Qian said: "Ilya Repin is like Tolstoy in painting, and Isaac Levitan is like Chekhov. Is this comparison OK? You know more about Russian literature than I do."

"That's a great comparison!" Chu Yuntian exclaimed. "I never thought about it like this. I once told Old Su that whenever I look at Levitan's paintings, I think of Chekhov's *The Steppe*, and when I look at Ivan Sishkin's paintings, I think of Turgenev's *A Sportsman's Sketches*. Hearing you say that, I'm going to consider Russian literature and painting together from now on. Luo Qian, when you think about problems, you really do shine a new light on them. This idea is great!"

Luo Qian looked happy and said: "It's nothing special. I was just inspired by what you said about literature." He stood up and continued: "Look at these pictures now, and I'll make you some tea."

Now, he would entertain his friend in the usual way – jasmine tea and Fuling pickled mustard – as they carried on their conversation.

Yuntian saw that during this period, Luo Qian's dark walls had acquired two more small paintings. At first sight, these two new works were quite different. One was abstract. In a crisscross of colour fragments, there was broken black and fuzzy greyish-blue and greyish-purple. Some warm colours like broken glass lit up the centre. He thought that the feelings behind this painting were a little different. There were some illusions and puzzles in it. The real interpreter of abstract works is the painter himself. Was there anything unusual in life that had touched him?

Another work on the wall was representational, but it too seemed to incorporate some special meaning. A bunch of white flowers were inserted into a crooked vase. The flower stems that should have been full of vitality were withered and had collapsed to one side. Was it calling for help because of its inability to support itself? Luo Qian had put a block of pure blue into the dark background of the painting, and together they formed a dark, cold colour that made him feel chilled to the bone. Morbid beauty was Luo Qian's consistent mode of expression. Although he did not know against what psychological background Luo Qian had painted these two paintings, he appreciated the simplicity, uniqueness, beauty of colour, sophistication of the brushstrokes and deep spiritual space in these two obscure paintings. He felt very happy. Recently, the Three Musketeers had all clearly improved – although they were not painting the same kind of paintings at all, and their aims were remote from each other. He felt they should find time to get together and have a discussion, to inspire each other's efforts.

Just as he was about to say this, he nudged a pile of oil paintings on the ground. The outermost one was larger than the others, and Chu Yuntian felt amazed when he looked at it. He didn't know whether it was the impact of art or of emotion. The impact was obviously vigorous, violent and abrupt, with a sense of tragedy. He had something of the same feeling as when listening to Beethoven's Symphony No. 5 in this room two years ago. He said: "This painting is really fierce, and confrontational. Surely this isn't one of yours?" He flipped through the pile of oil paintings. They were all landscapes done in the same style. The tone was gloomy and depressing. Something difficult to contain surged within the painting. He had rarely seen such powerful brushstrokes – he could almost hear the sound of the brush being scraped violently across the canvas. He felt a chill.

"Who painted this? Why haven't I seen it before? There's so much dust on it – it must have been painted many years ago." Chu Yuntian sat back in his chair and continued: "I'm sure this is no ordinary painting!"

Luo Qian poured Yuntian a cup of tea, looked at him and said: "Why do you think it is not ordinary?"

"There is a very strong emotion here – something that has to be expressed or it will explode. I can feel it. If the painter is not an eccentric or neurotic person, then he must have suffered greatly."

"You're quite right," Luo Qian said. Instead of going on, he sipped his tea slowly. He remained quiet for quite some while and then said in his steady tone: "This was painted by a friend of mine."

"Who? Have I met him?"

"Right now, my only friends are you and Luo Fu – no one else. He was a friend of mine more than ten years ago. He left this painting with me."

"Who is he? Where is he now?"

"I don't know." Luo Qian took another sip of tea and said: "You'll want to know how come he painted pictures like these. I can tell you the story, but you've got to keep it to yourself. Even if in the future you come to hate me, you can't tell anyone else. Do you agree?" Luo Qian's way of speaking was strange and mysterious. He didn't usually talk in this manner.

"Yes," Yuntian answered.

"I can only give you a brief outline. Let me explain. You'd better not interrupt me and don't ask questions."

Yuntian agreed, but he was confused.

The following is the tragic tale behind these paintings that Luo Qian told Yuntian –

. . .

"The painter's name is Qin Ling. He was a good friend of mine in middle school. We were both in the school's art club, but he painted better than me. He always won prizes at the city-wide art exhibitions for school-aged children. When he was a senior in high school, the Central Academy of Fine Arts had already picked him out and told him that he didn't have to take the usual college entrance examinations. He was directly selected into the Academy of Fine Arts. His drawings from life were wonderful, and his painting style was not what you see now. In those days his paintings were as bright as wind and water. There was a girl in our art club called…" and here he paused for a long time before continuing: "Her name was Wu You. She was lively, good-looking, cheerful and with a wonderful sense of fun. Quite apart from painting, she could also sing and dance, and her voice was really good. Everyone in the art club liked her, but she liked Qin Ling best of all. She adored him, and they'd been in the same class when they were in primary school. Their feelings were pure, somewhat like with you and Sui Yi…"

Having got this far, there seemed to be a warm brightness in Luo Qian's eye, but then for some reason, this turned into ice and snow. His eyes became cold and hard. He then said: "Do you really believe in such a thing as true love? Reality will tell you that love will change at the drop of a hat. No matter how beautiful love is, it can't be relied on." At this time, he seemed to have to stop for a while, so he picked up his small pottery bowl to take a sip of tea and let Yuntian drink at the same time.

Yuntian didn't rush him but waited for him to speak.

"Later, they got to know a man of some status. He was an official and also a painter. He was also some twenty years older than Qin Ling and Wu You. He was very kind and not at all on his dignity as an official. His house was huge, and he had a living room and a studio. His wife got sick and died, and they had no children together. He treated Qin Ling and Wu You like his own children. To begin with, they often went to hang out there, and they went so regularly that it came to seem like their own house.

"Gradually, Qin Ling realised that the situation was changing for the worse – that is, Wu You sometimes went to his house by herself, and she did so more and more frequently. Qin Ling also noticed that at first Wu You dressed up when she went to his house, but later she was very casual. When Qin Ling couldn't help himself asking Wu You why she was going to his house alone and stopped her from going again, Wu You burst into tears and said: 'It's too late. I've already agreed to marry him!'"

At this point, Luo Qian stopped abruptly. It was as if the film broke while the movie was playing. It was dark, and there was no sound at all.

Yuntian was silent and continued to wait. He felt that the story was unfortunate, difficult and sad. He was a little surprised that Luo Qian was so intense and emotional when he told the tale of his former friend. Was he really so close to this Qin Ling?

Gradually Luo Qian went back to this old story –

"That it was a terrible, shattering shock for Qin Ling, I don't need to tell you. It was useless to ask Wu You why she was doing this, what she was thinking, why she betrayed him. Wu You really did get married to that man." He looked ever more depressed, and his voice became ever lower as he said: "In the immediate aftermath, he was suicidal. He wanted to take sleeping pills, or he wanted to go and fight the man, and everyone had to stop him. But in the end, the thing that stopped his inner rage was painting. He actually calmed down while painting. Pictures kept him alive. That is the batch of paintings you were looking at just now."

He brought his story to a hurried conclusion. Could he not bear to go on, or was there nothing more to say?

Chu Yuntian listened to this story from long ago as if it had just happened in front of his very eyes. He glanced at the paintings lying on the ground. Yesterday's sadness seemed to still scream from them.

He asked Luo Qian: "Where is he now?"

"Who?" Luo Qian asked. He seemed to be in a daze.

"Qin Ling."

"I just told you, I don't know."

"Did he go to the Academy of Fine Arts in the end?"

"No, because he had a nervous breakdown over all of this, so he couldn't continue to study. He never even finished high school."

"Did he recover from this? Why don't you know where he is now?"

Luo Qian waved his hands, and his voice became a little stiff. "Didn't we agree at the beginning? Don't ask." He obviously had no wish to say anything further.

When he said this, Chu Yuntian suddenly understood that Luo Qian had been telling him his own story. Qin Ling was actually himself! The Qin Ling who had been destroyed by love was one and the same with Luo Qian sitting opposite him now. He was shocked and horrified! This friend of many years had been through such a terrible experience. Once the light of life goes out, who can turn it on again?

It never happens. Once the sun goes out, our hearts are always dark.

But why didn't he tell him this until today? It was because of what he had done that Luo Qian had cut open his closed-off self. Yuntian realised that he had no idea how to face his friend.

After sitting in silence for a long time, Luo Qian said the following words thoughtfully: "Sometimes love is like the passing clouds, while on other occasions it is etched into your blood and bones. That is why you should never hurt someone who really loves you. What is true love? It is when if she loses you, she will be left with nothing – or if you lose her, you will be left with nothing. If you hurt her, it is crueller than killing her. Killing a person is to destroy their body, and destroying a person's love is to kill their soul. When their heart is consumed by the flames, their whole person will turn into dust and ashes."

Chu Yuntian listened, but he didn't know whether this was about Wu You or whether it was meant for himself. Anyway, the message sank deeply into his heart.

CHAPTER 11

Luo Qian's words were about the truth of love. Chu Yuntian believed this, but he couldn't actually do it.

There were two candles in front of him. If you want one candle to give out light, you must blow out the other candle. He was in a dilemma.

He had gradually assumed the burden of guilt about betraying Sui Yi, and it was getting heavier and heavier. He felt ashamed of himself. For the past few months, although she didn't say anything, the atmosphere in their small attic room was dull and they seemed to find nothing to talk about. She had lost any interest in decorating their shared space; she didn't go to the shop any more to buy beautiful squares of cloth to sew together into something pretty. The flowers in the vase had died long ago and been thrown away. The empty vase was almost a symbol of their current feelings. All interest in life comes from social relationships. What had happened to the bright and joyful emotions that used to fill their attic room?

He had noticed that Sui Yi wouldn't let him kiss her. He used to always kiss her before she went to work, or after she came home. If he ever forgot, she would take the initiative and smile, tiptoe up to him and turn her face towards him. Why did she refuse now? Had she discovered something? Yes, when it comes to love, women's feelings are surprisingly sharp, subtle and accurate. She could assess exactly how much space she occupied in his heart. Furthermore, she no longer wanted him to hug her. She slept with her back to him all night. Once in the middle of the night, he felt her shoulders shaking. He asked her if she was cold. She kept her back to him and just raised her hand to wave away his concern, after which she stopped twitching. Soon after dawn, she got up to go to work. When he folded up his quilt, he discovered that her pillow was wet. It turned out that she had been secretly crying the previous night. Of course, he knew exactly why she wept.

He felt great remorse.

She had been under his protection since childhood, and they had grown up happily together. He forbade anyone to bully her, and he wouldn't bully her himself. He had never hit her. But now he was treating her more ruthlessly than any bully. No matter how he tried to be nice to her again, it was meaningless. Affection can be shared, but love can't. Love is exclusive. Maybe this is the purity of love.

Although he was determined to restore their relationship to what it had been before, his problem was that he couldn't blow out the other candle. He knew the depths of the girl's passion too well. What had happened between him and Yufei was her first love. Nothing is more intense and absolute than first love.

After returning the raincoat, she found she had lost her way to see Yuntian. Every day she longed for him, as a shipwrecked mariner scans the horizon for any sign of a sail. When her lovesickness grew too bitter, she called him on the phone or wrote to him and asked him to meet her in some quiet corner of the city. Every time they met, she looked at him with tears in her eyes and a smile on her face. Facing the infatuated gaze of her uniquely attractive, unfocused eyes, he couldn't hold out any hope of restoring his relationship with Sui Yi.

On the one side lay the innocence of childhood, on the other the infatuation of first love. He had no right to choose, nor could he choose. The reasons were nothing to do with the women concerned, but with himself. He was incapable of changing this reality; he could only endure it day by day. What he endured was not only his own distress but also the pain of the two women he loved. How could he deal with the mistakes he had made? Who could he ask for help? How could he ask that of Luo Qian? He knew that in Luo Qian's eyes, he was no different from the wicked Wu You, who had so cruelly hurt her true love and destroyed his life. How could Luo Qian help him? He also wanted to find Yufei's teacher Luo Fu, but how could he explain this situation to him? Would not Luo Fu despise him? If Luo Fu sided with his student, he would be sure to hate him.

Originally, Yuntian had the help of these two friends whenever he encountered difficulties. They were like the oars of a boat. Now he had no one, leaving him helplessly adrift in the water.

It was early summer when something suddenly appeared and something unexpected happened.

It was a weekend. In those days, it was common to have two meals a day at the weekend rather than three in order to save trouble and money. Yuntian and Sui Yi each read a book after breakfast. They had nothing to say to one another. Yuntian read for a bit before falling asleep. It was then that someone came up the stairs with heavy and fast steps. Yuntian was woken up by these pounding footsteps and got up to open the door. A young, bright and vibrant face appeared… Luo Fu!

Yuntian and Sui Yi were a little surprised. It was a long time since Luo Fu had last visited them. Yuntian felt awkward since for the last six months he'd more or less been avoiding Luo Fu because of his relationship with Yufei.

However, Luo Fu was not embarrassed at all; for him, everything remained the same. First, he said that the huge painting he'd produced with Yu Miao – 'Vast Heavens and Broad Earth' – had been acquired by a museum. However, the college was determined to keep their noses to the grindstone. After finishing their painting duty, they'd lost their big studio because the authorities were determined that the old building should be put to other uses. In accordance with the demands of their superiors, they were going to organise a 'Workers' Art Institute'. Students were to be drawn from the design arm of various factories.

Luo Fu said to Chu Yuntian: "Teachers are also being transferred in. I heard some teachers will be coming from the design institute at the Bureau of Light Industry! Wouldn't it be great if you were to come! We could meet every day." Luo Fu grinned foolishly.

Chu Yuntian didn't dare show how happy he was because he had seen the fixed expression on Sui Yi's face. If he were transferred to the art college, it would be all too easy for him to meet Yufei.

But just then, Luo Fu asked them: "Have you seen Yufei recently?"

The question was followed by a moment of emptiness. Sui Yi didn't speak; she just listened to what Yuntian had to say.

Chu Yuntian hesitated and said: "I haven't seen her for a long time. I guess she's preparing for her graduation exam."

Yuntian wasn't lying. He hadn't seen her much since the Spring Festival. Two months earlier, she'd sent him a book with a note slipped into its pages which said: "Flowers without fruit suffer painful blooming." After that, she had called him once on the phone and said she was preparing for the graduation exam – since then, there had been no news. He didn't take the initiative to contact her. He hoped that their affair would lighten up a little. If they weren't so intense, if things were more relaxed, it would be more comfortable for both of them. Of course, it would all depend on Yufei's attitude. As long as she was happy, that was all that mattered; he wouldn't hurt her by deliberately keeping away from her.

He was not expecting the news that Luo Fu announced. He said: "When you see her, you must congratulate her. She applied to the Exhibition Department at the Beijing Art Museum, and they've accepted her! She is going to work in Beijing!"

In that moment, he untied the burden that each of his listeners had been carrying on their backs. For Sui Yi, it seemed as though a huge stone that had been crushing her was lifted; and for Yuntian, it felt as if the ropes that bound him were loosened. They were both too honest and too open, that in the moment they did not know what it was that they ought to say. Therefore, the two of them both just said: "Wonderful! That's great!"

Afterwards, Yuntian felt increasingly certain that Luo Fu's sudden visit to their home was motivated by his desire to tell them the news that Yufei would be going to Beijing. He hadn't been to see them for ages and then suddenly turned up, and having told them that Yufei was going to work in Beijing, he left soon after.

If this was so, Luo Fu must know all about him and Yufei. In that case, the application to the Beijing Art Museum and being admitted must also have been achieved with Luo Fu's assistance. He was familiar with all the professional art units in Beijing. But how did she come to make such a decision? Her decision to go to Beijing meant that she must be determined to leave him – that was something Yufei had never shown any sign of wanting to do before!

That evening, Yuntian cycled over to the Xikai Church. When Luo Fu left that afternoon, he'd invited him to come to his house to look at his paintings that evening. The sky was quite dark, and the moonlight was bright. He saw the abandoned church standing silently and quietly like a barren mountain up ahead. Against the bright background of moonlight, it was as dark as ink, like the giant shadow of a monster. Few people were out and about. He suddenly caught sight of a figure standing alone by the small grove of trees over to one side of the church. At first glance, he knew that it was Yufei!

He went over to her. Yufei said: "Mr Luo told me to wait for you here."

He understood now that Luo Fu not only knew all about their affair but that everything that had happened today was arranged by him. Luo Fu didn't invite him to look at his paintings; he'd arranged for him to say an unusual goodbye to Yufei. He understood that this was the end of their relationship.

He respected her decision and didn't ask any questions. Yufei was the only one who spoke: "I shouldn't have blossomed in someone else's garden. Although everything that happened was beautiful, I'm sorry about Sui Yi, because I often forgot all about her. I'm also sorry about what I've done to you because I shouldn't have imposed my unrealistic fantasies on you. To tell you the truth, I can't stand this any more, and I'm sure you feel the same way! It's only by leaving you that we can live our own lives again!"

At this point, she became overwrought and her voice trembled, but she tried to bring it back under control.

Yufei then said: "I'm very grateful to Mr Luo. He helped me to get out of this dreadful situation." These last few words called to Chu Yuntian, as if he had entered the kingdom of heaven: "I envy you having such good friends. Mr Luo and Luo Qian have done an enormous amount for you, and for me."

After hearing these words, which really brought the truth to light, he felt that his friends were the genuine artists. With love, beauty and tolerance, they had repaired their own mistakes in life and pulled him back from the brink. And what painful self-sacrifice must Yufei have made that they were able to get out of this desperate, almost inextricable situation!

Then she came up and said softly: "Hug me! It'll be for the last time."

When Yuntian opened his arms to her, he smelled the familiar smell of her hair and body. But this time, he didn't hug her tightly. Although his heart yearned for her, he did this to make it a little easier for both of them, since they were virtually saying their final farewells. He just hugged her lightly and then let her go. He held her shoulders with both hands, turned her around and said to her back: "Go, Yufei! I will always wish you well."

Yufei's strength in the following moment was admired by Yuntian. Instead of turning back, she pushed her bike, which had been leaning against a tree trunk, over to the main road and then got onto it. She never looked back. Standing there, Yuntian felt as if he had lost some really wonderful things. These things disappeared into the darkness with her vanishing figure, and also disappeared into the time that had just passed.

CHAPTER 12

Two months later, Chu Yuntian was indeed summoned by the director and told he would be transferred to the art college to prepare for the opening of the Workers' Art Institute. This institution of higher education for workers, hastily launched in accordance with an order from on high, had no site allocated to it, so it was temporarily borrowing an empty two-storey old building from the art college. The large upstairs room had once been the studio where Luo Fu painted his 'Vast Heavens and Broad Earth'. Apparently, the students at this institute would be designers drawn from various factories under the auspices of the Bureau of Light Industry. Yuntian's job was to teach Chinese painting and art history, which would be easy for him. He was very happy because henceforward he would regularly be running into Luo Fu since they'd be working on the same campus.

But would he also encounter Yufei? Over the course of the next couple of weeks, he didn't meet her once. Later, he heard that she had already left for Beijing. He felt a sense of loss and emptiness again as if a bird of sweet song had flown away.

At the same time, another bird beside him had not yet begun to sing. However, the food she was cooking had improved, and the items on the cabinet were arranged once more in a striking and original way, and she went to the same fabric shop to buy pretty little squares of cloth again, which she sewed together to make fun things to decorate their room. At this time, he would praise her efforts, trying to please her and coax her to be happy, and implied in everything was an apology that he found hard to put into words. Nevertheless, he still felt that she was alienated from him. For example, when they slept together in bed at night, she still kept turned away. He would pat her on the back quietly, and she ignored him. It was not easy to get close to her again. It takes time to forgive a deeply hurtful mistake. No one can know beforehand just how long it will take.

How can a small boat that has nearly capsized at sea return to its harbour safe and sound?

One day, he took his students over to Qilihai to draw the flowering reeds. The reed flowers were in full bloom then, and from a distance the floating blossoms looked like great waves of snow, reaching all the way to the horizon. The scene was spectacular and unique. He had always had a special fondness for reed flowers: the last wildflowers of late autumn. He admired the character of this overlooked and unpopular wildflower. From the beginning of autumn until the cold winds began to blow in the early winter, it tenaciously demonstrated a kind of endless tenderness in its vitality. The stems of reed flowers are very thin, and the panicles are soft and light, so why do they never break? Like him, Sui Yi loved the reed flowers. There was a time in their lives when every autumn they rode far away to the southern suburbs to see the billowing, delicate white flowers. He would bring an easel so he could paint from life. Every time Sui Yi would pick a few and take them home, arranging them in an old, dark vermilion ceramic vase that stood in the corner of their room. When he thought of these days, he couldn't help asking his students to help him pick a lot of reed flowers and bring them home. He put bunches of these long and fluffy reed flowers all over the attic.

As soon as Sui Yi came back from work and entered the room, she sighed in amazement. Hadn't they both always loved these silvery white, bushy flowers? Suddenly she felt a tenderness from the past overwhelming her. She was moved – and that is the best feeling in the world. At that moment, Yuntian hugged her from behind with his long arms, and finally he got to hold her tightly. She didn't refuse.

Then, their happiness of days gone by was back again, and the wounds to the psyche were healed, and the scent of each other's bodies had become the most intoxicating perfume in the whole world!

At the end of that year, heaven gave this pair of young people who had finally reconciled a gift that they had been waiting for too long: they had a child, a beautiful girl! Children are angels that strengthen the family. How wonderful life is with angels in it!

Of course, Chu Yuntian had not completely forgotten Yufei. He was not a man who lacked commitment. When he thought of her by chance, in his heart he secretly blessed Yufei. However, he no longer got news about her, and he would never take the initiative to contact her. If he contacted her again, that would hurt her, and it would also hurt Sui Yi all over again. He knew this perfectly well, and his mind was made up.

Gradually, during his time on campus, he learned something about Yufei's past that he had never known before.

He was told that Luo Fu had been very fond of Yufei. After she graduated, he wanted her to stay as his assistant in the department. Later on, for some reason, things suddenly changed. Yufei went to Beijing, and Luo Fu had arranged this for her. There were all sorts of different reasons ascribed to this inexplicable decision, but Chu Yuntian knew that all this was thanks to him.

Afterwards, Yuntian realised that Yufei must have been Luo Fu's favourite student; otherwise he wouldn't have wanted her to stay after she graduated. When Luo Fu found out that she was having an emotional affair with him, he would no doubt have been furious. With Luo Fu's temper, he must have wanted to find Yuntian and give him a good hiding. But instead of doing so, Luo Fu had changed his mind and sent Yufei to another city, thus calmly and satisfactorily resolving a big problem for Yuntian.

He clearly remembered that day when Luo Fu had come over to his house and told them that Yufei was going to work in Beijing. It was as though he'd helped them extricate themselves from the huge net entangling their bodies.

He now understood why Yufei said that she envied him his good friends on that day when she'd broken up with him.

Chu Yuntian thought a lot about Luo Qian's secret efforts in this matter. That day when Luo Qian had told him about the tragedy he'd experienced: wasn't it a euphemistic exhortation and warning to him? Moreover, Luo Qian was the only person who could have persuaded Luo Fu to put their friendship first and restore the beauty that would otherwise be lost from life, or perhaps it would be more accurate to say restore the original beauty of their lives together. He did this for Yuntian's sake, but also for the sake of Sui Yi and their family.

After this unseen storm, the Three Musketeers became like three great trees living together, their branches ever more tightly intertwined and their roots deeper.

After lunch one day, when Yuntian was sorting out his teaching plans in the office, Luo Fu came running in and said: "Luo Qian just sent someone to deliver a message to ask us to go round to his place this afternoon."

"What's the matter?" Yuntian asked. "He's not often so peremptory. Is he ill?"

"I asked, but the messenger didn't say," Luo Fu said. "If you don't have classes this afternoon, let's go as soon as possible."

"I'm not busy," Chu Yuntian said. "Let's go now!"

They hurried off on their bicycles. Along the way, they guessed wildly what could be the matter, and their guesses were wrong. The moment they got to Luo Qian's house, they felt something was different. They didn't know whether something was missing, or something had been added. When they looked more carefully, all the paintings on the wall were gone, replaced by an odd-looking banner. The atmosphere inside the house immediately changed. Luo Qian sat there motionless, and his face was darker than the room. His eyes were a little blurred and his expression was gloomy. It was obvious that something terrible had happened.

"Who did this?" Yuntian asked.

Luo Qian said in a low voice: "A group of people came this morning."

"Who?" Yuntian demanded.

"It was the Street Reform Committee, and there was a local police officer with them. They said that someone had accused me of listening to banned music, so they came here to search the place. They took all my records and the record player, and they also said I was painting forbidden paintings. They said they couldn't understand what I was painting and asked me to explain."

At that moment, they noticed that the corner of the room where the record player originally stood was now empty, and the dark green military blanket that covered it had been thrown on the floor. With the record player gone, it felt like heaven was missing a corner.

Luo Fu asked: "When they said they couldn't understand your painting, what did you say?"

"I said my paintings weren't finished," Luo Qian replied. "I told them I can't paint, but that I was practising. They didn't understand a goddam thing, so they couldn't really tell me off. They just told me I wasn't allowed to practise like that, and that I shouldn't hang anything so weird on the wall. They told me I had to have quotations from Chairman Mao up there and that I must put one up immediately."

"Just forget about it," Luo Fu said. "I'll find you two beautiful landscape paintings from the college to replace them."

Luo Qian didn't say a word. Chu Yuntian knew that Luo Qian had his own ideas about interior decoration and would never willingly hang someone else's paintings in his house.

After a moment of silence, Luo Qian whispered: "The paintings are gone, the music is gone, and our salon is gone. The fact is, whenever I listened to music, the volume was always very low. Who can have denounced me? Whoever it was must also have recognised the pieces I was playing…"

Chu Yuntian said: "The worst informants are always those with expert knowledge." He tried to comfort Luo Qian. "Let's think about what to put up on the wall. You're only allowed to have something with a quotation on it, but you can't have this one. It's too much like our office. I'll help you make a much smaller one, dark red with little characters. The nails in the wall are still there, so whenever you want to look at your paintings, you can hang them up and then take them down later. The key to the salon is people. As long as we are here, the salon can survive. If we want to listen to music, we'll go with Luo Fu to find Yannian. "

"I bumped into Yannian on the street a few days ago, and he said he would give us a special concert," Luo Fu chimed in.

Luo Qian knew perfectly well that Luo Fu was making this up as he went along to make him feel better, but this did not lessen his sense of despair. The dull, tense atmosphere in the room did not let up.

Chu Yuntian knew that he had not only lost their salon, but also his sense of security. This was Luo Qian's deepest worry. He was being watched. In that era, once something happened to bring you to official attention, you would be watched, and that meant you could be under constant observation. Thus, the paradise of the spirit that he had worked hard for many years to keep hidden from the world outside had been destroyed.

How could he save himself?

After this, Chu Yuntian went to see Luo Qian every few days. Sometimes he sat down and chatted for a bit, and other times he lent books to Luo Qian. Before all of this happened, it seemed that Luo Qian was the calmer and more determined of the two. However, after Luo Qian told Chu Yuntian about his experiences, especially his nervous breakdown, Yuntian was more than a little worried about him. The shock he'd received was unexpected and cruel to Luo Qian. He'd spent so long in seclusion, hiding away, unknown and ignored, so as to be purely himself and live only through his art; once this world had been destroyed, how could he bear it?

Since this incident, he became more silent than before. Yuntian tried his best to break through this crushing silence. He lent him a very good book: Fu Lei's translation of Hippolyte Taine's *Philosophie de l'art*. Two days later, he returned it to Yuntian. It seemed that books could not calm him, nor could they give him a way out – he had not emerged even a fraction from his shell. He even said: "Fu Lei admired Taine as a man who 'lived for ideas'. Can we live for ideas now?" With that, he smiled bitterly at Yuntian – a truly frightening smile.

Chu Yuntian said to Luo Fu: "We absolutely must find a way to get him out of this state. He has always locked himself away in his own little world. But now that there's a problem, he can't get out."

They agreed on this, but there was nothing they could do.

A month later, the situation changed in a very odd way.

It was a Sunday, and the weather was fine and sunny. Sui Yi took her daughter to the former Victoria Park. The old park in the centre of the British concession was their favourite garden. Although it was quite small, it had the feel of a classic English garden, especially in the northern quarter, where it abutted the grey and white castle-like Gordon Hall. Chu Yuntian had planned to go with them, and he'd borrowed a camera to take some pictures of his wife and child. On their way home, they stopped at the Kiessling Restaurant to have a meal. Since admiring Western mores was anathema at that time, they had to eat their dinner with chopsticks. Little Yiran loved the novelty of Western food, especially the last course, which was ice cream. However, Yuntian was worried about Luo Qian, so he decided to go round and see him.

Thinking of Sui Yi's lovely smile when she waved him goodbye with their daughter, his heart overflowed with happiness. If Luo Qian hadn't secretly helped him out when he nearly shipwrecked his life, dear little Yiran would never have been born. He thought he had to do his very best for Luo Qian.

However, as soon as he walked into Luo Qian's house this time, he realised that the atmosphere was completely different – it was cheerful! He saw that Luo Qian had knocked a window into the wall opposite him. Now that this space was open, the trees outside were lush and green, and they formed a rich, transparent curtain. Yuntian felt the breeze rustling through the leaves outside against his face, and it made him feel relaxed and comfortable.

"When did you make that window? With a window there, the whole place feels quite different," Yuntian said. "I didn't realise you had a tree outside your back wall – that's really nice!"

Luo Qian seemed a different person, with a smile on his face. He looked at Yuntian with his small eyes narrowed and said: "Isn't it? Go over and have a look round the other side." A mysterious look came over his face.

Yuntian approached the window and was surprised to discover that it was a trompe-l'oeil painting! The wooden window frame was painted, and so was the scene outside. He'd used some semi-abstract colour blocks and broad and free strokes to conjure up the deep shade of overlapping green leaves outside the window, with lighter patches where the sun shone through.

"I change the scenery in my house every day these days. Yesterday it was windy outside. Today, it's sunny and the sun is full of light, shadow and shade," Luo Qian explained.

"It's amazing... You can change the scenery outside your window every day at will!" Yuntian said.

"Yes, I can paint whatever I need!"

What a magical imagination! Luo Qian's window was not only the window to his house but also the window to his heart. He was constantly changing the scenery outside his window and thus it constantly reflected his state of mind.

Two days later, Yuntian returned to Luo Qian's house. This time, through the open window, he could see a glittering river shrouded in fog. Here and there it was shrouded in mist, but he could still make out the shape of the river winding its way into the distance. A few days later, before returning home from work, Yuntian went to his house to see if by any chance the window on his wall had again changed its scenery. As soon as he entered, he saw that the river was gone; it was replaced by a faint, dreamy springtime vista...

He had never painted so often or so much. The window on the wall really had become a window into his heart. Yuntian remembered that he had emerged from his earlier tragedy thanks to his artist's brush, and this time he again depended on his brush!

The only thing that can save an artist's soul is art itself.

Yuntian told Luo Fu the good news. Luo Fu wanted to see this miracle too. The two of them went to Luo Qian's house together. Luo Fu did see the window painted on the wall, but there was no scene beyond; it was dark like the night sky, with no stars and no moon, as black as ink, like a bottomless pit. Luo Fu glanced at Yuntian because he didn't know what this meant, but Yuntian's heart was filled with silence and desolation.

Yuntian thought, this is probably the most incredible work that would ever be excluded from the history of painting.

CHAPTER 13

A year later, in the middle of summer, it was still very hot and difficult to sleep. No one among the millions of people in the city could have had the slightest premonition that a huge and devastating disaster was coming.

It was unusually hot that year. Yuntian asked someone to nail together a small bed made from some wooden strips and boards and put it right next to the small window in the eastern wall. Sui Yi got some gauze strips from the hospital and sewed a small mosquito-proof net for Yiran, which covered her daughter and the small bed. Sui Yi slept in the bed, and Yuntian spread a mat out on the ground and lay on top. It would be too hot to sleep next to each other.

In the middle of the night, Yuntian had just fallen asleep when his body was violently jolted upwards from the floorboards, until he was lifted some two or three centimetres in the air, and then with a crash he fell back to the floor. He jerked himself upright and saw a bright blue light flash across the sky outside the window. At that moment, the skylight in the roof was frighteningly bright. This was nothing like the lightning that you see before a thunderstorm. His mind flashed back to an exhibition about the Haicheng earthquake in Liaoning Province he had seen some weeks earlier; he knew that the ground would give off an unusually strong 'earthquake light' right before it struck. He shouted in alarm: "Sui Yi! It's an earthquake!"

Almost at the same time, the attic shook violently. When Yuntian tried to get to his feet, he couldn't stand upright. In the darkness, there were all kinds of things falling and breaking around him. Instinctively, he rushed over to Yiran's little bed and sheltered his daughter with his own body. He didn't know where Sui Yi was and shouted to her. The sound of the house collapsing around his ears drowned out his cry. He felt as though the earth itself had turned into a storm-tossed sea – it was as if they were in a wildly swinging boat that would capsize at any moment. He could hear the attic roaring just before it collapsed. Suddenly, there were two terrible, heavy rending sounds above his head, and he quickly realised that the roof had fallen in. The ground was still shaking ferociously and undulating beneath him. No one could control nature when it exploded. He felt helpless, and he was sure they were all going to die. Any moment now, the end would come.

But in this despair, the earthquake ended abruptly. It was as if he'd been careering along in a runaway car, in absolute terror, and just before impact the brakes had engaged, and the car had come to a halt. In fact, all major earthquakes will start and stop suddenly. In the instant after everything stopped shaking, there was total silence, as if everyone and everything around was dead, and that was followed by cries for help from all around. Yuntian called out to Sui Yi, and he heard her reply weakly from not far away: "Where's Yiran? Save her!"

"I've got her," Yuntian said. "We're both fine. How are you?"

When Sui Yi heard that her daughter was alive and well, she felt her strength flooding back. She said she was fine, too. When he realised that his family was all right, Yuntian immediately pulled himself together to ascertain the situation around him. The building next door was on fire, and the red light from the flames reflected into his house. He could see that the roof was at a crazy angle, and the room was full of dark shadows; all the original supports had come down. He saw someone get to their feet among the shadows – it was Sui Yi. At that moment when they found each other alive, they realised they could not have lived without each other. Sui Yi rushed over to take Yiran. Yuntian said: "No, I'll hold her. It's going to be difficult to get out of here. Quick, find some shoes, put on your clothes and follow me. We must get out of here right away. There may be aftershocks at any moment. Come on!"

When he went downstairs, he saw the terrible damage inflicted by the earthquake. All his neighbours downstairs had run out, and the big wall on the side had collapsed, taking the windows with it, while the building on fire directly opposite was burning in a terrifying way, and the dazzling light of the fire shot across, as if their building was also on fire. This appalling fire lit up the frightened eyes of his family.

Yuntian and his family ran out of the building and went straight to the grove of trees opposite. He handed their daughter over to Sui Yi and told them to stay there and not move. He was a clever, quick-witted man. He ran round the building and soon found a large, empty wooden crate at the back which he dragged to the woods, positioned upright and told Sui Yi and their daughter to hide inside. Then he returned to the building, found an iron jug, filled it with tap water and gave it to them. Afterwards he went to fetch his bike and said to Sui Yi: "I'm going to go and find your mother, Luo Qian, and Luo Fu. I'm going to check that they are OK, and I'll try and find us something to eat!" He told her: "This place is right away from the buildings on both sides. It's quite safe. There's nothing to be afraid of. Wait here for me, and don't move! Don't worry. Survival is the main thing, and I'll sort everything out!"

Then he rode out of the grove.

When Yuntian passed by Huangjia Park and turned onto Luoyang Road, he fully appreciated the devastation and terror that the earthquake had unleashed. At that time, nobody knew that the epicentre of the earthquake had been at Tangshan, and they did not expect that an earthquake could be so severe. Maybe Luoyang Road had been right on the fault line, because the buildings on both sides of the street had been utterly destroyed. In the thin mist of dawn, it looked like the ruins left by a prolonged bombardment. The telegraph poles were twisted and bent, lying across the street. After the strong surge of the earthquake, the street had been buckled into mounds, and huge cracks were running this way and that, which made Yuntian think with horror of the crazy rolling of the ground during the earthquake. Some people were searching the ruins for their families, and someone was shouting. One by one, anonymous dead bodies were laid out in rows on the street. There was no cloth to cover their rigid forms, and their faces were frozen in the expression of the moment when they met Death. Yuntian was more and more worried about Sui Yi's mother and brother. Their home was not far away from here.

The alley where their family lived was called Songzhuli. The houses were all regular bungalows and small courtyard residences, with main streets at both ends of the alley. Their home was at the opposite end of the alley. When Yuntian came to the alley, he felt overwhelmed with joy in a way that surprised him. Most of the houses at the end of this alley, where it joined Luoyang Road, had fallen down, but the other end was fine, not badly damaged at all. It almost seemed as if someone had arranged it that way. Sui Yi's mother's house was at the other end, and that was practically a miracle!

In fact, all catastrophes – whether in warfare, natural or man-made disasters – are full of such coincidences; the unlucky can experience extreme misfortune, while the lucky can be amazingly fortunate.

Fortune had chosen Sui Yi's mother's family. From the outside, it looked as if only the gable of the house had been damaged. Certainly, there was nothing much wrong here. He pushed open the door and Sui Yi's mother and brother were out there in the courtyard. He told them that Sui Yi and their daughter were both well, but he also said: "Our house has been destroyed!"

Sui Yi's mother burst into tears and invited them to come and take shelter with her. She said that as long as everyone was alive and well, they could make do. Right up until the moment Yuntian said goodbye, Sui Yi's mother kept repeating that she had to see Sui Yi and little Yiran right now, today, and she was crying as she spoke. Yuntian promised to bring them round and rode away on his bike.

. . .

On leaving Songzhuli, he cycled around behind the church because the road there was better. Along the way, he saw street after street destroyed by the earthquake, with all sorts of strange and shocking sights. In the row of buildings behind the gymnasium, all the walls along the road had collapsed. Every room from the first floor to the fourth was exposed in broad daylight. The scene in each room could be seen clearly from the road, like sets on the stage.

Behind the church, the humble shanties that abounded in the area where Luo Fu lived had all been utterly destroyed by the convulsions. The collapsed houses lay in ruins, blocking all the narrow roads that ran between them. Yuntian left his bike outside and climbed over mountains upon mountains of debris to make his way over to where he was going. The tragic scenes along the way were unspeakable.

When Yuntian caught sight of Luo Fu, he was horrified. Luo Fu's head was wrapped with a white cloth strip and his waist was encircled by a white sash. When he saw Yuntian, he ran over to him, crying loudly as he hugged him. His house had collapsed, and his parents had both been crushed to death. He'd been quick to get out of the house and into the courtyard, and then the building had crumbled behind him. Death had just been one step behind.

Although Luo Fu was adopted, his parents had treated him like their own son. For someone of deep feeling like Luo Fu, it was unbearable – he would say something and then start crying. When he gradually calmed down, he said to Yuntian: "What on earth did you do to your leg?" It was then that Yuntian realised he himself had been injured in the earthquake, but in the moment of greatest crisis he hadn't even noticed that he was in pain. He told Luo Fu what had happened to him. Luo Fu listened and told him to hurry back to get his wife and child to some place of safety. He had two cousins – actually they were his own older brothers – who would help him with the funeral; in addition, they would have some people coming in from the funeral home over on Guiyang Road. Yuntian saw that among the people standing in the yard were his two brothers. He knew both of them, and went over to say a few words of condolence.

Yuntian announced he was going to go and find Luo Qian. Luo Qian's house had also been wrecked, and half of it was in danger of collapse; who knows whether he'd managed to survive. So they all agreed, Yuntian should try to locate Luo Qian and then take Sui Yi and their daughter round to her mother's house. Then he was to come back and attend the funeral for Luo Fu's parents.

When Yuntian set off, Luo Fu wanted to escort him. Yuntian insisted that he should not do so. When Yuntian clambered through the earthquake-damaged ruins, one foot sinking way down, the other raised on high, he looked back and saw Luo Fu standing far away at the very top of a pile of masonry, with a white cloth strip wrapped around his head, watching him go and wiping away his tears. Yuntian also started to cry.

While he was riding his bike, he got to feel a little hungry. He realised that even though it was now midday, he hadn't had anything to eat, and his wife and child must also be starving. But right now, finding out whether Luo Qian was alive or dead was the most important task ahead of him.

When he arrived at Luo Qian's courtyard, the scene before his eyes was horrifying. The old building in front of Luo Qian's home had completely collapsed in the earthquake. You couldn't see at all that it used to be a building; it looked like a huge pile of wreckage… a barren mountain. The collapsed building had also caused further damage, crushing various trees around it. Luo Qian's hut lay behind this building. It couldn't be seen for the devastation – was it buried underneath? Yuntian was appalled. If the main building was in such a terrible state, he did not see how Luo Qian could possibly have survived.

Two people were standing talking in the yard, both of them residents. They said that at least three residents had died when the building fell in, and there was at least one person buried somewhere underneath, and their family was out right now trying to find someone to save them.

Yuntian stopped listening to them and hurried around the ruins. The first thing he saw was that half of Luo Qian's house had collapsed. In the shock of the moment, he threw his bike aside and ran over, only to see someone sitting on a huge lump of cement and red brick. When the man looked up, it was Luo Qian! Before he could say a word, Luo Qian remarked with a bitter smile: "Aren't we amazing? We've survived even this!"

"Yes, I've just seen Luo Fu too!" Chu Yuntian said.

Unlucky Luo Qian had been fortunate when the earthquake struck. The shockwaves running through the ground had hurled him from his bed to the ground and rolled him to the far side of the room. Just at that moment, the roof at this end had collapsed and hit his bed. He had escaped disaster by a miracle. Who could not thank God for this grace?

When Luo Qian discovered that Yuntian's attic had been destroyed and his wife and child were still waiting for him in the woods outside the building, he told him to go back as quickly as he could. No one needed him more than his wife and child. Luo Qian said that someone had just come from his factory, and on learning of his situation had assured him that someone would arrive at any moment to help him build a temporary shelter. Workers were good at doing that kind of thing. Yuntian and Luo Qian had been friends for more than ten years, but now for the first time he heard that he was employed in a factory, where he had workers as colleagues.

Just as Yuntian got on his bicycle and was about to leave, Luo Qian thought of something and called out to him. He took a handful of money from his pocket and stuffed it into Yuntian's pocket. Before Yuntian could refuse, he shouted: "Go back quickly. They must be starving." He pushed Yuntian hard to get him moving.

Yuntian took out the money from his pocket and found dozens of yuan. This might well be every penny he had. He kept ten yuan and tossed the rest back at Luo Qian before quickly riding away.

Yuntian bought some pancakes on the road and tucked them into his trouser pocket. When he turned onto the road leading to the synagogue, he saw that his home had been damaged beyond recognition. Of the three Western-style small buildings with their red pitched roofs, the middle one had the upper half burned out. Although the fire had been extinguished, it was still belching black smoke. The building on the right was still standing, but the roof was tilting eastward as if it were about to fall. The roof to his house on the left had disappeared, and his attic room had been smashed beyond all repair – his heart sank at the sight.

His wife and child were still waiting for him in a large wooden crate among the trees. They jumped out happily when they saw him. Yuntian was very surprised to see them; their faces, big and small, were black and coated in grime. At first glance, he worried that they were injured, but it turned out that it was just the filth that had fallen from the roof in the earthquake. He hurried back to the yard, took a bucket of water, washed their faces and hands, and then took out the food. He had not imagined them to be so hungry that they just wolfed it all down and smiled at him, as if they'd eaten something far more delicious than anything they normally got at home!

Yuntian asked little Yiran: "Is this better than the Kiessling Restaurant?"

Yiran nodded hard and smiled foolishly, too busy eating to speak.

Subsequently, Yuntian told Sui Yi about what had happened to her mother and younger brother, as well as to Luo Qian and Luo Fu. Sui Yi wept while she listened. Yiran asked her mother: "Are Uncle Luo Qian and Uncle Luo Fu dead?" Sui Yi waved her away and burst into audible sobs.

Yuntian told Sui Yi that the first thing they needed to do was make sure that everyone had something to eat and somewhere to sleep. He had to make sure that she and Yiran were safe. His idea was to send Sui Yi and Yiran to Songzhuli Alley off Luoyang Road – they could stay with her mother and brother. He wouldn't live there himself. Luo Fu had just lost both his parents and he was all by himself; he'd made up his mind that he'd go with Luo Fu to the art college and ask them to arrange some accommodation on site. There was a canteen at the college, so getting something to eat was no problem. At the same time, he could come back regularly and keep an eye on their attic. Now there were so many houses that were open to the four winds, their doors gone, their walls gone – someone had to keep an eye on things and save anything salvageable among their belongings.

Whenever something major happened, Yuntian would decide

what they should do; and Sui Yi trusted his judgement on these matters. That was what they decided.

Yuntian wanted to risk going into the tumbledown building to find some necessities for Sui Yi. She didn't want him to go, but he insisted. When he climbed the stairs leading to the top of the building, he felt a little strange. The stairs were blocked by wooden beams and sheets of corrugated iron, and there were bricks and cement lumps everywhere. How did they get down from the top last night? When he reached the attic, the most shocking thing was that a very strong beam had collapsed right on top of Yiran's little bed, but it hadn't crushed it. It turned out that right before the beam fell, a piece of cement had come down, and so when the beam dropped, it landed right on the cement block. He remembered that during the worst of the shaking, two loud noises sounded right above his head – they must have been made when the beam and cement block fell. The concrete block supported the beam, leaving a safe space for them to survive – that is why he and Yiran were still alive. He felt a cold shudder of fear pass over him. This was a terrifying scene to look back upon.

He did not dare to delay. He knew that some bags were hanging behind the door. He grabbed a large canvas bag and stuffed all sorts of necessities into it – clothes, towels, wallet, handbag, watches, photos, a small ceramic vase, Yiran's rag doll, a book lying on the table and so on. Most things he could not take because they lay under heaps of bricks and rotten wood. When he was about to go out, he caught a glimpse of the calendar on the wall. On the top it said 28 July – the darkest page for the suffering Chinese people. He felt moved and tore it down, tucked it into his pocket and ran out as fast as he could.

When Sui Yi saw everything Yuntian had found in the ruins of their house, she was pleasantly surprised, as if she had never expected to see any of them again. When Yiran saw her rag doll, she held it tightly in her small arms. The doll seemed to represent survival to her, so all her fears and hurts were swept away. This made Yuntian feel that he had really achieved something.

The next step was to take them over to Songzhuli Alley. When they were settled there, Yuntian rushed over to Luo Fu's place. The funeral had to be done immediately because the weather was so very hot that bodies could not be left unburied for long.

The next day, they took the remains of Luo Fu's parents to the funeral home in Beicang. Luo Qian also came for the funeral proceedings. When dressing his parents, Luo Fu carefully placed their favourite items by each body. His mother had her favourite horn comb, which she used every day when combing her hair. The *Ocean of Words* lay next to his father, as thick as a brick in its black binding. Luo Fu whispered to Yuntian in tears: "My father's family had thirty *mu* of land, so when he was young, he was assigned to the petty landlord class. He never got over the terror of it all. He never dared to so much as say a word. He loved reading, but he was afraid that he would get into trouble because of it, so he just read the *Ocean of Words*. He told me that without this book, he wouldn't have survived."

Only then did Yuntian understand the real reason why Luo Fu's father had read the *Ocean of Words* every day for twenty years. A person who only read one book in his entire life; what an amazing event in the history of human reading. When the *Ocean of Words* slid into the crematorium oven with the old man, Yuntian prayed silently that the fire would burn every last vestige of this stupid reading, and that when he got to heaven he could read whatever he liked…

After the funeral for Luo Fu's parents was over, Yuntian rushed back to his small house, climbed up the stairs and saw that now it all looked even worse. There had been another violent aftershock just before dark yesterday, followed by heavy rain all night, and his roofless home was now in an even more dreadful state. What with more bricks smashing down and the pouring rain, pretty much everything had been destroyed. He spent more than half a day trying to rescue something. Little had survived and most of that was damaged. Many of their favourite things, the things associated with their happiest memories, had been smashed, and many paintings had been ruined. Who could understand how Yuntian felt at that moment? Without his paintings, he really was left with nothing!

After the Cultural Revolution had robbed them of everything they owned, he and Sui Yi had carefully constructed this little asylum from scratch, one thing at a time, but now it too was gone, and they had lost everything once again. When he counted it up, exactly ten years separated these two terrible events.

Was this their fate? Was it destiny?

Yuntian's heart had become very dark. He seemed to have understood what fate is. Fate is something that happens to you, and you can't prevent it. That was true for him, and also for Luo Qian. Why was this not true for everyone? Why did some people escape? All this had nothing to do with a person's status or wealth, because there would always be a higher power that decided things for you. Whether you accept your fate or fight against it, you cannot stop it, because it was ordained.

However, even though people know in their hearts that they cannot go against the will of heaven, and that they will fail whatever they do, they will still struggle, resist and fight back. Why? Is this also a basic instinct for living creatures?

The art college treated Yuntian and Luo Fu pretty well. Huge disasters always arouse the best in normally numb human nature. The college arranged for Luo Fu to live in the staff dormitory, while Yuntian took a night shift and slept at the college too. Eating and sleeping there were not a problem. There were beds and bedding in the duty room, so he hardly counted as homeless, and he was free to do whatever he wanted. Yuntian was very pleased with these arrangements. Over the next few days, he tried to locate his friends and see if anyone wanted his help. Only two of them were beyond assistance.

One was Mr Xu from Xinhua Middle School. During the earthquake, Mr Xu got up in a hurry, but he found it impossible to stand firm, so he fell and broke his hip; now he was confined to bed. Usually, he was surrounded by crowds of his former students, but right now nobody had the time or energy to help him. There was no way to set the bone properly either, so he was lying in bed in agony, just waiting. The other was Su Yousheng, the writer at the Yu Opera Troupe. Old Su's one-hundred-year-old house was built like a rock; nothing and nobody had been injured in the earthquake. But he said something that made Yuntian feel as if the sky had fallen in! The nearly two thousand books he had in his collection were in fact stored at the home of a friend of good origin, but in the earthquake, the place was destroyed and the whole family had been crushed to death – not one was lucky enough to survive. Old Su only found this out when he went to visit his friend some ten days later. He was told that the bodies had been pulled from the rubble and cremated, and a whole heap of rubbishy books had gone to the dump. A wealth of classics of human civilisation had been destroyed!

Old Su, who always used to be so chatty and cheerful, was now silent.

Chu Yuntian would never again go to Zhishi Street to borrow or return books, nor would Old Su ever talk and laugh again in the empty room on the second floor of his building.

Life can change in an instant, and things will never go back to being the way they used to be.

Yuntian and Luo Fu helped Luo Qian's colleagues to rebuild his house. Luo Qian's colleagues were a very straightforward and plain-speaking bunch. In their eyes, Luo Qian had lost a hovel, and they were building him a nice home in exchange. With all the work they put into it, the place was a lot prettier than it had been before. However, Yuntian felt that it lacked the atmosphere of the former home.

More than two hundred and forty thousand people died in Tangshan, the epicentre of that great earthquake. Although Tianjin was more than two hundred miles away, due to its dense population and the number of old houses, more than ten thousand of its residents were killed, and the millions who survived were left traumatised. No matter whether their houses were well-built or not, no one dared to sleep at home, and they all constructed earthquake-proof huts so they could stay outdoors. These low and crude shanties were cram packed into all the open-air spaces in the city: school playgrounds, parks, factory yards, the streets themselves. In such a situation, who would care whether Luo Qian's house was festooned with quotations from Chairman Mao or his forbidden paintings? The walls of his new house were plastered afresh and dazzlingly white. He couldn't stand it. He covered the white walls with a layer of grey, so the room became quieter. The hand-painted window on the front wall was no longer necessary – without him being aware of it, his life had changed. That was how everyone felt at that time. After a series of terrible upheavals, the future was just a vast, empty blank. No one knew what they should be drawing on it.

That day, a massive demonstration was held in the streets, as they marched to "Smash the Gang of Four". Chu Yuntian had never cared much about politics. But on that day, he walked along with the rest of the marchers and joined in loudly and sincerely when they shouted their slogans. Did any of this really matter to him?

CHAPTER 14

Chu Yuntian now had a feeling of disillusionment that he had never experienced before. Even at the beginning of the Cultural Revolution ten years ago, when he and Sui Yi had just been married for nine months and they got thrown out of his father's old house in Mu'nan Road to live in an attic, he'd never had this sense of let-down, even though at that time they'd been alone, empty-handed and lost all that they possessed. Now, a decade later, he'd been 'thrown out' by the earthquake all over again. What was worse than being homeless was that his paintings had been destroyed! What made him feel so desperate was that the day after the earthquake, after the funeral for Luo Fu's parents, he climbed up the badly damaged building again to try to rescue anything that had survived the disaster. Thanks to a strong aftershock, he found that his home had vanished. The sloping roof was gone. He stood in the room and there was only the blue sky and white clouds above him. Only two or three long wooden columns pointed up at the sky like masts. Rainwater and dust had mixed together to form a filthy paste that besmirched everything. The cabinet he used for storing paintings in one corner of the room had been smashed into a pile of broken wood chippings, and scrolls had been reduced to pulp by the pouring rain. From surviving fragments, he could still identify which ones had been his favourite paintings. All gone! All the history of his development as an artist, every jewel he had produced in the past ten years, and every footprint in his journey of painful exploration had come to nought! He had nothing left, and he himself was nothing!

In the painting classes at the college, there were times when he should have been demonstrating for the students, but when he picked up the brush he suddenly felt that he couldn't paint. He had no interest any more in painting. He had never been tired of art before, but now he could not summon the slightest interest in it.

His students were worried because they could see he was struggling. They had all worked for years in various factories and they knew how hard life could be, but they thought that their teacher's misery was because he'd lost everything to the earthquake – they simply could not understand his emotions. The female students quietly gave him towels, clothes, food stamps and ration tickets for cloth, while the male students volunteered to help him rebuild his home. However, while the material damage could be made good, it proved impossible to restore the tenor of his mind.

Within a few weeks of the earthquake, every district in the city began to make things safe; they demolished crumbling buildings, took down dangerous walls and removed debris. At that time, all housing belonged to the state. Everything was arranged and allocated by the state. Therefore, when a house fell down, it was naturally up to the state to repair it. Various housing management departments installed tie rods to strengthen the walls of old houses and stepped up the restoration and reconstruction of damaged buildings. Yuntian's students worked very hard; in the space of just ten days, they'd cleared all the wreckage from the earthquake out of his house. Among the heaps of broken bricks and tiles, if some small, intact object was unearthed, it gave him a burst of joy. This feeling of wonderment was very much the same sensation as making an archaeological discovery. Later, he called these remnants of destruction "excavated cultural relics".

One of the biggest gains was that, among a heap of columns, a student found the painting that he originally had hanging on the wall. The three dark red pitched roofs that you could see in the painting were gone; this surviving painting represented a part of his life, a witness and memorial to the history of the city. This small discovery gave him no small comfort.

The students helped him pack and transport the few things he had left to the college for temporary storage. At the same time, they stacked the old wooden columns from the attic in the corridor of the second floor. When the building was restored, they could put them right back where they had been to support the roof. He thought that Sui Yi had always loved those wooden pillars so much; he didn't want to make her feel that she had lost too many things.

However, when he cleaned out the attic, removing the unstable walls and broken corrugated iron sheeting, he realised that the attic would never be repaired. The roof and walls were wrecked, and only the floor was left intact. In fact, this floor was also the roof of the second floor. Standing on the bare boards, he began to worry that the housing management department would simply not bother to rebuild his house. Shortly afterwards, he heard the disturbing news that the housing management department had decided to "shave down" the building. That is, they would keep the first and second floors, and a layer of cement would be slapped on top of the second floor to create a flat roof. Now, he really was homeless!

He had to summon up all his reserves of strength to save his little attic. Moreover, he didn't want the news to get back to Sui Yi, lest she become anxious. He had a lot of friends, and after asking around, a young man named Guo Cong who used to listen to his stories informed him that it was a certain administrator named Li who held the power of life and death over his attic. This man always had a smile plastered across his face, but he was as hard as nails underneath; asking him for help would not be easy. His great weakness was an addiction to nicotine. As long as he was plied with good cigarettes, it was always possible to find room to manoeuvre. He had been born with one sightless eye, so everyone called him One-Eyed Li.

Chu Yuntian went to find One-Eyed Li. Mr Li smiled and said: "I knew you'd be coming to find me. Your house was destroyed down to the last brick – how can it be repaired? What you want isn't for us to repair your house… you want the state to build you a whole new place to live. Do you really think that's acceptable?" His very first words left no room for compromise.

Chu Yuntian said: "You can't want me to become homeless,

surely? If you are going to leave me with nowhere to live, you have to assign me another house."

"How many buildings were destroyed in the earthquake?" Mr Li demanded. "You aren't the only homeless person round here – I've got at least a hundred on my hands."

Chu Yuntian took out a cigarette. At that time there were three brands of cigarettes on the market, each of different quality. The inferior brand was called 'Battle', the medium one was called 'Forever Red' and the superior one was 'Evergrande'. Yuntian had specially bought some Evergrande, and Mr Li's eyes lit up upon seeing them. Yuntian took out two, gave Mr Li one and stuffed the other in his own mouth. He lit Mr Li's cigarette and his own. He didn't smoke, so he choked on the first puff and immediately started coughing. Mr Li smiled and said: "If you aren't used to it, you can give them all to me."

Chu Yuntian was a simple and straightforward man, lacking in guile. He stretched out his hand and gave Mr Li the full pack of Evergrande cigarettes. Seeing how generous the young man was being, Mr Li was glad to make his acquaintance.

From this day on, Yuntian went to find Mr Li almost every day. He was a very busy man, but Yuntian would search all over for him, begging him for help, wearing him down. The key was keeping him supplied with cigarettes. Every single time One-Eyed Li got a pack of Evergrande cigarettes from Yuntian, and each pack cost three *jiao*. Most people simply couldn't afford to smoke that brand every day. Sui Yi noticed this with some surprise: why did Yuntian always seem to be so short of money?

One day, One-Eyed Li finally said to Yuntian: "I can see you are being honest – you need somewhere to live. I've talked to my superiors on your behalf, and they've agreed. They'll build a simple house for you up on top of the second floor."

Chu Yuntian almost kowtowed to him. He hurried to the nearby grocery store, emptied his pockets and bought him another pack of Evergrande cigarettes. Then he ran to Songzhuli Alley, hugged Sui Yi and Yiran, and shouted: "We've got a house."

That evening, Yuntian rushed round to Luo Qian's house and told his friends about his brilliant achievements over the past month. He was not expecting that Luo Qian would ask him: "Do you know what 'a simple house' is?"

Yuntian didn't understand.

Luo Qian explained: "The walls on all four sides are a single layer of bricks thick, and on top you get a roof of wooden planks. No plaster, no tiles – they'll just put a single layer of tar paper down. It'll be a temporary shed, cold in winter and hot in summer. Is that what you want?"

"If I don't agree, I'll be homeless," Yuntian said.

Luo Qian knew that Yuntian was in no position to argue. He said: "Don't worry, I'll help you keep an eye on the construction work."

Before the beginning of winter, Yuntian's castle in the air had finally reappeared, but it was altered beyond recognition. The old crimson roof was gone, and in its place was a crude, flat-topped brick house; when looking up from below, you could hardly see it. And not only his building, but the scenery of the whole area had completely changed. The original three small buildings adjacent to each other had been profoundly altered. The middle one caught fire in the earthquake and had to be knocked down. The one on the right, like his own, had also lost its roof and been turned into a flat-topped building. In fact, this had always been part of the plan for 'risk reduction' in the wake of the earthquake. However, One-Eyed Li made the most of this opportunity to extract ten or twenty packs of Evergrande cigarettes from him, and would even have taken his bike, but fortunately he was quick-witted enough to say that his family needed the money and therefore he'd had to sell it. In fact, he temporarily hid it over at Luo Qian's house to keep it in his own hands. In his dealings with One-Eyed Li, there were both gains and losses. His gains included a better understanding of how cunning other people could be – he learned some practical survival skills that he'd been lacking in the past. Among the losses must be counted the fact that he'd picked up the bad habit of smoking. Of course, the other reason for smoking lay in the heavy pressure he was under and the many troubles that afflicted him during this period.

That day, he took Sui Yi and Yiran to see their new home. It wasn't cold, so the windows were open. Yiran rushed in and ran about, jumping for joy. Sui Yi's face clearly showed her disappointment. This was no longer the deep, simple and unique cave it had been in the past. She felt it looked like a ward in her hospital, pale and boring. Chu Yuntian explained to her that the wooden columns they'd stacked in the corridor on the second floor when cleaning up the earthquake wreckage had been taken away by the housing management department for use as building materials. All the corrugated iron sheeting on the original roof had been smashed in the earthquake. The sheeting had been imported from Germany a hundred years ago, and there was no way to replace it. The skylight had been removed because it would be unsafe in a flat roof. But whatever he said, without the original columns, sloping roof and skylight, all poetry had been driven away from this place by utilitarianism.

Chu Yuntian kept explaining this to Sui Yi, over and over again. She came to understand that he was trying to make himself accept the reality before them and alleviate the heavy damage inflicted upon her by the earthquake. She looked up at Yuntian. His tired face looked a little rough… even a little older. When had he developed those pouches below his eyes? He was still a very young man, so how could he have aged all at once? She realised that for the past six months, he'd been under massive pressure with resolving not only the issue of the destruction of their home but also the difficulties of many other people as well. She remembered something he had said: "Women are the palm of the hand and men are the back of the hand. The back of the hand is born to protect the palm."

She felt a warmth flooding through her heart. She hugged her tall husband and said: "I'm very happy."

A new life began for them.

Thanks to the help of his friends and students, there was no shortage of daily necessities in their little hut. But Yuntian knew that Sui Yi needed more.

Sui Yi didn't need luxury, but she had to be surrounded by beauty and things that made her feel alive. She collected some old gauze strips at the hospital, dyed them into stripes of light blue, pink, pale green, grey, pale yellow and light brown with Yuntian's painting materials, and then sewed them into a gauze curtain and hung them up in the window. In this way, the desire to rebuild their lives came back to her again. At this time, they were both just a little over thirty.

Yiran still missed her corner behind the column. Yuntian used the bracing in their house to create a tent around her small bed made from canvas. Children like to keep their secrets hidden. She finally had her own house-within-a-house which she loved very much. Yuntian also found this inspirational. He set up a five-foot-high bookcase in one corner, and two shelves were nailed to the wall to hold more books, as well as tasteful works of art and framed photos. He now also had his own space. Sui Yi said that since there were three blank walls, there was one wall for each of them, by which she meant the Three Musketeers. She went in person to ask Luo Qian and Luo Fu for their paintings. Luo Fu gave her a magnificent landscape oil painting of great rivers and forest-covered mountains. She liked it very much. Luo Qian's painting was in his unique style: a wet, dark alley after the rain, with white flowers fallen to the ground, a little melancholy – and she liked that even better.

Hanging on the front wall was the old painting Yuntian had 'unearthed' from the ruins after the earthquake; that is, the sketch he painted when he sat on the riverbank opposite the Qiangzi Canal when he had just moved in. Beyond the bend in the peaceful waters and the trees, three old red rooftops could be espied. This poetic sight was no longer to be seen, and the red roofs would henceforth only be a memory. The Qiangzi Canal had now been filled in, and the willow trees along its bank cut down so that it could be used as a road, with cars and trucks blasting up and down it all day every day. Was this painting not more than just a poetic commemoration of the past? Was it not a sad memory, recording a history of helplessness?

Sui Yi said that she found a sense of satisfaction and a sense of security in these three paintings.

However, the Three Musketeers now had less time to meet than before.

Luo Fu's art college was in a state of uproar. With the end of the Cultural Revolution, the art world was thrown into chaos. After so many years of restraint, people's brains had atrophied; now that they were required to think again, they couldn't do it. The change in policy brought some old painters back from local farms just in time for the great earthquake, which traumatised them all over again. Luo Fu took Yuntian to meet Tang Sanjian, an old painter who had worked on a farm for seven years. Mr Tang had been the director of the Department of Traditional Chinese Painting at the college before the Cultural Revolution. After seven years on the farm, coming back was almost like being born again. When Yuntian visited him, they sat together for a long time, but no matter what Yuntian said to him, he just replied: "OK." Now, Mr Tang was only prepared to paint plum blossoms, and more than half of his paintings were entitled 'Smiling Amid the Thorns'. Yuntian didn't know whether to laugh or cry. He felt constrained and bored, and eventually respectfully said goodbye.

Luo Qian also found himself in trouble. After the earthquake destroyed the main building out in front, the mountain of rubble had to be removed. But once it was taken away, Luo Qian's cabin was exposed to anyone passing by. What happened next was even more annoying. The cleared space and the original courtyard together formed a small plaza, which drew many people to build temporary buildings and earthquake shelters there. More and more constructions were put up until eventually they ended up door-to-door with Luo Qian's house. Luo Qian's feeling of being hidden away disappeared; after work, he no longer wanted to go home.

Now if the three of them wanted to get together, they would go to the forest near the back entrance to Shuishang Park out in the western suburbs of the city. This place was originally discovered by Yuntian and Luo Qian. At the beginning of the Cultural Revolution, they wanted to meet and talk, so they'd intended to go to the park. However, at that time, parks were held to be places where the exploitative classes enjoyed themselves, and so they were all closed. They found this deserted place just outside the back entrance to the park. There was a large forest of poplars here, and beyond lay beds of wild reeds, spreading as far as the eye could see, bringing a delightful freshness to the air. The most pleasant thing was the thick grass growing in the forest, like a fragrant green blanket. Being far away from other people made this place safe. They lay on the grass and talked, relaxed, enjoying the freedom.

They used to come here every autumn. Now it became their 'salon' to replace the loss of Luo Qian's house.

The Three Musketeers spread out and lay on their backs.

"A few years ago, we were regulated to death and didn't have any freedom to choose the subject of our paintings," Luo Fu said. "Now, no one cares, but I don't know what to draw."

Chu Yuntian, with his head resting on the grass, joked: "It seems that you are domesticated, not wild. If people don't feed you, you don't know what to eat." He was looking up at the shining white clouds moving slowly in the gap between the trees above as he said this.

Luo Qian, lying off to one side, seemed to be asleep, but now he spoke up: "You'd better stop doing those duty paintings in the future, and save your time and energy for your own work." What he said was directed at Luo Fu.

"There's no such thing as a duty painting any more." Luo Fu turned over and sat up. "I'm in a different position from you – because I was working for the college, I had to paint whatever was allocated to me. But even when I was working on those duty paintings, I was still thinking about my own work."

"That's good," Luo Qian said. "You have to stick to your artistic vision, no matter how difficult that is."

"It's not difficult to paint your own paintings, but who will admire them?" Luo Fu said.

"Is it necessary for other people to admire them?" Luo Qian asked. "Art is a matter of your own spirit and ideals. One's own recognition is enough."

Luo Fu felt a little confused. Luo Qian's words were indisputably true, but in real life they were illusory and pointless. He looked at the silent Yuntian and said: "Have you always painted to your own artistic vision?"

Unexpectedly, Chu Yuntian said: "I don't know what is the matter with me… I can't paint any more." His eyes were indeed a little confused when he looked up at the tree canopy and clouds above.

"Why?" Luo Fu asked him.

Yuntian didn't answer.

Luo Fu asked Luo Qian: "What do you think the problem is?"

"Only he can find the reason. It's not necessarily a bad thing if he can't paint. Maybe he's coming up to a point where he has to choose, or maybe the choice hasn't appeared yet."

Luo Qian's words aroused some indistinct feelings in Chu Yuntian's heart. Yuntian felt that he had to take up the conversation and said: "I feel now very much like I did at the moment when the earthquake stopped shaking. In that instant, everything was silent and confused. What should we do? But just then, the survivors all started to scream."

"I've heard that big changes are on the way," Luo Fu said.

Luo Qian said: "Whatever changes, we will remain the same."

Chu Yuntian said: "I'm afraid it will be hard for us to remain unchanged."

They each had their own reasons for saying this.

Afterwards, they fell silent, and each pondered their own position.

The breeze passing through the poplar forest was a marvellous sight. The tops of poplar leaves are waxy, so when the sun shines, they are dazzlingly bright. When the wind blows, the thousands of poplar leaves rustle like countless little clapping, glossy green hands. Only the applause of poplar leaves can make such a wonderfully pleasant sound. In a slight breeze, it is like the boundless earth whispering. In a gale, it is like the roar of the tide. They were intoxicated by the sound of the leaves.

"Are you watching the movement of the leaves?" Luo Fu asked Yuntian.

He said: "I've been looking at the clouds moving across the sky through the branches of the trees."

"Are you thinking about how to paint the clouds?"

"I don't need to paint them. The wind is like a Rodin in the sky, sculpting the clouds afresh every day."

"That's beautiful." Luo Qian, lying on the grass, suddenly raised his head and said to Yuntian with a smile: "I like the way you are now. Don't change."

CHAPTER 15

As the river thawed, all the boats began to move. They sailed around, but they didn't know where to go. When the cage was opened, all the birds were stunned. Looking at the vast, empty and boundless sky outside, where should they fly? Horses having slipped the bridle, run away as fast as you can, but where are you going?

Such was the feeling of the times; this was something that everyone experienced in the late 1970s.

They were just three young people with artistic dreams among the millions that lived in this city. They had no social capital, and no one knew who the hell they were. Facing an unknown future, what did they want to do? What was important and what was not?

Luo Qian always seemed to live in his own world, while Luo Fu paid more attention to the changes in society. Compared with Luo Qian and Luo Fu, Yuntian was the more worried, concerned and yet hopeful about the trends in this unstable social situation. This was because he was interested in literature, and literature is directly connected with society and cannot be separated from thought.

Sometimes life just repeats, sometimes life changes every day. Now they saw the latter. Yesterday is different from the day before yesterday, and today is different from yesterday. Their thinking couldn't keep up with the changes right before their eyes.

The biggest change for Yuntian was that the policy of restoring people to their original positions began. His father had already returned from Jiangxi cadre school. To begin with, he was living in his work unit's dormitory, with four people crowded into one small room. The other three men smoked, and his father hated smoking. He wanted to take his father away from the reeking, choking smoke to his own home, but he refused to live in the same place as his son and daughter-in-law. Later, there was a gratifying hope that his family's house on Mu'nan Road would be returned to them. His father was a famous cardiologist, whose skills were in high demand, so restoring him to his old position was a matter of priority. There was some talk that Sui Yi's house would also be returned to the family, but her father had passed away, and various other households had moved into the place in recent years. These people were being very troublesome: either they were refusing to move, or they were demanding a huge amount of money to go. The whole thing was a nightmare. At that time, they were used to being submissive and did not dare to fight hard. They had to wait. Hope is better than hopelessness.

Then one day, Luo Fu suddenly mentioned something to Yuntian.

He said Yufei had come to Tianjin after the earthquake. Her house by the Hai River was damaged, so she came to collect her mother and take her to live in Beijing. She didn't come to see Luo Fu, but she'd phoned him. Luo Fu had told her about what had happened to him, Yuntian and Luo Qian during the disaster. She said time was too tight to be able to see any of them. She'd asked Luo Fu to say hello to Yuntian and Luo Qian but hadn't said anything else. At that time, Luo Fu had just lost his parents and was homeless, so he'd forgotten her simple message.

Yuntian heard this unmoved. After such a terrible disaster in which so many people had died, and with the changing of the times, the past was naturally over. Life is made up of one damned thing after another.

Over the past six months, Yuntian had been teaching a technical course in Chinese painting to the students at the college. In his view, the techniques of landscape painting are the most complex in traditional Chinese painting. Therefore, starting from landscape painting, he divided the technical side into three different topic areas: trees, stones and water. In painting trees, you had to master linear strokes; in painting stones, you had to master pointillism; and in painting water, you had to learn to control your brush and lay down precise washes. Of all of them, painting water is the most difficult, because water is dynamic, flowing and ever-changing. At first, he took his students to sketch on both sides of the Hai River, but it was very upsetting for him to walk from the Sancha Estuary to Junliang because he felt that the great waterway there – created by the gathering of many rivers on the North China Plain – had lost its former vitality. There was little water there now, and it ran slowly, so it was not really appropriate as a subject for art. Yuntian dragged some funding out of the college and took his students to Shanxi and Shandong to draw the Yellow River. He didn't know why, but when he stood by the Yellow River, he was shocked and moved by it, so he would start shouting.

The Yellow River really does come crashing down, with a roar like ten thousand horses at full gallop. It breaks through the clouds and mist, carries thunder and lightning in its wake, raising a sharp, cold wind like a blade, and spraying splashing foam high into the sky. Torrents, huge waves, dangerous sandbanks, rocks, whirlpools… What surprised and puzzled him the most was that there was a mysterious, violent, rebellious and dangerous quality hidden within it. In the rolling of the waves, the deafening roar and the relentless struggle, he seemed to see some black holes of disaster, scenes of suffering, heavy repressions and overburdening. He could hear a voice calling. Was it a cry of despair, a plea for help or a bellow of rage?

Looking around, there was a desolate vista, one of wild mountains and chaotic clouds.

He thought, isn't the Yellow River our mother river? Why do you always think of the difficult history of our nation when you see her? Why isn't the Mississippi like this? Or the Volga? Or indeed the Danube, Rhine or Thames? Does this suffering come from herself, or is it imposed by our terrible history? He began to project all the confused feelings he had about the life he'd experienced onto the waters. He suddenly found a passionate desire to paint the river!

The third day after their return to the college was a Sunday. The classrooms were all empty. He jammed together four student tables and covered them with an eight-foot length of rice paper. He seemed to have no design prepared, but he couldn't wait to place his long-handled brush, dipped in ink, against the surface of the paper. With a flick of his wrist, an emotion surging in his heart was released. A huge, towering wave rose up in the river, followed by layer upon layer of ink upon paper, bursting wave upon wave from his mind. The bitterness of social conflict, the struggle to survive, the sudden advent of disaster, the abyss of suffering, the helplessness of circumstances, and the lonely, noble persistence of his heart were all integrated into the form and soul of the river.

When painting, Yuntian would completely forget himself, even forgetting that he was painting. In the empty room, he moved freely, swaying about. As he swayed, the handle of his brush trembled in excitement and kept banging against the water bowl, and the splashing ink sprayed across his clothes and face.

When he finished painting the lofty, spiritual feelings he'd resolutely held to in his heart, he saw that far off in the distance in the river he'd created there was a blurred, brilliant and rippling play of light. He was fascinated by this. He was amazed at himself.

He seemed to have given rise to a magical realm that had never existed in his work before. He suddenly merged with the invisible, grand and rapidly surging social tide behind him.

It felt sublime.

Real artistic creation is sublime; every single time.

This was a magical qualitative change, which happened entirely by chance. Every artist looks forward to achieving such a level. At the same time, an era of unprecedented change was quietly approaching.

PART TWO

中

LIGHTNING PIERCES THE BLACK CLOUDS:
  LET MY SONG NO LONGER BE
  IMPRISONED WITHIN MY HEART!

CHAPTER 1

Two years later, Yuntian and his family moved back to their old house in Mu'nan Road to live with his father. Since the house faced north, the garden was right at the back. This was an English-style house, built in the 1930s, and like other buildings in the Five Avenues district of the city, it was in a detached row running east to west. In the 1940s, most of the buildings had been constructed in the simple eclectic style then fashionable in the West. There weren't many classical buildings like the one Yuntian's family lived in. It had a high, expansive, dark grey pitched roof, along with wrought-iron railings and heavy stone foundations. A Virginia creeper, covered in small leaves, grew all over the walls. In the summer it was green, in the autumn a fiery red, while in between those two seasons it was mottled and blotched: very painterly! The architect who designed this building was probably a foreigner; as to who the original owner was, nobody seemed to know.

Yuntian's father bought this place in 1943. At that time, the Five Avenues district was flourishing as never before. Prominent figures both in and out of favour, powerful people hoping to get even richer, and all kinds of talented people interested in Westernisation flocked there. Tianjin guarded the capital – it was right at the forefront of contact between China and the West. This was a place where you could enjoy the comforts and conveniences of Western-style living in a way that was still unimaginable in most parts of

China – hot and cold running water, telephones and electric lights, central heating in the winter – it was like being transported into paradise. With all the rich and powerful people who flocked there, they would need good doctors. Yuntian and Sui Yi's fathers had both moved to Tianjin in the special circumstances that then prevailed. In those days, half the doctors of the Five Avenues district lived right there on Mu'nan Road, and most of them were like Yuntian's father, graduates of the American-backed Peking Union Medical College: that was one of the first Western hospitals in China. Those medical students would remain famous right through to the 1980s; really fine doctors one and all. Although Sui Yi's father wasn't a graduate of the Peking Union, he'd studied abroad in England, was a specialist ophthalmologist, and he too was a top-rate doctor. The two families were close, they often got together, and so Yuntian and Sui Yi had played with one another as very young children.

Yuntian had grown up in this house, and here he'd lived with Sui Yi when they first got married. At that time, his mother was still alive, but he was an only child, so after he married there'd still only been four people living there; they'd had a lot of space to spread out. There were three rooms on the first floor: a living room, study and dining room, with bedrooms on the second floor. Yuntian and his wife hadn't occupied the second floor, since they were living in quarters on the mezzanine where a separate bathroom was located right next to the bedroom. This had been a guest suite originally. Living separately from one another, they didn't impact each other.

Sui Yi often visited the house as a child, and later she lived there. She liked the atmosphere, the peace and quiet. People didn't speak loudly, and occasionally there was the sound of music. Yuntian's father and Sui Yi both worked in the hospital, so occasionally there was a slight smell of boric acid at home, something that did not happen in ordinary families. The smell reminded her that she had come home.

Ten years ago, they'd lost everything in the Cultural Revolution, and now in an unbelievable moment, it had been returned to them. On the first occasion that Yuntian returned, the house was filthy and full of rubbish. Standing in the middle of the room, he burst into tears. He thought of his mother, who had died the year his father went to Jiangxi cadre school. His mother had loved the old house more than any of them, but in the end she would never be returning.

After they all moved back, his father said that he was too old to want to climb the stairs. He asked Yuntian, his wife and child to use the bedrooms on the second floor while he took up residence in his study on the first floor. Only Sui Yi could guess the reason for his decision. If her father-in-law had returned to his old rooms, he would be constantly reminded of the past, remembering his late wife, stirring up the pain hidden at the bottom of his heart. Therefore, Sui Yi paid special attention to making sure her father-in-law was looked after. Every time Yuntian's mother's birthday or the anniversary of her death came around, she would try to comfort her father-in-law in various ways. She was a cautious and practical woman who could help people out with the minimum of fuss. She was also thoughtful and kind, so that her father-in-law could be cheered in a way he'd never expected. Now, with the addition of clever and sensible little Yiran bouncing around, Yuntian's father said that if his life were to end now, he could die truly happy.

That made Yuntian and Sui Yi demand that he knock on wood, to take back this unlucky remark. That evening, they fined him by making him drink half a glass of red wine at dinner. Father drank the wine and said with a smile that he took back these words he shouldn't have said – nevertheless he had a heart attack only one month later and died shortly afterwards. Yuntian's father had been in good health; why should he have a sudden heart attack? Later, they discovered that he laboured too hard at the Jiangxi cadre school. He'd had two heart attacks there, but with prompt treatment he'd survived. He had not allowed the people at his work unit to inform his family. In that era of suffering, no one wanted to put their burdens on the backs of their loved ones. Sui Yi wondered whether her father-in-law's unlucky words that day might have been a premonition about his body. If he'd told them the truth, she would have paid more attention to him. He was a cardiologist and should have had a good understanding of his own person.

Now, the house felt too big and desolate.

When the sunlight passed through the tall fir trees in the courtyard, it turned into patches of light and shadow. It entered the window and refracted through the house. It was very beautiful and quiet. She appreciated the truth of one of Yuntian's sayings: Light brings architecture to life. Light can refer to brightness or darkness, to clarity or haziness – all these qualities lie within its compass. When she was still living in the wooden attic room over by the Qiangzi Canal, she had clearly felt that the sun was a living thing. It came walking through the house once a day, showing off its beauty and charm, and then it would depart, just like the late owners of this house – her gentle father-in-law and her kind mother-in-law. Who would now ensure that this empty old house would continue to have the vitality, mellowness and joy that it had always possessed?

She was completely unprepared – the old house entered the era of Chu Yuntian. What era would this be?

Yuntian was at work on a large painting in his studio, but Sui Yi didn't know that this would transform their lives. Was he aware at some subconscious level that society was just about to change? With his sensitivity, his inexplicable passion and his own artistic impulses, he painted something that drew on his deepest feelings.

Yuntian once again was thinking of the Yellow River – the mother river. No other natural feature had such a profound symbolic significance for the country. But he did not paint the Yellow River as he had a few years ago, the rough waters reflecting profound suffering. Then his brush was stiff and dignified, and his ink murky and sticky. This time, he painted the thawing of the ice and the sudden rush of water. His brushwork was filled with a sense of relief and excitement! He showed how amid the boundless snow, the frozen river suddenly cracked, and there was a strong nascent force beneath the solid ice, magnificent and irresistible. Then, with a deafening roar, the cold black waves forced their way through the vast expanse of hard ice, surging forward. The river had thawed, spring was coming, and the world would soon be new.

For the ten days or more that Yuntian was working on this painting, Sui Yi didn't enter his studio. She did not want to interrupt his concentration and disturb his state of mind. When he finished, he called her into the studio to look at it, and then she went in. Facing this huge new work, she was so stunned that she didn't speak for a long time. She understood that his paintings no longer expressed his feelings in the same way as the works of the ancient literati, nor were they just landscapes or scenic views. He expressed the common aspirations of the people of that era through his paintings.

She was proud of Yuntian, but she didn't express her feelings. She loved him very much, but she'd never told him so.

When the painting was sent to Beijing for a nationwide art exhibition, it became one of the stars of the show. He'd encapsulated the way that society was thawing, and people were hungering for something new. Yuntian was now a darling of the art world; what is more, his reputation transcended the art world, and he became known to the man in the street. His painting was originally called 'February', but no one called it by its proper name any more. They all called it 'The Thaw'. In the beginning, he'd also wanted to call it by that name, but because of the prior publication of the much-criticised novel *The Thaw* by the Soviet writer Ilya Ehrenburg, he'd called it 'February'. Now, no one cared about those things; society was changing rapidly, and the relentless criticism that had been fashionable throughout the Cultural Revolution had been put aside. If it was called 'The Thaw', then let it be so. The major newspapers went a bit too far in their enthusiasm, saying that he had "opened the door to a new era with his brush" and "transformed Chinese painting in an unprecedented way".

Chu Yuntian felt a bit confused.

For quite a while afterwards, Yuntian spent more time in Beijing than in Tianjin. Various specialist work units asked him to give seminars, universities invited him to give speeches, and the media scrambled to interview him. He was not afraid of the exposure, because he was well-prepared and could think on his feet. Sui Yi smiled and said that all the skills he had learned when telling stories to younger people could now be pressed into service. The better he spoke, the more people wanted to hear him, and the more people came to invite him. During this period, as soon as he set foot back in Tianjin, a group of admirers would come out there to track him down. For the first time, he understood what it was like for celebrities who have nowhere to hide. He felt like a rabbit running on the grassland, hunted by a flock of eagles.

However, he still didn't understand that what society needs of you is not the same as what you need. Society will shape you according to its needs. The worker's institute that employed him had no ties to bind him now that he was famous, and there were plenty of specialist art departments trying to recruit him in the hope that, by bringing him onboard, they would become better known themselves. Various art colleges wanted him to teach. But he'd been at the art college for a while now and didn't like the complexity of interpersonal relationships in units that attach great importance to professional titles and positions. The Municipal Federation of Literature and Art also tried to recruit him, and he talked with them, only to discover that these people were far too utilitarian, which was out of step with his personal style. Later on, the city set up an Academy of Fine Arts and asked him to be a 'resident painter'. This he agreed to do since he only had to go to meetings once a week. The Academy didn't have an associated building, so the artists would paint at home during the week – and they only had to provide two paintings of "no less than four square feet of paper" to the academy every month to retain their positions. This gave him a great deal more freedom. He thought that in a socialist society, people can't survive without work units – a person without a work unit is a complete weirdo. Therefore, he transferred his affiliation from the Bureau of Light Industry to the Academy of Fine Arts. But by this time, nobody could care less what unit the famous Chu Yuntian was affiliated with. What they most wanted to know was what amazing thing he would do next.

He soon tasted the wilder side of modern times.

Everything became the focus of media scrutiny: his paintings, the story behind them, his family, why he'd named his daughter Yiran, his hobbies, his old house that seemed to have been transported from somewhere in Europe, his childhood, what he hated most, his views on the model operas, the theme of his next painting, whether he wanted to establish his own painting school, his personal motto, his secret for success… and so on and so forth. He had never been much interested in himself.

One day, a refined-looking middle-aged woman came to visit him and asked him if he was interested in writing poetry. This woman was the editor of a literary publishing house. Her name was

Cao Ying. Chu Yuntian said that he had written many old-style poems, but most of them were inscriptions on his paintings. He preferred writing prose poems, and he showed her some. Some had been written to Yufei. Unexpectedly, after reading a few pages, the woman clapped her hands in delight and cried: "Some of these are every bit as good as anything written by Gibran or Tagore, I dare say. You are a poet! Otherwise, you wouldn't be able to paint so well. Do you write much?" She seemed to have discovered a literary genius.

Yuntian said that he had a whole lot of manuscripts – some poems and some essays. There were loads of them, but they were out of order, and some had been damaged in the earthquake. The woman made an appointment with him. When they'd sorted out all the poetry manuscripts, there would be enough to make a pretty solid book out of them: four or five hundred lines in total. He named this collection of poems *Symmetrical Beauty*. He wrote a single sentence for the title page: "Beauty in the balance is equality."

This sentence had a special meaning at a time when autocracy had just collapsed.

As soon as the book was published, it was like adding firewood to the flames. A talented painter who can also write such meaningful poems must be a genius ignored by the times. If the Cultural Revolution had not come to an end, it would not only have destroyed those famous masters who'd died but also led to the continued neglect of who knows how many unknown talents. Because it was believed that he was an irrefutable witness to historical progress, he became the subject of even more intense interest.

Chu Yuntian's literary talent was first discovered by Cao Ying, so she naturally wanted to manage his career, dragging him off to meet with readers, holding various signing events and seminars. She would often come to his house and sit on a white rattan chair under the tall fir tree in the courtyard, drinking tea and chatting about literature. Cao Ying was an excellent literary editor. In among the seemingly relaxed gossip, she was secretly looking for the spark hidden in Yuntian's heart that belonged to literature, which periodically inspired his literary imagination and creativity. Soon an epistolary novel – *Love Letters* – had been conceived, written and published. This novel originated in the letters exchanged between his father and mother when the former was imprisoned at the May Seventh cadre school in Jiangxi during the Cultural Revolution. There were not many letters, but he'd read them and been deeply moved. But later, when he looked at them after his mother died and then again after his father had passed, he never found them again. There were only about ten letters in total, and they couldn't possibly have been posted – they'd all had to be secretly hand-delivered by trusted persons who would carry them back and forth. Some things they did not dare to say openly, so they'd used slang, or even risked a few words of English… but such was the reality of that time. Writing this kind of letter was still very risky. Whether they used slang or a few words of English, it would have caused enormous trouble if one of them had been found. Wasn't English a 'secret agent's code'? When writing *Love Letters*, Yuntian couldn't help thinking about his parents' hardships in those years and the loneliness his parents had endured when they secretly wrote these letters, which made him feel very sad. The most distressing thing was that both his parents had passed away before they could see what was happening now.

One day at dinner, when talking about Cao Ying, Sui Yi said to Yuntian: "In fact, Cao Ying was not the first to discover your literary talent. Guess who it was?"

Chu Yuntian was stunned. Yiran pointed to Sui Yi with her chubby little hand and said: "It was Mum."

Chu Yuntian smiled and said: "You understand how great your mum is!"

He was not expecting that Sui Yi would say sternly: "It was Luo Qian! Remember when you were nothing, he said several times that you had literary talent. He admired you and understood you…" She was silent for a moment and then asked: "How long since you last saw each other?"

"It's been more than six months," Yuntian said. "Last time, when Luo Fu asked us to go to the Beijing Art Museum to see his 'Five Thousand Years', I went round to his house twice. He wasn't there, and the door was locked. I left a note in the crack, but he just ignored me." Yuntian thought for a moment and said: "Has he been avoiding me because I'm too much in the news? He's very proud and doesn't want to take the initiative to approach me... I guess I can understand that."

Sui Yi didn't say anything. Was this silence a kind of condemnation?

If you suddenly become prosperous, how should you treat your poor friend from the past? Maybe you didn't deliberately ignore him, but he felt the situation to be awkward and uncomfortable. What to do? This is a difficult topic. If you don't deal with it seriously, everything in the past will gradually disappear into history until it is silent.

CHAPTER 2

Yuntian didn't expect that so many amazing and talented people would rush into his life all at once.

It was a brightly coloured era.

A new life, the future that you could create for yourself, the opportunities that came, the unexpected luck, every kind of possibility that seemed to turn reality upside down… Everything was in motion, amplified, illuminated by an invisible force and constantly changing its course. It seemed as though he was standing at a great crossroads, branching out in all directions, and whichever road he looked down, there was hope for him. Yuntian felt that the hordes of fans who came to shake hands with him every day each brought him something hitherto unknown. Where did all these people come from? Before, they must have been hiding somewhere, but now with the sudden hoopla they had all emerged at once. On second thoughts, surely some of these people must be wondering where he had come from. Had he crawled out from the grass, from under a rock or from some mouse hole? He smiled at the idea.

Just like the weather when it turns warm, those underground, repressed lives were now filled with light, shining everywhere. No wonder they were scrambling out into the sunshine!

Among the various individuals who popped up around him at this time, some came out of admiration, some wanted a painting or a book out of him, some were the kind who'd seek out any sort of 'celebrity', some were caught up in the excitement, and some wanted to make use of his name, or ask him for favours. He was not interested in any of this. He was only interested in people who could talk to him, or who loved art and talent. This was also the underlying principle for him when making friends. For him, art was always supreme.

What interested him most about the academy he now belonged to were several of the young painters. Especially Yu Changshui, who had graduated from the Shandong Academy of Fine Arts and was originally from Binzhou. Most people from Shandong are simple and honest. Yuntian liked his informal manners; those who hold too fast to etiquette can't ever amount to much. His hair was long, his clothes casual and his buttons were never done up properly. He was even more untidy than himself. This man had a poor memory, and his work was always rough; however, he had a good understanding of subtle changes in brushwork and ink. Although Yu Changshui had not yet produced a single work of high quality, his refinement and calm in painting made Yuntian value him highly. If you tried to talk about life, society or people with Yu Changshui, he was not interested at all. When the conversation turned to brush and ink, he would be very relaxed. In this, he was like Yuntian. Although there was a ten-year age difference, Yu Changshui felt friendly with Chu Yuntian because they shared the same lighthearted, cheerful temperament. The communication between artists is all based on intuition. It felt right, and therefore the two of them were happy in their dealings with one another.

One day, Chu Yuntian had just arrived at the academy, when he bumped straight into a young man charging out. If he'd been an old man, he would have been knocked off his feet. Yuntian was about to get angry, but the young man just said: "I'll apologise to you later," and ran off. Why was he in such a hurry? He wondered whether this young man might not be the academy's newest recruit, Fei Liang.

After a while, the young man returned to apologise. It was indeed Fei Liang. He felt the back of his head in embarrassment as he bowed to Yuntian. He explained that there was a residential block behind the academy, and from the window he'd spotted a child climbing the balcony railing. He was horrified but didn't dare to shout. He was afraid that this would end with the child falling off, so he had run over there to save it. He ran so fast that he nearly knocked Yuntian head over heels.

Chu Yuntian said with a smile: "You nearly killed one to save one."

From then on, he became friends with this brave young man. Chatting together, he discovered that Fei Liang originally came from Jingzhou in Hubei Province. Since his girlfriend was in Tianjin and the academy was recruiting, he applied and was accepted. Fei Liang painted landscapes and flower pieces, and he particularly enjoyed working on a huge scale. At that time, the main hall of government buildings and offices all needed gigantic paintings to hang there, and this was his speciality. Fei Liang was a hard worker; his brushwork and ink lacked spirit in some ways, but he was very good indeed at constructing these large paintings with massive heaps of rocks, heavy mountains and weighty rivers. Chu Yuntian said to him: "I'm not good at painting big pictures."

When Fei Liang heard that, he looked almost embarrassed. He said: "Your 'The Thaw' is a great painting, and it will be mentioned in the history of art forever. How can the rest of us compare?"

It turned out that Chu Yuntian was regarded as a god by these young people. When they became acquainted with him, they would go round to his house from time to time and ask for advice on painting.

Chu Yuntian got to know Yu Changshui because of his painting, while in the case of Fei Liang, he'd met the man before seeing any of his work. Anyway, regardless of how they'd become acquainted, he had a good impression of both of them. As for the famous painters from this city – and indeed from all over the world – they passed through his daily life like smoke or clouds; he couldn't remember what they looked like, let alone their names. If an artist's paintings were unusual, then he would remember them. However, these new friends were quite different from the old friends of many years ago. There was nothing like the spiritual interdependence of the Three Musketeers in past years. Although Yuntian's literary works proved highly influential, he did not set foot in the literary world. Yuntian had been in contact with some writers, and he felt that they were a little reserved, not as frank as painters. He had been living among painters since he was young, and he loved painting landscapes because they expressed his admiration for nature. He couldn't stand the false pride, snobbery and cliquiness of some writers. This was the reason why he always kept his feet firmly planted in the world of painting.

His artistic friends never cared about other people's social status and fame, but only his works, talent, artistic feeling and originality. Talented people were always held dear to his heart, while he would ignore those who found it difficult to live up to their fame. He observed self-restraint; he did not criticise others openly, but he kept to his own high standards in his heart. Although Yuntian had now been lauded to the skies, he continued to carry about him the strong sense of independence that had come from all those years in the wilderness. On the other hand, thanks to having been well brought up, he would not be rendered arrogant by success, nor would he selfishly disregard anyone else's feelings, making them feel awkward.

Over the past few years, he'd travelled widely and got to know more and more people. 'The Thaw' was the symbol of that era and his signature piece. Everyone wanted to get to know him and take a picture with him as proof of their acquaintance. This happened so often that sometimes he felt overwhelmed, but on other occasions he became a little proud: after all, this was a manifestation of his importance. Every day, sandwiched in with the bundles of his regular mail, were flirtatious messages from young women. Sometimes he would read them, smile and throw them aside. The warning he had received from Yufei many years ago was still embedded in his heart. He had sworn not to let Sui Yi suffer any more injury.

The year before last, Sui Yi had quit her job in the eye hospital and concentrated on being his assistant in work and life. She helped him with his writing, transcribing manuscripts, picking up and seeing off visitors, taking care of Yiran who had just started school, washing, cooking and cleaning the house. She arranged the rooms in a quiet and comfortable way and even mowed the courtyard all by herself. Everything was nice and neat. Sui Yi's mother wanted to help, but they were careful not to put their burdens on the fragile shoulders of their parents. If they had a free day, they would go and collect Sui Yi's mother and younger brother to spend time together, enjoying in their company one of the greatest pleasures in life: a family reunion.

As Yuntian met more people, he discovered that there were talented individuals everywhere. Now that society had opened up, everyone was feeling less depressed – at least Yuntian very rarely felt depressed again. But after all, he was in a minority, or perhaps he was just one of the lucky ones. He understood that if 'The Thaw' had been painted a year earlier or a year later, it would not have had such a powerful impact. Its symbolic significance in representing the feeling of the times was something more than its artistic qualities. Moreover, after all, there must be other extraordinarily talented people out there, still buried behind the counters of shops or out in the vast wilderness, and they had not yet found their opportunity. Who would discover them? Who would acknowledge their genius?

Once Yuntian returned from an event in Luoyang, he crossed the Yellow River Bridge from Sanmenxia City to see the Hukou waterfall. Standing on the wet, high cliffs and hard rocks, he watched the river fall straight in front of him, descending into thunder, waves and torrents, lifting the sea and turning the sky. The stunning momentum silenced Yuntian. He stood there in a daze for an hour and a half. The spray and mist soaked his clothes, but he didn't notice it until his companions pleaded with him to go. If you leave too late, they said, it will be dangerous on the mountain roads. But before they had gone any great distance, the sky grew dark, and it began to rain. They had to go to Jiangzhou to find a hotel to stay in.

When they entered the hotel, they were very hungry and wanted something to eat. The hotel clerk said that the dining room was full, so they would have to eat in their rooms; Yuntian and the others would have to make do. The clerk was very attentive and soon brought them hot food. While eating, they heard some people talking loudly outside, as if quarrelling. They went out to have a look. There were about ten people in the dining room, standing around a huge table that had been produced by pushing eight square dining tables together. From a distance, they could see a man waving his arm as if he were painting. When they came closer, they realised he was indeed painting. Yuntian motioned to his companions to stand silent and watch; they should try not to disturb them.

Chu Yuntian looked at the painting and was amazed. This man had painted the Hukou waterfall. Obviously, he had just been there in person and had been impressed. He couldn't wait until he'd got home to paint it, so the moment he arrived at the hotel, he'd spread out his paper and set to work. Yuntian quietly walked up behind the man and craned his neck to look at the painting on the table. He was surprised. The strength, heroism, passion, wildness and arrogance in the picture grabbed him at once. He seemed to hear the man shouting and singing wildly, releasing the boundless vitality of nature. He had never seen such a remarkable waterfall painting, nor such unrestrained expression. This man clearly had profound training in traditional painting techniques combined with a personal vision. Who could this talented man be?

He kept painting with his head down so Yuntian couldn't see his face clearly.

But at this time, someone had already recognised Yuntian, and quietly walked up to the painter and whispered in his ear. The man didn't seem to hear. He was still intoxicated by his art. When the man finished his painting, he threw down his brush and looked up. Yuntian didn't recognise him at all. He was about fifty, of average height, thin and strong. His face was wrinkled and his hands too, like the cankers on an old elm tree. He had the look of someone who had experienced terrible vicissitudes. His hair was grey and frizzy, and he was going a little bald. His manner was also unusual. When the onlookers praised his work, he said: "After I finished painting the middle section where it is all spray and foam, I thought that this place should be wet and splashed with ink! That would make it sufficiently wild!" Then he said: "Let's go back so I can paint another one!"

Yuntian felt that this man ought to be a friend. His painting and his words were everything he could have hoped for.

At this time, a man came up and asked if he was Chu Yuntian. Yuntian nodded. The man immediately pulled over the painter and introduced them to each other: "This is the famous Mr Chu Yuntian, and this is our great Huangshan painter, Mr Yi Liaoran."

It turned out that these people were all painters from Anhui Province. Chu Yuntian had never heard of this man's name. The world is so big that you should never underestimate the possibility of hidden dragons and crouching tigers. Yi Liaoran stuck out his hand at Chu Yuntian and said: "Oh, I didn't expect that Mr Chu would be watching just now when I made a fool of myself. I'm quite embarrassed."

"Not at all!" Chu Yuntian replied. "Your painting is wonderful. I haven't seen anyone paint water like this! You've captured the movement, momentum and spirit of water!" He spoke as he felt.

He wasn't trying to be polite; he was saying what he really thought. It was like a fan to the flames and Yi Liaoran now came to life. Yi Liaoran turned out to be a man of great sympathetic qualities, so he patted Chu Yuntian on the shoulder like an old friend and said: "You are a pure artist!" Then he pushed Yuntian towards the painting and said: "Tell me what's wrong with it. You know, I made a special trip to Beijing to see your 'The Thaw'. You know more about painting water than I do."

Inspecting it carefully, Yuntian said: "The mountain in the distance has potential, not only horizontally, but also vertically. These small trees, done with only a few strokes and yet so well-shaped... it is clear that you have learned the technique of Song painting."

Yi Liaoran carried on as if Yuntian had hit some vital spot. He was very excited and said: "That's very impressive. You have spotted my trump card, but you have an even deeper training in Song painting than I!"

Half of the assembled group didn't understand what they were talking about. How many people today know and have studied Song painting?

Chu Yuntian said to the people who came with him: "Artists in the Song dynasty would paint tiny trees in the distance whereby they would look and feel like big trees. Ma Yuan and Xia Gui were particularly good at this. Literati paintings produced in the Ming and Qing dynasties don't have this skill. You see, in Mr Yi's painting, isn't it obvious that those trees in the distance are actually huge?

If you draw small things in the distance so that they look big, your picture will appear expansive."

Then, Yuntian turned his head and said to Yi Liaoran: "You just said that the middle section is very good with the ink splashed about. The water around you is very well painted and more specific. There should be an empty place in the middle. It should be completely open, or maybe you should even paint nothing there. That leaves space for the imagination, and your painting will then be even more powerful!" When he gave voice to his idea, he was very frank, as if this were an art seminar.

It is only when real artists are gathered together that they can have fun talking. Yi Liaoran excitedly asked someone to pull over a table and got the hotel to produce some hot and cold dishes for them, and a bottle of Fen wine. He had to make friends with Yuntian. For his part, Yuntian liked this warm-hearted Huizhou painter and sat down at the same table with him. Yi Liaoran was fond of drink, unlike Yuntian – however, Yi Liaoran wasn't going to make him do something that he was uncomfortable with, and just said: "I'll give you a toast!" Then he raised his glass and poured the wine down his throat, as if toasting was just an excuse to drink. Both he and Yuntian smoked, so the two men kept passing cigarettes to each other until the table was surrounded by smoke. Yi Liaoran pointed to the smoke and said: "These are the clouds of Huangshan. Wherever I go, they follow me."

Everyone laughed. Yi Liaoran didn't have much capacity for wine, and pretty soon became drunk. Suddenly, he pointed to Chu Yuntian and said: "Do you want to paint a bit? Show us something new." He didn't care that he was just a country nobody and his companion was a famous artist; he spoke as one friend to another.

Yuntian never stood on his dignity, and besides, he'd had a nip or two of the wine and was feeling tipsy. He waved his hand and said: "If we are going to paint, let's paint! Give me some paper!"

A piece of rice paper was spread across the table. With just a few brushstrokes, Yuntian created several powerful boulders in strong ink. Between these lines, all the blanks that had been left behind were the flowing waters of the spring. Then he used a fat sheep's-hair brush to lay down a thin wash, and a smooth clear flow came pouring across the paper. It was wonderful to see Yuntian when he was painting. The clear, swift-moving current seemed to flow straight from his heart. As the current twisted and turned, the apparent vagaries of his brush showed the richness of his talent – onlookers were amazed. Then Chu Yuntian put his brush down, and in that moment the painting was finished.

Before Yi Liaoran could speak, Yuntian turned towards him and said: "This painting is for you!" Then he picked up a different brush and wrote four lines:

Stone is stubborn and spiritual,
Water is soft and strong.
How about human nature?
Let us leave it to mature.

Three people present said that they all understood the metaphorical meaning behind these lines.

Yi Liaoran said to Yuntian: "Although I couldn't really capture the Hukou waterfall in my painting, I've tried my best." Then he said: "I would also like to write a few words on my painting. I know you are a poet, so please could you come up with something for me."

Chu Yuntian knew that most painters of this generation were not well-versed in poetry. In the circumstances, nobody could be surprised. So he politely said: "I can't just come up with something on the spot. How about you use the two lines from Li Bai – 'The Yellow River drops from the sky down to the Eastern Sea; Its thousands of miles are written into the hollows of my heart.' It's very appropriate for the atmosphere of your painting."

Everyone agreed that this would be perfect, and Yi Liaoran wrote the words on his painting.

They gave each other examples of their calligraphy and went off to bed. The next morning, they shared a meal of Shanxi noodles and oatmeal honeycomb rolls, and then said goodbye to one another in front of the hotel, though they felt reluctant at the idea. Chu Yuntian admired the talent and independence he had observed in this remarkable man from Huizhou, his untamed quality and his arrogance. Yi Liaoran appreciated Yuntian's broad-mindedness and elegance, his great talent and his lack of snobbishness, for all that he was very famous already.

Two people, coming from opposite directions, one from the north and one from the south, nevertheless find that they have gained the same things from their journey: one was the wonderful sight of the Hukou waterfall, and the other was to unexpectedly acquire a close friend.

CHAPTER 3

Early in the morning, Luo Fu placed two colourful suitcases in a conspicuous place in the living room.

After the earthquake, his family's home in the shanty behind the church had been left in ruins. Those rickety houses and old homesteads had long been dilapidated and in a state of disrepair, the bricks crumbling and alkaline. When the earth shook, they simply fell apart. Repairing them was tantamount to rebuilding them from scratch, and given the government's financial circumstances, that posed some difficulties. For a long time after the ruins were cleared, it was left as a large, empty space and gradually became a paradise for children to play football, play and fly kites. Luo Fu was not in any hurry; anyway, his parents were dead, and he had no family left. "When he got to eat, the whole family got their fill."

He lived at the college, where there was a classroom for his teaching, a studio for painting, a canteen for eating, a dormitory for sleeping, and a group of students to keep him company. This was a life that he enjoyed. The art college was one of the places where you could always keep up to date with the news and the latest gossip. As a result, although always filled with vitality, his work seemed to put on an amazing growth spurt, like a tree that had received a shot of fertiliser. He produced a series of remarkable masterpieces at this time: 'Five Thousand Years', 'Ploughing Deep' and 'The Shout'. In particular, the old farmer depicted in 'Five Thousand Years', still strong and powerful under the weight of history – a figure described as "the backbone of a silent people" by the critics – was even compared to Luo Zhongli's 'Father'. This painting was indeed the finest of Luo Fu's works. The most important thing for any artist is his masterpiece, which is his ID card. Luo Fu's exceptionally realistic style and expressiveness enabled him to depict "our ancient nation's strong and unyielding backbone, which has gone through all manner of vicissitudes, while still holding firm". For a time, this 'backbone' was held to be symbolic of contemporary painting. This made the leaders in charge of culture in the college and the city speak up on his behalf and demand that government begin to actually do something about housing for earthquake victims. As an outstanding talent, he was assigned a three-bedroom apartment on the ninth floor of one of the high-rise apartment blocks then being constructed for the first time around the city. He would have a living room, a bedroom and a studio. By the standards of the time, this was a pretty generous offer.

Once a person has shown themselves to be lucky, good things just flow in. Soon afterwards, he was sent by the Ministry of Culture to participate in a delegation of artists to the United States. He had just been halfway around the world, visiting places from the west coast of the United States to the east coast, with a side trip to Chicago. Today was his third day back home, so he excitedly asked Chu Yuntian and Luo Qian to come round.

The Three Musketeers hadn't seen each other for quite a long time. Luo Fu had never forgotten his 'friends of poverty' of yesteryear. In those days of icy winds and cold blasts, they'd gathered together to keep warm. Now it was sunny and bright, so they should be even happier in their association. Together, they could turn yesterday's bitter dreams into today's tangible reality.

The door opened and two old friends came in. Yuntian was wearing a dark blue windbreaker with a wide collar flopping down on his shoulders, the ends of the belt hanging down behind him. He was in the prime of life and looked handsome and well. Luo Qian came wearing the overalls he usually wore when he painted, and his black coat was daubed with oil paint in various colours. Both were smiling. If you paid attention, they smiled a little differently. Yuntian's smile was relaxed and familiar, while Luo Qian's smile was a little forced.

At that time, artists rarely got to travel overseas, and for Luo Fu it had been his first experience eating foreign food. In this, he was different from Yuntian. Yuntian was born in the foreign concession and grew up in a classic English-style house on Mu'nan Road. His father had studied at an American medical college and worked in a foreign hospital. His family naturally incorporated some Western customs and culture into their daily lives. Luo Fu was born and bred in one of the local shanty towns, and on this occasion, he'd had the unimaginable opportunity to spend some time overseas – it was like living on another planet for some days. He seemed to have been overcome by the sudden shock of exposure to a foreign culture. Today, his linen shirt, fine leather jacket and thick jeans were all things he'd brought back with him from abroad. His hair curled naturally, but now he used hair gel to fix it. Yuntian said with a smile: "You've been transformed into an American overnight!"

Luo Fu's first sentence was in English: "Please have a seat!"

It was a joke, but he was also feeling pleased with himself. He was still young, and when he was pleased with himself, that elation was also a kind of inner joy.

He couldn't wait to talk about the United States, so he did not even pause for his friends to start asking questions. At that time, Chinese people were most interested in the United States, and of the Three Musketeers only Luo Fu had actually been there. So it all came pouring out… the skyscrapers, highways, supermarkets, jazz, traffic jams, hot dogs, urban graffiti, tattoos, strange social customs, peculiar museums, bizarre and fantastic art… he could hardly give voice to it all. To show his friends exactly what he had seen, he kept motioning with his hands and would draw things for them. And to show that he was now an expert on America and American art, he would throw in an English-language name or term from time to time. As he spoke, he ended up confusing himself. Finally, he said: "It'll take a day or two for me to explain everything. Anyway, the painters we used to know are completely passé. When I mentioned their names to the others, they laughed at me. They said they couldn't remember all these out-of-date people." At that point, his eyes flashed with excitement, as if he were the only one to understand these things.

"That's not surprising," Luo Qian said. "If you asked them about our painters, they might know Shitao or Bada Shanren, but that would be it. Which contemporary artist from China would they even know the name of? Would they know about Yuntian?"

Luo Qian's words made the warm atmosphere in the room turn a little cool. Was this because he didn't like to hear the boastful note in Luo Fu's conversation? But why did he mention Yuntian? In the old days when the Three Musketeers used to help each other out, as close as brothers, Luo Qian was the most admired among them, not only because he was a few years older, but also because of his integrity, far-reaching knowledge and deep thinking. Yuntian respected him, and Luo Fu too. However, in the past seven or eight years, Yuntian and Luo Fu had attracted great attention in artistic circles for their work, and only Luo Qian remained obscure. Of the three wild mountains, two were verdant, grand and dazzling. He alone was still desolate and silent. How could he remain unaffected? In the dark ages, now more than ten years back, they had relied on their love and confidence in art. Could they do the same now? At that time, there was no comparison, no differentiation, no critical evaluation and no social recognition, but now it was just the opposite. Art was no longer a personal hobby, but a career – a mechanism for social advancement. Who could withstand the snobbish eyes and evaluation standards of society at large?

Yuntian was a thoughtful man, so whenever he went to meet Luo Qian, he would be very careful and attentive, trying his best to maintain their friendly feelings of yore. Luo Fu was much rougher, and right now he was feeling really good about himself, so he was quite oblivious to Luo Qian's state of mind. He opened a box full of art publications; some were museum catalogues, and others were monographs on an individual painter. He took them out one by one and explained why they were important. From his tone, it seemed that he imagined that this was something only he understood. Luo Fu handed Luo Qian two volumes of paintings and said: "These are about Dali and Chagall. You must have a look at them. You need to know about them!" This was something he might have said to his students.

Luo Qian stood there, but he did not pick up the books. Yuntian responded quickly, immediately picking them up, and said with a smile: "I want to see this too."

Luo Fu had brought back a large number of picture books. A whole box, containing at least forty or fifty books, large and small. These volumes were now spread out across the sofa and tea table in the living room, which was very spectacular. These beautifully bound volumes gave off a strong scholarly smell. Luo Fu said: "If you want to look at these books, you can just take them away, as many as you like." He was feeling generous, like a Maecenas. Then he pulled out another suitcase, which was covered with colourful stickers from every city he had visited. Each one was like a badge, novel and fresh. He said: "I brought each of you a present." Then he opened the suitcase.

When he opened it, the room was filled with a pleasant smell, as if the case were full of rare treasures. Luo Fu took out all the gifts he had bought for his friends along the way. He gave Yuntian a tie because Yuntian had many occasions to socialise. This dark blue tie with purplish-red flowers was really elegant and formal; Yuntian liked it very much. His gift to Sui Yi was a small box beautifully wrapped with fine ribbons and flowery paper. He didn't want Yuntian to open it since it was a present for his wife, but he couldn't help telling him what was inside. He said it was a silk scarf which he had bought at the Metropolitan Museum. The design was part of Monet's famous work 'Waterlilies' in the Metropolitan Museum collection. He said that he was sure Sui Yi would want to wear it every day. Yuntian said with a smile: "She might not want to risk it!"

A gift for his daughter would always be even more pleasing than a gift for himself. When Luo Fu pulled a big Mickey Mouse out of a beautiful bag from Disneyland, Yuntian couldn't help saying: "Yiran is going to go mad about this! She's been watching Mickey Mouse and Donald Duck on TV." Luo Fu was very happy to hear this.

At this point, Luo Fu made a show of taking a dark grey paper bag out from the bottom of the suitcase. He handed it to Luo Qian and said: "This is for you. I'm sure you'll like it."

Luo Qian hesitated, as if he didn't want to take it. He removed a carton from the paper bag, the top of which bore some wording in a foreign language. Then he heard Luo Fu say: "English Windsor and

Newton's oil paints! The best oil paints in the world! As soon as you squeeze the paint out onto your palette, it's so inspirational! We've never had such beautiful colours!"

Unexpectedly, Luo Qian said: "It would be a waste for me to use such good paints. Keep them!" He tossed the paints onto the small cabinet beside him.

There was a little embarrassment. It was Yuntian who took up the conversation and said: "Why are you being so polite? It would be a shame to leave them to Luo Fu."

After they'd spent a while gossiping, Luo Fu was still engaged in telling all kinds of anecdotes about his trip. Seeing a faint look of impatience on Luo Qian's face, Yuntian said to Luo Fu: "We've been here for long enough. It's time to go. Anyway, your stories about a month away can't all be told in a day or two. Let's come back some other time."

Luo Fu took out a large plastic bag covered in brightly coloured patterns and put his gifts to Yuntian and his family inside. Yuntian put the paints that Luo Fu had given Luo Qian in as well. When they were leaving, Luo Fu said: "Oh, I almost forgot. There were those two books for Luo Qian."

"Let's talk about that next time," Luo Qian said.

Yuntian rushed forward to take the two books and put them in the bag. He said: "Give them all to me!"

Luo Qian was silent for a long time after they had emerged from Luo Fu's house. Yuntian noticed for the first time that Luo Qian's temples were greying. His heart lurched. He had not expected white hairs to have already begun to appear on his friends' heads. From Luo Qian's attitude towards Luo Fu today, he felt conscious for the first time of his overweening self-esteem. Excessive self-esteem is often a shell that people with a low opinion of themselves use for protection. Seeing that his ever-respected friend was showing an inferiority complex, Yuntian felt sad and helpless. He ought to have a heart-to-heart with him, but where to start? Would he refuse? To have a deep and meaningful conversation, they would have to tear down the barriers of self-esteem. Did such barriers – whether overt or hidden – also affect Luo Qian's relationship with him? Since he moved back to Mu'nan Road, Luo Qian had seldom come to visit him. When he invited him, he always said he was too busy. Was this an excuse to gradually alienate himself from Yuntian?

At the crossroads, it was time for the two of them to say goodbye. Yuntian wanted to take the oil paints and books that Luo Fu had given Luo Qian out of the bag, to give them to him. Luo Qian looked very indifferent and said: "These books you can find everywhere. I've seen all of them. I can't use the paint, so you might as well have it."

"What are you talking about?" Yuntian said. "I don't paint with oils. They were a present for you, so why don't you use them? The books I want to look at." With that, he shoved the oil paints into Luo Qian's hand. He thought Luo Qian had never been so tiresome.

Luo Qian then said something that surprised him: "Luo Fu is going in a different direction from us…" He stopped and then continued: "Or at least from me."

He did not explain.

Yuntian was startled, but Luo Qian had gone.

The next day happened to be a Sunday. Chu Yuntian and his family went cheerfully to Luo Fu, first to express their gratitude, and second to see his new house. Yuntian was carrying a bag of fruit; Sui Yi was wearing her new silk scarf with a design taken from Monet's 'Waterlilies'; and Yiran was clutching her Mickey Mouse which she would kiss from time to time. The family walked happily along the road, attracting glances from other passers-by.

Gifts make people happy, but they make themselves happier. "To tell you the truth, when I saw that Mickey Mouse at Disneyland, I thought straight away of Yiran," Luo Fu said.

Sui Yi asked Yiran to kiss Luo Fu in thanks.

Then he asked Sui Yi: "Do you like the scarf?"

Yuntian said with a smile: "She wore it all day yesterday, and almost wouldn't take it off to go to bed…"

"It suits you," Luo Fu said. "It's elegant and refined."

Yuntian said with a smile: "Are you praising Sui Yi or the silk scarf?"

Sui Yi said: "Luo Fu knows that I like Monet best. I admire Van

Gogh most, but I like Monet best. Monet has a kind of tenderness, and it is an all-encompassing tenderness – very moving."

"That is like Yuntian," Luo Fu said. "He has an all-encompassing tenderness, along with his talent and hard work. Otherwise, how would so many girls fall for him?" Having said this, he suddenly felt awkward and turned the conversation: "But Yuntian only loves Sui Yi."

"And me," said Little Yiran.

This made everyone laugh for a long time.

Then they talked about the United States. That was now Luo Fu's only topic of conversation and he talked for two hours on the subject, at which point they left, still feeling happy. Yuntian said in an off-hand way: "Let's go and see Luo Qian next time you're free."

"I wanted to talk to him about the art world abroad," Luo Fu said. "It really is another world. What we know about is just a fraction, from one hundred years ago." It seemed that he was not sensitive to Luo Qian's peculiarity of manner yesterday.

Yuntian said: "I want to remind you to pay attention to the way you talk to him. Don't treat him as if he doesn't know anything."

"But he doesn't know anything!" Luo Fu exclaimed. "He can't just close his eyes and ears. How open the world is now! I saw Chinese students studying painting at the Academy of Fine Arts in New York and Boston. I was amazed when I saw their work. In the future, our paintings will be the same – it's unimaginable!"

Yuntian didn't speak. He felt that the artistic viewpoints of his two good friends had now diverged too far from each other.

Sui Yi heard what they said. After their return, she said to Yuntian: "You should keep reminding Luo Fu that he needs to speak carefully. You don't want to hurt Luo Qian's self-esteem."

"I know, but right now art is all about expressing your own personal viewpoint, and everyone is quarrelling about it. The most popular literary magazines are *Works and Contentions* and *Popular Cinema*, and half the articles are about these kinds of controversies. Our Academy of Fine Arts is riven with quarrels, which sometimes go to extremes. If you have different viewpoints, all these disputes and conflicts may be a good thing. The more controversy, the more people think actively. And the firmer the opinion, the more it reflects your personality. If you isolate yourself, you will be abandoned by the mainstream. After all, things are different now!"

When Yuntian spoke, an image floated into his mind: the Three Musketeers went racing forward together and finally came to a place in the wasteland where many roads crossed. Although they had never held a grudge or quarrelled, they suddenly, and for no particular reason, scattered, without saying goodbye to each other. Instead, each rode off in a different direction and they went their separate ways.

CHAPTER 4

Life is like a river that constantly flows onwards, and time passes as the changing seasons, in never-ending variety. Things remain long after their owners have passed away, the glory days of yore will never return, and there is nothing you can do to stop this process.

When spring is about to depart, people feel deeply hurt and cherish it; when autumn colours wither and die, people mourn and bewail it. However, in the end, don't you have to helplessly watch them pass until they disappear?

The end of spring and the coming of winter may be the essence not just of the passing seasons, but also of life. Time can't stop, and more than life can freeze. Can you keep the hair on your head black forever or preserve your youthful and bright countenance from wrinkles? Even if you manage to retain them by sheer hard work, the passage of time will always carve a network of fine lines in your heart.

On your journey through life, how long can the best friends of childhood and youth accompany you? When you felt like-minded, when you were close, swearing blood-brotherhood, promising to live one for all and all for one, you thought you would never quarrel – that you'd be friends forever. However, with the changing of the times, new life goals, a different environment and the setbacks of personal destiny, these will all make your former companions drift away one by one. However, in return some people you had never met before will come into your life, becoming new friends, joining you, maybe even abandoning their own family and friends to be with you, to struggle and fight for a new world.

Life is like this. While these new partners move forward, side by side with you, your old friends will naturally become indifferent and alienated from you, as naturally as the sun sets in the west, and finally without you necessarily even noticing, they will withdraw from your life completely.

No matter whether you continue to care for them, in the long journey of life, there will be different companions at different times. You have to constantly gather new faces around you, to participate in your endlessly changing life – especially if you are full of new hopes and ideals, for then many new people with smiling faces will come jumping onto the scene.

Chu Yuntian occasionally remembered his friends of the past, just like when he climbed out of the ruins of the great earthquake, the first thing he did was to race around the city on his ramshackle bike, from one friend's house to another, afraid of losing even one of them.

Now, most of these friends were consigned to the past, though he continued to remember them.

Mr Xu's little gatherings of artists, which he often called to mind, were now as a yellowing old photograph, sandwiched in a page of his memory. Mr Xu had never recovered from breaking his bones in the earthquake, and he died three years later. The history of famous men is documented in writing, while the history of ordinary mortals may or may not be engraved in the memory of their fellows. But that period in these artists' lives once brought beauty to a lonely corner of the city – Yuntian would never forget that.

After the earthquake, there were two people he had never seen again. The first was Su Yousheng. Old Su once called Yuntian and said that he had been seconded to a unit in Beijing to write a history of the theatre. On the phone, Yuntian asked him about the books he'd kept at his friend's house; had he ever been able to replace them? Old Su laughed and said: "Don't worry about them. We can get to buy whatever books we want now, can't we?"

Listening to his cheerful laughter, it seemed that a heavy page of history had been turned. After he was transferred to Beijing, there was no news of Old Su. Later, officials at the Culture Bureau mentioned that he had been transferred to the Beijing Institute of Art, and his registered permanent residence also moved to Beijing. When he left Tianjin, he didn't even stop to say goodbye – not a word. Was he, like Luo Qian, afflicted with some kind of inferiority complex?

Psychological problems cannot be seen or touched, and there is no way to resolve them. But if you put them aside and ignore them, everything will be over.

Another person he had not seen again was Yannian. In 1984, Yuntian had gone to see some paintings on display at the gallery next to the Moscow Cinema on Jiefang Road. A man grabbed him from behind. He was very strong, especially his hands. He turned around and was shocked at the sight of a foreigner. Looking again, he shouted: "Is that you, Yannian?"

The man smiled and said: "Of course it's me. Longfellow! You're even more handsome than before."

They hadn't met for at least seven or eight years, but he remained unchanged; if anything, he looked younger. The curly hair on his head was glossy, and he looked much happier than before, as if a gust of wind had blown away all the misery from his eyes. He told Yuntian that he lived across the street and insisted on dragging Yuntian over to his house. He also waggled his fingers in a circle, as if he wanted to give Yuntian a gift. "Come with me," he said, "and I'll play something for you."

If he had never been to Yannian's home, he wouldn't have known that there was such a house in Tianjin, just like his attic room supported by a forest of wooden columns over by the Qiangzi Canal. Jiefang Road was called Central Avenue before 1949. A hundred years ago, it was the most important street in the foreign concession district. It started from the Hai River at its northern end and stretched south through the concessions of France, Britain, the United States and Germany. The financial, commercial, media and administrative authorities of each country were concentrated in this street. In front of many of the buildings there would be a row of tall, stone-carved columns or high steps, looking serious and dignified. The boundaries between the concessions of these four countries could be seen from the style of houses alone. Yannian's house was located in the former American concession, but because this was when the American Civil War was raging, it had been managed by the British concession. Many of the buildings there were in classic British style.

The house stood very high, with solid foundations and thick walls. The interior of the building was decorated with blue-grey marble. Curiously, the ceiling in the corridors was covered with Western frescos depicting flowers, birds and animals, all perfectly preserved. But since no one looked after them, and many cooking stoves had been set up out in the corridors, they smoked and burned all day, blackening the frescos. The marble floor and stairs had been badly damaged, indeed were pretty much wrecked, but it must have been a very beautiful house a hundred years ago. As for what it was originally used for, no one seemed to be quite sure. This was history, and history was not open for scrutiny.

Yannian opened the door and introduced Yuntian to his wife and son. Oh, he'd been married for quite a few years now. His wife and son both looked entirely foreign. His wife's name was Liu Ba and his son Vilya. Liu Ba was not tall and looked to be Russian. Their son was very cute with his curly blond hair and bright blue eyes.

However, Yannian's current abode was far smaller than his original room on Shanxi Road. Although the ceiling was high, the room was very narrow. At one end was a heavy door, and at the other end, a tall, slit-like window, which was further covered by cast-iron railings. The light in the house was dark and gloomy, like a prison cell. Yannian explained that he'd moved here after his mother died. First of all, this was because he and Liu Ba looked like foreigners. There'd been constant trouble when they were living on Shanxi Road near the old city of Tianjin. It was better to be here in the old foreign concession, where there were still some foreigners about, so they didn't attract too much attention. Second, they'd moved because of the piano. Yannian said that having a piano was more important than any house. Since the earthquake destroyed the building on Sichuan Road and the piano in the basement was crushed, he could not find a piano anywhere. At that time, he was almost driven mad, but luckily the piano here was 'waiting' for him.

No one knew how long the piano had been in this house. It had changed ownership a few times. Because the piano was too badly damaged and so heavy, no one wanted it. It was left here all the time. Later, one of the locals liked music and wanted his son to learn the piano, so employed him to teach. He was very happy when he came to teach piano here; not just because of the money, but also because it would allow his hungry fingers to touch the keys and thereby communicate with gods. But the son refused to learn. Yannian was afraid that he would never find a piano again, so he came up with a plan to exchange his two-room apartment for this tiny 'cell' and a broken piano that no one else wanted.

At that time, it is quite possible that there was only this one piano in the whole city. It was a miracle!

"This way," Yannian explained, "I can enter heaven whenever I like."

Yuntian was deeply moved. Those who devoted themselves to their art always did.

Yannian played for him the prelude in C major from Bach's 'The Well-Tempered Clavier'. Yuntian suddenly felt that he was no longer in a cell but sitting on white clouds floating in the air, enjoying the breeze, sunshine and eternal tranquillity of the universe.

Of all the arts, only music contains such magic.

In the evening, he told Sui Yi about his chance encounter with Yannian. Sui Yi suggested asking him to teach Yiran. Yuntian agreed that this was a good idea. They wanted their daughter to learn to play an instrument. Sui Yi said that music can soothe the soul. In her mind's eye, she could see an image of a small, black upright piano standing in a corner of the downstairs living room, and Yiran sat in front of it with her hair tied in a pink bow, just like when her mother taught her the piano as a child. Women are often more romantic than men.

Turning ideas into reality seldom happens overnight. They decided to buy a piano. Yuntian went to Yannian first, and he agreed to their plan. However, the next time he knocked on the door of Yannian's house, the man who opened the door was some old buffer with stubble on his chin. When asked, he said that Yannian had moved out a few months ago, and further questioning elicited the information that he had "returned home". Yuntian was sceptical and asked about the piano. The old buffer replied very simply: "That thing was useless. It took up far too much space, so I got rid of it!" It sounded like he'd just thrown it away.

Yuntian made a special trip to see Luo Fu, who told him: "I haven't seen Yannian since we went to see him after the earthquake. Didn't I tell you that his father was some sort of White Russian? Now that the Soviet Union has disintegrated, White Russians aren't unwelcome any more, so maybe he's gone back to claim family property or something."

People's lives together sometimes drag on for a long time, but sometimes they will be interrupted for no reason at all. It is all a matter of chance.

Yannian had evaporated from his life.

As long as you are moving forward, some people will fall behind and drop out; but someone else will catch you up and walk by your side.

Everyone's life is like this.

Those who leave quietly can disappear without you noticing; those who join in their stead are always bright, new, personable and charming.

In the 1980s, Yuntian was at the peak of his fame, and almost every day he met at least one new person – painters, journalists, editors, admirers, all kinds of strangers and intruders, friends of friends, acquaintances of acquaintances, and so on and so forth. Of course, some people just came to meet him and shook hands the once. But don't imagine that this kind of life is light, easy and fleeting – it may simply be the starting point of a whole new existence. Whether you can find something there of weight and value depends on yourself.

At that time, literary and art circles were going crazy. Almost every day, you would hear the name of a budding young artist, the title of a fabulous book that everyone was talking about or some strange new artistic theory. Philosophy, literature, aesthetics and literary theory translated from overseas were increasingly piled up on the cultural dock of Sino-foreign exchanges. Yuntian had been promoted to the position of vice president, and henceforth was in charge of discussion and criticism of theories and works at the Academy of Fine Arts. He organised seminars at least twice a month. There was one critic who worked at the Academy of Social Sciences, whose name was Xiao Shen – a strong, bearded and extremely talkative man, supposedly of Oroqen extraction. Xiao Shen was a bizarre character; at every meeting, he would express amazing new ideas, expound some previously unheard-of opinions on art and cite the names of many strange foreign thinkers. It made people admire him for his great learning and profound thoughts. Capable people are invariably the subject of envy. Some said that whenever he talked in a meeting, he was just trying to put the wind up the others – he was just making play of having read recently translated and published books before anyone else. Yuntian said with a smile: "He's making the most of his opportunities, then. At least it stimulates us to think."

In that unconventional era, no one was content with the status quo and no one could sit still. The sense of crisis was a driving force. On one occasion, Yuntian set the seminar topic as: "What is the eternal value of art?" When setting this subject, he was aware of a certain uneasiness. He wanted to get enlightenment from other people's words.

Recently, he had begun to experience a little hesitation.

Once, Xiao Shen said to him: "It's time for you to move on from 'The Thaw'."

These words were a touchstone for him. He had already become aware of this: he couldn't remain in thrall to 'The Thaw'. But how could he move on from it? A few years ago, when anyone mentioned 'The Thaw' to him, he had a sense of pride. 'The Thaw' was his masterpiece, and it had made him famous. Now he felt differently. It seemed that this painting was now just a medal pinned on the chest of a veteran to show his past military achievements. In fact, wasn't it a witness to his loss of creative vitality? He longed to reach new heights, but where were they to be found?

He couldn't discuss this with Luo Qian. Luo Qian and he no longer lived in the same world at all.

He would often talk about the matter with Yu Changshui, his young friend at the Academy of Fine Arts. He was breaking down barriers right, left and centre. Every time he came to Yuntian's house, he would bring along some completely different paintings, and fresh ideas. He liked to discuss artistic issues with Yu Changshui. Chu Yuntian was older than Yu Changshui, but they were good friends nevertheless.

Once, Yuntian asked: "Why do you keep working on all these experiments and innovations? I don't think you should innovate for innovation's sake. What are you trying to achieve?"

"I don't want to repeat myself. Repetition is stagnation."

Yuntian thought about this and told him a story. He'd once met Wu Guanzhong at an event in Beijing. Wu Guanzhong asked him: "Do you never repeat your paintings?"

"Never," Chu Yuntian replied. "I can't work unless I have something new to express."

Mr Wu nodded and said: "I've never repeated either." He was silent for a moment and then asked: "Why don't you repeat yourself?"

Chu Yuntian said: "Literature is never repeated. A writer cannot write the same article or even the same sentence over and over again."

Mr Wu smiled, nodded and left.

After Yuntian said this, Yu Changtian said: "You're right. Repetition is death for an artist. This is also a problem that modern Chinese painting must face. A French artist once asked me why all Chinese paintings look the same?"

"Why do you think that is?"

"That's a huge question, one that touches upon history, philosophy, aesthetics, customs and national character. We can discuss it later. Right now, I just want to say that refusing to repeat ourselves is not a matter of artistic vision, but psychological need. Painters in the Yuan dynasty transformed their work from what you see in paintings of the Song dynasty because they wanted to "document their pure thoughts" – at least, that is what Ni Zan said. Writers want to write because they always have their characters alive in their minds, with their uncontrollable emotions and difficult thoughts, and that puts pressure on them… they have to write. If they don't write, they won't be able to eat or sleep – that is why they have to put pen to paper. If there is no such pressure, what would we write? Why bother?" Then he said the following to Yu Changshui, to get him to think about what he was doing: "You can't write for writing's sake, or innovate just for innovation's sake. Wouldn't you agree?"

Yu Changshui nodded, before going off into a world of his own.

Yuntian liked talking like this. Through conversation, he could always go deeper into a problem, or clarify some vague feeling in his mind.

Although there was no crisis yet, he had begun to worry about the future of his artistic endeavours.

A person with infinite strength, after a lifetime of effort, may still have ended up moving the wrong thing. If you finally realise this when it's too late, it behoves you to alert others.

Yuntian needed his friends. A true friend is not a cheerleader, but someone who, when you reach a fork in the road, can help you see which way you need to go.

One day, Yuntian had just come back from a visit to Japan when he received a call from Yi Liaoran. The voice coming down the line was hoarse but excited. He was obviously a bit drunk but certainly not slurring his words or anything like that. He asked Yuntian to visit Huangshan. He'd been painting the mist-covered slopes of Huangshan and wanted him to see his work. From his proud tone of voice, it was clear these paintings were very good. If he was so excited about his own paintings, they must be really special. The next day, Yuntian bought a ticket to Huangshan and took Yu Changshui along. As soon as they got to the exit, he could see Yi Liaoran and several people from the Huangshan painting academy standing there waiting. Yi Liaoran stood in the middle with his legs apart, his arms crossed and his hair standing on end – he looked quite extraordinary.

As soon as they arrived, they went to Huangshan. Yuntian was eager to see the paintings, and Yi Liaoran was equally eager for him to see them.

The first sight of them shocked Yuntian. These paintings were all either four- or six-foot square. In addition to ink, he'd used little touches of dark green and ochre pigment. The dry brush scraped and rubbed the paper, and then washes of colour had been overlaid. The shapes and shadows of clouds, pine trees and mist had been painted when the Xuan paper was still wet, so the ink had run, the brushstrokes blurred, but the form and spirit were present. The areas of paint showed lofty peaks, while the blank spaces were as ethereal as a dream. The mist floated across the cliffs and ravines, in the deep valleys and streams, hidden and yet revealed, present and absent, unpredictable. He was impressed with how Yi Liaoran had conveyed the density of clouds and mist, as thick as snow or as thin as gauze. In the mist, the peaks, trees and rocks behind were half hidden and yet still discernible. Who else could have painted such a magical scene? No wonder he was so excited on the phone yesterday.

This was not just the beauty of Huangshan recreated on paper; it elevated the scene to a fairyland on earth.

Chu Yuntian couldn't stop himself from saying: "Other people paint the Huangshan they can see – you paint the Huangshan of your imagination and your dreams. Others paint forms where you paint the spirit. To tell you the truth, these paintings are wonderful!"

Yi Liaoran suddenly threw his arms wide and clapped his hands. He took a few steps forward to hug Yuntian and then burst into tears. He then grabbed Yuntian's arm and said: "Let's go and get a drink!"

At the table, Yu Changshui kept pushing away and blocking every attempt to get Yuntian drunk, downing cup after cup in his stead. But Yuntian was so happy to see the truly outstanding talent of this man from Huizhou that he couldn't help raising his glass a couple of times and pouring the wine down into his stomach.

Although they were drinking, they were by no means befuddled. Both Yuntian and Yi Liaoran agreed to cooperate on a group of paintings. When it came to the theme, Yi Liaoran said: "I have a good subject. Let's paint the four things mentioned in Cheung Ming-man's song – the Yangtze River, the Great Wall, Huangshan and the Yellow River!"

Yu Changshui chimed in: "What a good idea! The four symbols of the Chinese nation. If you want to paint them, you'll need a big canvas!"

Chu Yuntian got excited, stood up and said: "The Yangtze River and the Yellow River, one to the north and one to the south, are two cradles of our people. Huangshan is the greatest mountain in China, and the Great Wall is the greatest building of mankind. Besides, two of them move and two are stationary. Huangshan and the Great Wall are static. The Yellow River and the Yangtze are dynamic!"

"Or to put it another way," Yu Changshui said, "two are horizontal and two vertical. Huangshan and the Great Wall are vertical, and the Yellow River and the Yangtze are horizontal!"

Bang! Yi Liaoran thumped the table. He was even more excited than Yuntian. His hoarse voice shouted: "Let's paint! Yuntian will paint the Yellow River and the Great Wall. I'll paint the Yangtze and Huangshan!"

"In terms of colour, the Yangtze is blue, the Yellow River is mud-brown, Huangshan is green and the Great Wall is rosy with the occasional vermilion highlight."

"Your Yellow River and Great Wall are warm. My Yangtze River and Huangshan are cold."

The two of them chatted away, almost as if they could see these paintings in front of their very eyes.

This made everyone present feel happy and full of pride. Together, they raised their glasses and consumed all the wine in them, going on to empty every bottle on the table.

Yuntian had never experienced such feelings before. Painting a picture under these circumstances seemed as heroic as going into battle.

Yuntian and Yi Liaoran kept their promise and each of them painted in his own home. To maintain some kind of visual harmony between the four paintings, and keep them informed of important developments, Yu Changshui kindly acted as a go-between. At the end of the following spring, they were exhibited at the Beijing Art Museum. 'Landscapes' hit the world of art like a clap of thunder, and crowds flocked to the exhibition. This was to prove Yuntian's second spring after 'The Thaw'. At the same time, a new talent from Huizhou came to public attention for his marvellous facility with ink – and that was Yi Liaoran.

CHAPTER 5

To outsiders, having begun his 'second spring', there seemed to be nothing that Chu Yuntian could not do.

He made this spring last for more than a decade, and right up to today it remained beautiful and bright – that was sufficient to demonstrate his undoubted abilities. On the one hand, he received a constant stream of visitors every day, which put him under a lot of pressure; on the other hand, even more honorary titles were bestowed on him. The bottom shelf of his bookcase was where he put all these letters of appointment. What bothered him the most was that he could not just refuse all these pompous stupidities, but if he accepted them, he would have every waking moment filled with other people's boring ideas of fun.

Sometimes he had to wear the mask and put in an appearance with a bit of false bonhomie – adding some gloss to other people's staged events. Celebrities belong to society; they are a part of social life. This is true all over the world.

When there was turnover in the China Artists Association, he was given the title of vice chairman. This honour involved attendance at a series of events, speeches, award ceremonies, ribbon cuttings, preface writing, calligraphy for book titles and other such duties, as well as being expected to accompany officials on the rostrum with a fake smile. This was something he had never contemplated when he was sitting with the other Three Musketeers in their salon. It was ridiculous, but it was now a duty that he took very seriously. Although it may be vulgar, you can't place yourself outside the world in which you find yourself. You imagine that the result of your efforts will be more and more room to manoeuvre, but in fact you find yourself increasingly at the mercy of others. You may be arrogant and aloof and keep yourself to yourself, but can you really cut yourself off from all human contact? Are you prepared to become a recluse? Can you really live in a busy city as though you were far away in the mountains? Luo Qian was like that. However, did Luo Qian genuinely accept his way of life with peace of mind? Or was he just hiding his sense of inferiority with overweening self-esteem?

No one knew what Chu Yuntian felt in his heart when it seemed as though he had everything he wanted.

Once, Sui Yi said to him: "You're getting a little vulgar."

He responded with a smile. Even Sui Yi didn't understand the meaning of his smile.

The deepest distress that he felt came after the end of the 'Landscapes' exhibition, when he realised that one part of his life had drawn to a close. He had a sense of something having come to its natural end.

From 'The Thaw' to 'Landscapes', he had produced a kind of landscape painting that had never existed in the past; that is, he had sublimated the grand spirit of a particular era and integrated it into a natural scene, investing it with historical and humanistic significance. But where should he go next?

Chu Yuntian had a writer's sensitivity to the world around him and a writer's capacity for analysis. Therefore, he could feel that a profound change was underway in this rapidly developing society. In the process of rapid marketisation, people had come unmoored from their values and lacked the pureness of spirit that they had had before. Impetuousness, utilitarianism, money worship, hedonism, individualism, vulgarity, fashion and popular culture had gradually come to dominate their lives. The materialism of consumer society made people stop caring about purely spiritual things. At the same time, both artistic circles and the literary world were blindly caught up in imitating Western modernism and had completely lost their way. He felt that he could not grasp this era; he could not get hold of its spirit and soul. He could not comprehend the way that society had fragmented and splintered into ever more bizarre patterns.

On one occasion, he discussed his ideas with Yu Changshui and Xiao Shen. Xiao Shen might sometimes put things in extreme terms, but his analysis was sometimes surprisingly accurate and deep. He was that rare person who can think. At the time, Xiao Shen didn't say a word. The next day, he brought him a book: Frank Furedi's *Where Have All the Intellectuals Gone?* A few days later, he went to Britain on an exchange visit and happened to visit Cambridge. When he had lunch with three professors at the university, he said he wanted to talk to them about intellectuals. One of the professors smiled and said: "I am amazed that there should be Chinese people interested in talking with us about intellectuals! Mostly when you come to Cambridge it is to talk about cooperation and projects with us."

They were not interested in talking about the problem either. It is a serious issue when no one cares about philistinism. Had the right to speak in the era of globalisation been given over to the powerful, leaving no room for intellectuals to say a word?

Against such a background, was not painting facing a new dilemma? At least he felt more and more clearly that his original road had come to an end and was now a matter of the past.

He was examining himself, and this period of introspection was important.

One ought to notice things about oneself before they become obvious to others. He who loses consciousness of himself experiences another kind of death.

Facing the mirror, Yuntian knotted his tie and put on a silver-grey jacket. His suit was paired with a dark blue tie flecked with purple flowers against a snow-white shirt, very smart and refined-looking. He was feeling very handsome and relaxed. Self-appreciation put him in a good mood. Mostly he hated wearing a suit because he always associated them with putting on a show for other people; they made him feel constrained. He said a tie was like an animal halter. But today was different. Today, Luo Fu was holding a solo exhibition of his paintings. He was invited to attend the opening ceremony and give a speech. He wanted to do his best for his old friend, so he had to take it seriously and give a good performance.

Just after the car arrived at the gate of the Art Museum on Jiefang Road, he saw through the window that there was a lot of traffic and crowds of people. As soon as the car drew to a halt, someone opened the door from the outside. The first face he saw, bending over and grinning from ear to ear, was Luo Fu. He wore a very fashionable plaid overcoat and no tie, his hair as curly as ever, so he looked like a fashionable cowboy, and smelled of cologne. Luo Fu pulled his friend out of the car. Yuntian felt a little confused amid the crowd, some of whom he knew and many more that he didn't. Various reporters took pictures of him with their cameras, as people called out his name.

Luo Fu pulled him through the gate. The opening ceremony was held in the lobby. At least sixty or seventy large flower arrangements were standing against the wall, each one of them taller than a man. How had Luo Fu managed to assemble so many well-wishers and supportive work units? Luo Fu said to him: "The exhibition is inside. Let's get the opening ceremony out of the way first and then go and see the exhibition. Everyone is waiting for you!"

"Whatever you want," Yuntian said. Then he walked along with Luo Fu, shaking endless hands stuck out at him from the crowd.

When the guests of honour were introduced by the master of ceremonies, it became clear just how highly ranked Luo Fu's invitees were, and how many celebrities from all walks of life he had managed to corral. What Yuntian didn't understand was why so many bosses of well-known large enterprises had come to support him.

When the master of ceremonies invited Yuntian to speak, he made a big play of the various honorary positions he had assumed. Although Yuntian didn't like people to do so, today was all about Luo Fu, so he was prepared to admit the necessity. When the time came for his speech, he had not seen the exhibition and did not know anything about the contents, but he was sure that Luo Fu would have included his best-known pieces, so he started by talking about 'Five Thousand Years', 'Ploughing Deep' and 'The Shout', praised his talent and creativity, and then finished up with some flowery well-wishing for the future. Yuntian had always been noted for his outstanding eloquence and he spoke well, but he realised from the reaction of the audience that his speech was alien to the focus of the exhibition. When he looked around the hall, he realised that his speech was irrelevant. This time, Luo Fu was only exhibiting modern abstract works – his art had undergone a complete transformation. Yuntian hadn't visited his studio for a long time and so was unaware of this revolution. Chu Yuntian wasn't quite sure how to feel about this, but he could appreciate his boldness and courage, and he admired his openness, his rough and bold talent in essence, especially when it came to colour. When some reporters interviewed him on the spot, he didn't know how to evaluate this sudden burst into modernism on the part of his old friend. Yuntian was surprised that Luo Fu had got so far in one jump. Was this a change in artistic outlook or simply a matter of following fashion? Anyway, in today's art world, anyone who wants to attract public attention can make themselves a trendsetter.

He heard Yu Changshui say to Luo Fu: "You really are charging a fortune for 'The Red Age'!"

Chu Yuntian realised at that moment that there was a price listed alongside the title on the little plaque placed at the bottom right of each painting on the wall. In such a formal context, it was an innovation to openly set a price for his work. Looking at the painting carefully, it was a little absurd. It consisted of a red square on a beige canvas; and while the colour was nice and bright, there was nothing else to it. It was just that the red square was angled on the square canvas so that it looked about to fall off. There were two or three wild and powerful strokes on that side of the picture and that was all, with the signature line at the bottom in black written in a foreign language. Yuntian couldn't understand it. At that moment, when Luo Fu turned away to speak to one of the other guests of honour, a low voice behind Yuntian said: "This painting is pretty much a reproduction of Kasimir Malevich's 'Black Square'."

When Yuntian looked back, it was Xiao Shen. He just shook his head.

· · ·

At the exhibition, Yuntian saw many artists from the Artists Association and Academy who had made the journey from Beijing especially for this occasion. Some were very familiar and others he was meeting for the first time. At that time, people handed out business cards when they met. Soon, Yuntian had a stack of cards in his hand. He asked Luo Fu if he had invited Luo Qian and said that he ought to see his paintings. "I sent him an invitation and said you were coming," Luo Fu replied. "But he said he had other things to do today." Then he smiled and added: "I don't know what's the matter with him, he's getting more and more peculiar."

Yuntian noticed that a woman kept reappearing around Luo Fu. She would be standing there for a while and then go away again, and every time she whispered something in his ear. The woman was tall, almost as tall as Luo Fu himself. She looked beautiful, very well-dressed, with strong eyebrows and a lot of make-up. At first glance, she appeared both energetic and capable. Was she the organiser of the exhibition? Luo Fu tugged at her arm and introduced her to Yuntian: "This is my friend, Hao Jun."

While Yuntian searched for something to say, the woman spoke up: "Luo Fu often talks about you. You are his idol." Before Yuntian could respond, she waved and disappeared into the crowd. An open, lively, very outgoing woman. That was Yuntian's first impression of Hao Jun.

Yuntian wanted to ask Luo Fu about her, but just then he called someone else over: a short man in his forties, dark-skinned and coarse-featured. He looked a wheeler-dealer type. When they had been introduced, the man's name turned out to be a little vulgar: Xu Dayou. Luo Fu explained that he was the manager of the Purple Clouds Gallery in the Liulichang district in Beijing. He had a lot of experience in arranging art exhibitions and a wide range of contacts, so he could always get sponsorship. He had been invited to curate many art exhibitions in Beijing. This exhibition was all Xu Dayou's doing. Luo Fu went on: "Mr Xu has always wanted to get to know you and would be delighted to hold an exhibition of your work!"

"We all admire you greatly," Xu Dayou said, "and we actually have one of your greatest fans working for us at our gallery."

"Who would that be?" Chu Yuntian asked casually, a little curious, but the occasion was not one where he could insist on an answer, so he just treated it as a joke.

The day after Luo Fu's exhibition opened, Yuntian flew to Guangzhou with Yu Changshui. A cross-straits exhibition of calligraphy and painting was being held there. Yuntian particularly wanted to see the work of one famous artist from Taipei whose traditional Chinese painting had been widely acclaimed in the West. He had brought Yu Changshui thinking that he might learn something and make a few friends. In Guangzhou, he met and talked with the famous master from Taipei, and the two of them got on extremely well. He had a lot of presence, and unlike southern people he had a cheerful temperament and a loud, clear voice – both he and his paintings were on a grand scale. But his painting technique was not profound; he would just crumple up some rice paper and then brush it down with a dampened brush so that the ink was sometimes thick and wet, and sometimes thin and dry. Using the texture of the crumpled paper, he would get a variety of interesting effects and it also gave the picture an abstract quality. Compared with traditional painting methods, this kind of painting did indeed have an entirely original visual effect, absent from traditional Chinese painting and also from Western painting. That's probably why Westerners were interested in his work. However, Yuntian was a very learned man, and he knew that Huang Yongyu used this painting method as early as the 1970s. Later, when IM Pei designed the Fragrant Hill Hotel, on completion he asked Zao Wou-ki, a Sino-French painter, to produce two large paintings for the lobby, and he also used this method. First, crumple up the paper and then paint it. In Yuntian's eyes, any innovation based on technical effect is just a superficial skill, so he didn't delay much in Guangzhou. He only stayed for two days before flying back.

When he had dinner that night after returning home, he happily told Sui Yi what he had seen and heard during his southbound trip. Sui Yi listened with a smile and said: "While you were away, Yufei came to see you."

"Who?" He was confused.

"How many people do you know called Yufei? Your old student."

"What did she want?"

Yiran asked her mother: "Was that the beautiful woman who came the other day?"

Sui Yi ignored Yiran, but said to Yuntian: "She's still very pretty but a little plumper than she used to be."

Yuntian felt awkward. He tried to keep himself calm and asked: "What's she doing here?"

"She was helping out at Luo Fu's exhibition," Sui Yi explained. "Didn't you see her?"

"Luo Fu didn't say a word and I didn't see her," Yuntian replied. "If I'd seen her, I would have mentioned it. Luo Fu did introduce me to one of the exhibition organisers, but that was some guy called Xu Dayou – he's the manager of the Purple Clouds Gallery in Beijing."

Sui Yi was still smiling. "The day before yesterday, she was here with Xu Dayou. He's Yufei's husband." Then she looked to see his expression.

Chu Yuntian was surprised. He didn't know what to say. He just stared at Sui Yi.

"Luo Fu brought the two of them round for a visit," Sui Yi continued. "He said to give him a call when you got back, because they might not yet have returned to Beijing, and they want to arrange an exhibition for you. I think you should go and see them." Her voice was quite expressionless, as if she were just conveying the information and that was all.

Because of the past, he didn't know what to do.

"Can I come too?" Yiran asked.

Yuntian said yes, and Sui Yi also agreed.

When there are misconceptions between husband and wife, a child can just sweep them away like a fan.

Yuntian and Luo Fu talked on the phone. Luo Fu said that luckily enough Yufei and her husband were still there since they would not be going back to Beijing until the day after tomorrow, so they agreed to meet at Luo Fu's house the following afternoon. All that

Luo Fu said in addition was: "They can help you sell your paintings."

Yuntian was not interested in selling his paintings. That was how he was different from most other painters. So, when he went to see Yufei, was it just because she was an old flame? He couldn't be sure himself. The situation all those years ago put him, Sui Yi and Yufei in a real dilemma, but thanks to the help of Luo Qian and Luo Fu, everyone had emerged unscathed. He was determined not to look back. However, once it was all over, he occasionally reminisced to himself about those days. Of course, he had no intention of reawakening their stupid affair. However, some particularly exciting moments from the past, once over, had become unforgettable scenes. For example, their first kiss while he had held two Japanese ceramic bottles against the wall with his arms, the way she would wait for him no matter how long it took when they had agreed a date, their mad passion in the heavy rain, the melancholy that showed in her slightly unfocused eyes… they were like chapters in a novel he had read, which had somehow become etched into his memory. Every time he called these incidents to mind, he wanted to know how she was doing now. That was all. And now here she was. Was arranging an exhibition for him just an excuse to see him again?

Could his sentimental, romantic streak be reawakened?

Yuntian told himself that he was only going to see her once, and that was going to be an end to it.

The following afternoon, Yuntian took Yiran to Luo Fu's house. By this time, Luo Fu had become very rich. Even the sofas and curtains had been changed, and everything was now refined and exquisite, luxurious and somewhat nouveau riche. When they entered the room, Xu Dayou and Yufei were already seated in the living room. Seeing him come in, they all stood up. When Yufei stood up there was a slight movement that twisted her waist, reminding him of how much he had once cared about her. And it was Yufei who said the first words: "Our great painter has arrived. We have been waiting for a long time!"

This sentence instantly separated the past from the reality before them. The embarrassment that he was on the verge of feeling simply vanished. Xu Dayou took out another pack of cigarettes and handed them around, and they chatted as they smoked. All of Chu Yuntian's prior intensity of feeling seemed to have vanished.

There was also a three- or four-year-old boy there, who was Yufei and Xu Dayou's son. He was a round-faced, bullet-headed child, very dark-skinned and strongly built. Xu bared his teeth in a smile: "Everyone says our kid looks just like me… he doesn't take after Yufei at all!"

"If we have a daughter," Yufei chipped in, "she can look like me." Her tone was frank and forthright.

Yuntian felt a little surprised. This was not at all like something the old Yufei would have said; she had been a gentle, introverted and slightly shy girl. He glanced at her. She was indeed plumper than she used to be and very good-looking, but when did her long face grow so round, and where did her pointed chin and long eyelashes go? When he looked at her, the unusual, dreamy expression in her unfocused eyes seemed to be lacking. Then she said to him: "As any good art dealer would say, I would like to be your agent. I used to be your student, and I know your paintings better than anyone!"

Yuntian smiled. All at once, he returned from the distant past to the present, from imaginary days of glory to naked reality. What followed was a practical conversation with Xu Dayou in which they hammered out the details. From what came next, Yuntian realised that Xu Dayou was ignorant about art. At most, he knew the names of Li Keran, Huang Zhou, Fu Baoshi, Zhang Daqian and other popular artists who sold well, but he didn't know anything else. Whenever he was at a loss, Yufei came to the rescue. They operated like business partners. Yufei used to be a girl full of spiritual yearnings who cared about good taste. Why did she choose to marry this money-grubber? What kind of experiences must she have gone through in her life, and why did she turn her back on her old principles to pursue profit at all costs? Yuntian felt a little disappointed in her. Of course, it had nothing to do with him.

When Xu Dayou mentioned that someone wanted to exchange a Mercedes-Benz for his painting 'The Thaw', Luo Fu went so far as to say that if he didn't like the deal, he could make a copy of the original and swap that, at which point Yuntian decided that it was time to bring the conversation to a close.

At the same time, Yiran was also growing a little impatient. She couldn't stand the constant racket being made by Yufei's son as he threw things about, and no one seemed to pay the slightest attention to the child.

This time, when Yuntian and Yufei said goodbye, it really was a final farewell, since henceforth their paths would lie in different directions. He didn't dislike her. He had seen too many people destroyed by life, so he stuck to his principle that circumstances should not be allowed to crush his artistic vision.

CHAPTER 6

When a person's life is beautiful and full, they may still secretly worry about making mistakes and losing all that they have gained. This does not necessarily mean they are concerned about being envied or having someone plot against them. You can never have complete control over your own life and therefore there will be accidents, no matter what you do to prevent them, and sometimes you can't predict what will happen at all.

For example, Sui Yi felt that she was the happiest woman in the world when she married Chu Yuntian. She and Yuntian had grown up together and she had never wanted anyone else. She liked Yuntian's family and knew his home like the back of her hand, including the sound of birds singing out in the garden. Yuntian's parents had watched her grow from a lively little girl to a gentle young woman, and she had also watched Yuntian's parents age from the prime of life to becoming frail and hesitant. She seemed to have been part of his family since birth. However, less than a year after her marriage, the force of the Cultural Revolution drove her out of this house and into the tiny, strange attic room overlooking the Qiangzi Canal. With her husband who she had grown up with like a brother, she had made great efforts to bring beauty into their small room, transforming it into a 'little piece of heaven', but the earthquake had destroyed everything. She had lost everything twice over, and then from nothing she had built up something, returning all over again to where she had originally begun.

However, life is fair. Although fate had disrupted her life repeatedly and ruthlessly, it had also given her sweet fairy fruit again and again. Was this because of her pure and simple character, being submissive, never complaining, and always trying to make the best out of life within its limitations? Was it because she loved her family and home too much? Or was it because she always used her love of beauty and goodness to improve upon a dry and boring reality?

Sui Yi believed that her life could not possibly be improved upon now. She had nothing more to wish for, but she just hoped that God wouldn't take it away again.

She liked this old English-style house, the gigantic fir trees and the lawn, and she enjoyed chatting with Yuntian, sitting out on rattan chairs under the trees. Those white rustic-style armchairs were elegant and pleasing to the eye in the green garden. She never planted flowers in the garden, since she preferred plain, natural greens, and the grass gave her quite enough: from spring to autumn, it was always hosting various tiny flowers of different colours. The neighbouring houses also had gardens with big trees. There were many birds in this area, and from time to time they would fly into the house. The smell of all this greenery penetrated deeply into the house, and even more deep than that was the unique smell of the old house. It gave people a feeling of antiquity, of peace and quiet.

In this old house, she would sometimes call to mind the writings of Charlotte Bronte or Jane Austen. Girls of her generation who liked to read had all been obsessed with their books.

Yiran was growing up and had already reached the age where she had become more silent and reserved. She was deeply influenced by her mother. She wasn't interested in make-up at all, but kept a clean face and didn't care about fashion like most girls. Instead, she liked to sit with a book in her hand, reading quietly. As she had suggested, half of the living room was given over to bookcases that reached from floor to ceiling. The other half was hung with her father's paintings. However, her first choice was not 'The Thaw', but the old painting rescued from the ruins after the earthquake – a sketch of three red pitched roofs. Although the picture was small, it was of great significance for the whole family. It embodied so many unforgettable memories; it was where they had all come from. In Yiran's view, it was very important to hang paintings significant in their lives in the living room.

A small concert grand piano was placed obliquely in one corner of the room, and Yiran would sometimes play it. After Yannian disappeared, Sui Yi had invited a piano teacher from the Conservatory of Music to teach her for a while. In Sui Yi's mind, the sound of a piano playing was part and parcel of the old house.

Yiran looked so much like her mother. Her beautiful eyebrows, small, bright mouth, well-shaped nose, and smooth forehead gave her a gentle and refined air. However, she took her physique from her father, including her very long legs, so that when she was a teenager, she was slim as a reed. Growing up in a family like that, it was only natural that she worshipped art. She didn't study painting with her father, but she was very interested in art history. She would often discuss the history of Chinese art with him. When it came to Western art, she often argued with Luo Fu about it, but she didn't dare to talk to Xiao Shen. Sui Yi had begun to think about where she might go and study art history overseas and planned to send her abroad as soon as possible to begin her studies and visit museums. To learn art history, she would need both Chinese and foreign languages.

Once Yiran had started middle school, Sui Yi didn't have to go and pick her up after class, so she devoted her entire attention to housework. She cared too much about whether everything in the house was in its proper position, and often changed the decoration of the rooms so that her beloved home would give its inhabitants a different impression. Yuntian said she was an "unrepentant aesthete". Of course, the most important thing was to make Yuntian comfortable in terms of food and clothing. She cooked his meals, washed and ironed his clothes, sent his letters, shopped and tidied the garden, with all the diligence she had developed during the many years their life had been hard. She never complained, regarding this work as nothing more than her proper task. She ate the leftovers, having picked out all the most delicious bits with her chopsticks and put them into Yuntian's bowl. It was natural for her to do so.

Her friends laughed at Sui Yi and said she spoiled Yuntian too much. In fact, Yuntian treated her like a little sister. Whatever problems were thrown up, big or small, he would deal with them on her behalf.

No one could have said which of them was more dependent on the other.

Sui Yi understood that what happened with Yufei was not that Yuntian fell in love with her, but that he was a very romantic man, and he would like to make his life seem like something out of a novel. He didn't really want to leave her. But if she left him, he would be unmoored, his soul as lonely and adrift as a solitary cloud.

That day, when Yuntian came back from Luo Fu's house with Yiran, their daughter was complaining furiously about how the black-faced Xu Dayou wanted to swap a car for 'The Thaw'. "How dare they!" Sui Yi shouted. "Even if they bring a mountain of gold, you shouldn't sell it – not unless they are going to donate it to an art museum in the future!"

Chu Yuntian was very moved. It was Sui Yi who took his art seriously. No ordinary woman would have that kind of appreciation of his work. Of course, he was also pleased with his daughter.

Although they were now well-off, they maintained a low profile. They agreed with the saying: high profile and low profile are just different ways to live. High-profile living means you live to show off to other people; low-profile living means you live for yourself. They didn't like showing off and parading around, throwing their weight about and attracting attention. They never envied anyone else's wealth. They only cared about beauty, because beauty was a fundamental need for both of them.

Beauty has nothing to do with wealth. Beauty may be a bunch of pretty flowers, a moving piece of music, an elegant play of colours or an object placed in the perfect position. This kind of everyday beauty is something you cannot expect all your visitors to appreciate, but as long as you know it is there, that is all that is necessary.

Ever since she was a baby, Yiran had agreed with her parents' motto: the enemy of beauty is not necessarily ugliness, but vulgarity.

Keeping yourself away from all vulgarity is a matter of education, and also a kind of self-cultivation.

That was the secret behind this family's unusual qualities.

By adopting this approach to life, Chu Yuntian and Sui Yi had never deliberately pursued wealth. His income was enough to live on. Occasionally he might sell one or two paintings, but that was because people came to find them. Yuntian never took the initiative to sell his paintings, nor would he send them to an auction house. Sui Yi wasn't in the least bit greedy, and luxury goods meant nothing to her. She had been with him for decades, and she was used to letting him deal with his own affairs. She believed he was right. She remembered one thing he said –

Yuntian had a friend, a talented old painter with the romantic name of Qu Fangge. The name 'Fangge' was a quotation from one of Du Fu's poems: "When singing in the daytime, you must pour yourself some wine." There was always a pot of wine on his painting table, so he could drink while painting. His favourite subjects were Buddhist and Taoist immortals, eminent officials from history, and he was particularly good at fine ladies. He had well-honed traditional skills, with excellent placement of pictorial elements and strong lines, something in the manner of Chen Hongshou in the Ming dynasty. His paintings were very expensive and popular with collectors.

One day, Yuntian went to see Qu Fangge. He was angry, breathing heavily, huffing and puffing into the wispy beard on his chin. When asked what the matter was, he informed Yuntian that a person who had been helping him sell his work had cheated him out of a batch of his paintings. The old painter told Yuntian that he was so angry the night before that he didn't sleep for the first half of the night, and the second half was filled with nightmares. There were all kinds of ghosts and demons running around in his dreams.

Qu Fangge was a man of some character. He said that all the demons and monsters in his nightmares were extremely ugly, some treacherous, some strange, some cunning, and some bony and desiccated. He said: "I want to paint their hideousness! Didn't Luo Liangfeng, one of the Eight Eccentrics of Yangzhou, do a marvellous painting of ghosts? I am going to paint one too, and then paint the demon-queller Zhong Kui so he can catch and kill all these horrible ghosts!"

"Great!" Yuntian said. "Your painting is exquisite in the antique style. But with all due respect, the subjects you choose for your work have too long been stereotyped. If you do this painting, something new will emerge and your style will change. Go ahead and paint it. I can't wait to see it – I am full of anticipation!"

"OK, you wait and see! This picture is already taking shape in my head," Qu Fangge said confidently.

A few days later, Yuntian heard that he had finished painting. He went round to his house and asked him: "Where is the painting? I want to see it. Is that OK?"

"Of course! Come this way," Qu Fangge said, and he pulled Yuntian into his studio.

All he could see was an eight-foot-square painting hanging on the wall directly in front of him. Yuntian felt something was wrong, and when he looked at it more closely, the painting turned out to be one of 'The Twelve Beauties of Jinling' representing the major characters in the eighteenth-century novel *The Dream of the Red Chamber*. Qu Fangge had painted this theme at least a hundred times, and the composition was almost identical in each case. Yuntian said with a little surprise: "Didn't you say you were going to paint ghosts?"

Qu Fangge laughed and then he told Yuntian the truth. He patted him on the shoulder and said: "Brother, you don't understand this. If I changed my style all of a sudden, without any warning, people would just think it is a fake. Do you know how many forged works there are in circulation right now with my name on them?" He stretched out his right hand, pressed his thumb and index finger together and exclaimed: "At least eight thousand!"

Yuntian didn't say another word. He felt a little sorry for the complacent old painter. When he got home, he told Sui Yi about it. "Once a painter is held hostage by the market, he no longer has any freedom." Then he added: "If you paint pictures, you can do whatever you like. Once you start selling your paintings, you have to listen to other people."

This was one of the reasons why Yuntian had been distancing himself from the art market.

When the market got hot, Yuntian naturally became cold. He was content with the tranquillity brought by this 'cold', so he could concentrate on research, painting and writing, and live a simple if cultivated life.

But his achievements forced him to become socialised. A socialised person has many friends, at least on the surface. In fact, these friends are scattered – they come and go like the figures on a magic lantern. It is difficult to make real friends. Although Yuntian didn't take his social status seriously, others did, and they kept away from him. And so loneliness, like a ghost, sometimes came to him. Fortunately, he had Sui Yi. Although she couldn't understand his innermost thoughts about his chosen profession and converse seriously with him, her strong moral values meant that in some respects she was in a position to advise him – she made an excellent confidante. Over the years, he had become accustomed to asking for her opinion whenever he'd painted something particularly well; and whenever he felt proud of something he'd written, he would ask her to read it first.

Right now, his interest was in painting.

He didn't like the studio to be too bright. He preferred to spread out his paper where the trees threw heavy shadows.

With his brush just touching the white rice paper, he drew a vigorous line of ink, just like a strong tree trunk. Then some branches, long and short, spread out from this trunk; some clear and powerful, others twisted and hesitant. When a long line stretched out smoothly across the paper, he felt almost as though it were his imagination racing ahead. Then at a certain point, it suddenly split into two branches, each one heading off into unknown territory. At that moment, he realised that what he was painting was not a branch, but a representation of the thoughts in his head.

When people think, all kinds of thoughts can coexist, some chaotic and some orderly, intermittent and interspersed, complex and tangled. Confused and lively thoughts can shoot through this mess, like a branch making its way through the tree canopy, until it has found its own place – taking the foreground in his picture.

All of a sudden, he spotted a gap in the tangled and interlaced branches. There, a vivid, playful branch stretched out and called him: was this the clear-thinking thread finally appearing?

It had never occurred to him that rational thinking might lead to such a magnificent image. He called for Sui Yi to come and have a look, for he wanted her first impressions.

Sui Yi looked at the painting; he looked at her expression.

He noticed an expression of amazement gradually cross her face. She said to him: "I think you are painting more than just a branch…?"

She was very perceptive.

He was so moved that he put his left arm around his wife's shoulder and told her about the wonderful feelings he had when painting this picture. Later, when it went on exhibition, he called this painting 'Levels of Perception'.

CHAPTER 7

After entering Luo Fu's life, Hao Jun seemed to have grown a pair of wings. He really needed those wings because he felt as though he were flying. Everything seemed to be up in the air.

Not only had he realised his ambitions; some ambitions that he would have been afraid to hold in the past had emerged into the light and come to fruition.

Hao Jun was a woman full of energy and vitality. She would never be satisfied with the status quo; she was always going to keep on striving, to have the courage to ask for more, to fix her eyes on her goals and to go after what she wanted, never tiring. She said that sitting is better than lying down, standing is better than sitting, walking is better than standing, and running is better than walking. She was quick, confident, with a good memory and decisive judgement – having made up her mind, she would go right ahead and do it. She liked to have several things on the go at once, and she would get everything done absolutely perfectly. She was like a great tree, with roots deep into the earth, forming a huge web, absorbing the water and nutrients into itself, while its branches stretched out to the sky in another huge web, to catch all the sunshine and breezes going past. She was never going to slow down or rest on her laurels; she would always be launching herself as fast as possible towards her next goal.

For all that she worked so hard, she never seemed fatigued, only more cheerful and energetic. Her hair was black and glossy, and her skin pale and soft. This was a result of her constitution and the energy given to her by abundant food and material wealth. Her dark hair set off her swan-like neck, and her deep-set eyes made her forehead seem higher. She must have looked adorable when she was a child.

Her beauty was of the kind that comes from dramatic features, so she did not use make-up to make her more elegant, but to make herself more strikingly eye-catching. She was very concerned about brands of clothing; whatever she wore and whatever she held in her hands was intended to attract attention.

She had studied design in the School of Arts and Crafts, and after graduation she joined a private design company to such excellent effect that she was promoted to vice president a year later. Having been engaged in design work, she knew all about visual impact. She wanted to make sure that she herself created a strong visual effect, so no matter where she was standing, she would jump out at first glance. This was another aspect of her character.

The previous year, Luo Fu had spotted her the moment he set foot in an event hosted by the Technology Department at the College of Art, but he didn't know that she had gone to the college that day because she wanted to meet him. She had heard his name and made all manner of inquiries about him. She needed such a man, just like a cannon needs a fortress giving it a wide field of action. She was still unmarried at the age of twenty-seven because she had been waiting for someone like Luo Fu to appear.

So, in their relationship, from the very beginning, Luo Fu was the prey, and she was a very experienced huntress. As a result, the oblivious Luo Fu happily entered the attractive and comfortable cage she proffered him.

Luo Fu lacked the ability to make a life for himself, but Hao Jun supported him easily enough. He had ambitions that he had no idea how to achieve which would soon become a reality when confided to her. She also had the ability to enlarge Luo Fu's vision, expand his reputation and double his wealth. He admired her, trusted her and left her alone. However, an obstacle to their happiness arose when she decided they had to move out of their apartment which was no longer good enough for him. Luo Fu could not stand living with other people; he had to live in a house all by itself. She then fell in love with a large villa in a new development southwest of the city, which was all white, overlooking the water in front of the house, with a huge wooden dock. She said the place looked just like the houses on the Mediterranean coast in the south of France. However, the price of this villa was very high, and they simply couldn't afford it. Their only option was to sell Luo Fu's paintings: 'Five Thousand Years', 'Ploughing Deep' and 'The Shout'. The previous autumn, Xu Dayou's exhibition of Luo Fu's work at his gallery had fallen rather flat. First of all, in those days there weren't so many buyers for modern art. Second, oil paintings were harder to sell than traditional Chinese paintings. However, these three paintings were not only painted in a highly realistic style; they were regarded as modern classics and so were bound to sell at a high price. Hao Jun designed a wonderful special auction to sell them. She wanted to make the auction a cultural event. Even the master of ceremonies for the occasion was a famous face from TV hired at a steep price. More important, she even found buyers. The location was a five-star hotel in Beijing.

Hao Jun said that the auction would not only give him the money to live properly but would also build on his past reputation so that the glory of yesteryear would continue to shine today.

When Luo Fu heard that, he was happy enough, but after he took the paintings out of the cabinet where they were kept, he felt reluctant. Those brushstrokes, so full of vitality, still had the power to move him. An artist's paintings are his lifeblood – this feeling is one that only artists can understand. Moreover, the paintings were part of his personal history, something that could never be repeated, a rare glory and a source of pride, witnesses to the fact that he had once stood at the pinnacle of his profession – they were more him than he was himself. He could not bear to sell them!

Chu Yuntian was the most firmly opposed to any sale. Yuntian scolded him: "How can you possibly be so mercenary as to sell your lifeblood? Have you gone insane?"

Luo Fu hesitated, which made Hao Jun angry. As she said: "Chu Yuntian has that big house over in the Five Avenues district. Of course, he doesn't have to worry about a thing. If he had to live in our chicken coop, I refuse to believe he wouldn't sell all his precious paintings."

Hao Jun's most powerful technique was to make concessions now to gain advantage in the future. She said she would give up the whole idea; even though it was only one step away from success, she wanted to put an end to it. She also wanted to break up with Luo Fu and never see him again. They might be living together now, but at least they weren't married. She was resolute and generous. She said she would never ask for anything from Luo Fu, but just walk away. She carried on as if she were the innocent party in all of this; everything she had done was for his sake and had nothing to do with her.

At that moment, Luo Fu collapsed. He couldn't live without Hao Jun. He needed her with him, to talk to him; he loved her and cared about her, and he couldn't do without her – he couldn't explain it. Anyway, without her, his world wouldn't turn. He tried every means to bargain with her, suggesting that they might keep one and sell the other two – for example, they might keep his most important work, 'Five Thousand Years'… but Hao Jun wouldn't give an inch. He thought she was going to destroy everything, but she said she wanted him to have a new life with unlimited prospects. "'Five Thousand Years' is your painting whoever owns it," she told him. "Just think of the 'Mona Lisa' – even after ten thousand years everyone will know it was painted by Leonardo Da Vinci. What can possibly change that?"

Luo Fu was at the end of his tether. Finally, he just left everything up to Hao Jun to decide. He didn't tell Chu Yuntian about the decision for fear he would oppose it. He didn't say anything to Luo Qian at all, since by this time they hadn't been close for many years.

However, when Chu Yuntian read in the newspapers that Luo Fu was going to sell 'Five Thousand Years', he remembered that the day Luo Fu came back from the United States, when he and Luo Qian had gone to see him, Luo Qian had said: "Luo Fu is going in a different direction from us…" He had thought it was his lack of self-esteem speaking. Now he realised that Luo Fu really was moving in a different direction.

· · ·

Hao Jun was a very capable woman. The results of the auction that day exceeded even her expectations. She was six years younger than Luo Fu, so she had not experienced with him the passionate era of Reform and Opening Up when everything and anything seemed possible in the world of art and literature. She was surprised and puzzled by the extraordinary enthusiasm shown for these three classic works. At the end of the ceremony, they took the trouble to see off each of the guests of honour. Luo Fu turned around to see his three paintings hanging on the wall all by themselves. He suddenly realised that these paintings now had another owner and no longer belonged to him. He felt a little empty, lost, confused and sad. His eyes pricked with tears and his vision blurred. On this occasion, there was no one to notice such a reaction. He quickly raised his hand and wiped his eyes. At the same time, he called over a photographer and asked him to take a photo of him with the three paintings as a souvenir, which was also his final farewell. Then Hao Jun shouted from off to one side: "Who wants to take a group photo with Luo Fu and these three paintings? Come on! It's a rare opportunity!"

Luo Fu suddenly felt a deep gulf open up between Hao Jun and himself.

A man walked past him, and it so happened there was no one else nearby when he said: "Chu Yuntian is your real friend."

Luo Fu was a little puzzled at this off-the-cuff remark. The man was in his fifties, tall and thin, with a slight frame. He was wearing a pair of gold-rimmed glasses and had a gentle expression. Luo Fu had never seen him before in his life. Why would he say this to him? By the time he decided to ask, the man had already left.

Chu Yuntian was depressed for many days after finding out that Luo Fu had decided to sell his best paintings. For years, whenever Yuntian was depressed, Sui Yi would try to help him cheer up, although some of the methods she used were quite childish. One day, Sui Yi said she had an idea, but she didn't know if he would agree or not. Yuntian asked her to explain.

She said she wanted to ask Yuntian to sell his own pictures to buy Luo Fu's work. Of course, he was not to sell his most important pieces, and he should only buy one of the three works Luo Fu had put up for auction. Sui Yi spoke carefully when she mentioned her idea because she knew that Yuntian really cared about his paintings and never repeated them.

Somewhat unexpectedly, her idea blew away the melancholy clouds oppressing Yuntian's heart, and he smiled. After the two of them had discussed it, they went to find Yu Changshui. They trusted him to help with this kind of thing. He had all kinds of friends in odd places and so was kept well informed.

Yu Changshui was deeply moved by what Yuntian and Sui Yi proposed. "Since you sell so rarely, if your paintings appear, many collectors will want them. But Luo Fu is selling his best work, famous pieces, and that means the price will be very high. You may have to sell more than two paintings to make his price."

"I don't care if I have to sell a few of mine for one of his," Chu Yuntian said. "But I can't let him sell all his best works down the river."

Again, Yu Changshui was moved. He asked: "Which one do you want to save?"

"I want to save 'Ploughing Deep'," Chu Yuntian said.

"I agree," Sui Yi said. "Although this painting appears to just depict the landscape of the loess plateau, it is very meaningful. This is land that has been worked to death for thousands of years, and yet it is still cultivated every year."

Chu Yuntian glanced at Sui Yi. He appreciated her understanding of the painting.

"I also think it's best for you to keep that painting," Yu Changshui said. "To tell you the truth, most buyers are after 'Five Thousand Years' and it would be difficult to afford it. But I have to find out what the estimate is, and I don't even know which auction house they've sent it to."

Chu Yuntian asked Yu Changshui to inquire about the reserve price and also to find someone to buy his own paintings. However, it was a little difficult for him and Sui Yi to choose the paintings they wanted to sell. The really good ones he did not want to part with, and he was afraid he would not find a buyer for those that were a little inferior.

"If you really want to do this good deed," Sui Yi said, "you have to be willing to make sacrifices."

In the end, Yuntian selected several of his very best paintings and made preparations to recover some of the losses of his temporarily confused friend. Although Luo Fu was a talented artist, he lacked cultural knowledge and historical vision, and he had been led further astray by his vulgar-minded partner. In this way, Yuntian had to make sacrifices, not only for his friend, but also for the sake of art itself.

Yu Changshui had done a good job. He found out that the auction house Hao Jun had contracted with was the Yahao Company of Beijing. They had a pretty good reputation for specialised calligraphy and painting auctions – this was an awful lot better than Xu Dayou and his Purple Clouds Gallery.

He had also found out that the reserve price for 'Five Thousand Years' was one million yuan, and that 'Ploughing Deep' and 'The Shout' were half a million each. These prices were sky high for the early 1990s, so many people doubted whether they would be sold. But the more they wondered, the more attention the sale would get. Yu Changshui had also found several buyers for Yuntian's paintings, each of whom would be paying about one hundred thousand yuan for a painting four feet square.

It was time for Yuntian to make the cut.

In the end, he saved 'Ploughing Deep' for Luo Fu at the cost of five of his own beloved paintings.

When Yu Changshui brought out 'Ploughing Deep' and handed it to Yuntian, he looked at this familiar painting and was moved afresh by the passions of that era when they were still struggling out from their spiritual shackles. How could such a painting be allowed to fall into the hands of profit-minded dealers and collectors who regarded art as just another kind of valuable for them to hoard away? Once locked away in these people's secret cabinets, they may never again see the light of day.

Yuntian handed the painting to Sui Yi for her to look after. "Only the three of us know about this," he reminded them. "When Luo Fu misses his paintings so much he starts to cry, that's when we give it back to him."

After this, Yu Changshui had even more respect for Chu Yuntian and Sui Yi.

Yu Changshui knew that there were too few people like them in this world, and he couldn't even begin to match up to them himself.

A year later, Luo Fu sent out wedding invitations. He married Hao Jun at that big house with a wooden dock outside.

Chu Yuntian's whole family went along to congratulate him. To show that he was sincere, Yuntian wore the silver-grey suit again. Sui Yi wore a light brown tweed dress with narrow grey-green vertical stripes, with a loosely tied cinnabar-red scarf around her neck. Compared with the gorgeously coloured, flashy costumes worn by Luo Fu and Hao Jun, they were as autumn lotuses next to summer peonies, but Hao Jun felt better. She said to Sui Yi: "Do you not go shopping often? Many brands are offering new-season ensembles which are very eye-catching. I'll go with you one of these days."

Sui Yi smiled gently.

A love of beauty is a kind of self-cultivation, which is not something that everyone can appreciate.

Chu Yuntian gave them a bronze statue ordered from the Rodin Museum in Paris. It was a reproduction of Rodin's masterpiece, 'The Thinker'. After this gift had been opened and placed on the table, half of the guests were artists and loved it; and half of them knew nothing about art and didn't like it. Luo Fu liked it very much, and Hao Jun only smiled.

Hao Jun had decorated the two-storey villa with luxury, care and a lot of effort. When people suddenly have money, they inevitably want others to see that they are getting their money's worth. It was all red sandalwood and pear-wood cabinets, large dining tables in heavily carved baroque style, leather sofas and reclining chairs, colourful wool carpets, dazzling crystal chandeliers, and imported Louis quelque-chose clocks, while all kinds of bright and glittering small knickknacks and objets de vertu were scattered about the place upstairs and downstairs, and a ceramic black dog more than one metre high was placed at the foot of the stairs. Hao Jun wanted to make their home look like a five-star hotel, so the floors, door-frames, windowsills, stairs and handrails were all made of Spanish marble.

Hao Jun kept asking the guests: "What do you think? What do you think?"

She wanted to hear their praise, see their surprise and envy – she wanted to feel proud of having money. At that time, everyone seemed to want to be filthy rich.

Chu Yuntian felt a little uncomfortable. Subjectively, he had made sacrifices in silence in order to show his admiration for his friend's art, but objectively he was sponsoring their vulgar lifestyle in a way he didn't like at all. Sui Yi saw what he was feeling from his expression. She said to him: "None of this matters. What he has lost here, you have preserved."

With that, she called Chu Yuntian back to his true values.

CHAPTER 8

No matter how clear your origins, the possibilities ahead are hazy and obscure. There are no signposts, so most people just follow the crowd. However, art is a career that calls for an individualistic spirit, and your road is one you have to explore by yourself. In these wild thickets and rocky outcrops, you and your shadow are alone together, sometimes hesitating, sometimes anxious, sometimes depressed. If you are a real artist, you will never be satisfied with yourself, nor will you spare or cosset yourself. Any earthly praise or reward does not count because it comes mixed with all kinds of vulgar schemes. It is history that really validates the meaning of art. Xiao Shen told Yuntian that he had once seen somewhere or other a letter from Gauguin to Pissarro. At that time, Gauguin had already been living for a long time in Tahiti, far away in the South Pacific. He wanted to find the primitive frankness among the local people that had disappeared in modern civilisation. But on that remote island, he lived alone, poor and sick. Due to the language barrier, he could not communicate with anyone, let alone see the value of his own efforts. Therefore, he often doubted himself, wondering if he had made a terrible mistake. He was in agony.

In his letter, he told Pissarro in despair that he wanted to commit suicide. But from the point of view of today, this was the golden age in which Gauguin produced his finest artworks.

In today's noisy metropolises, crowded with millions of people, would any artist be willing to bear such solitude?

In art schools across the country, imported avant-garde art replaced socialist realism as the dominant trend. However, in China, the avant-garde was not an artistic trend of thought, let alone a school, but a fashion. Almost all the genres and patterns tossed out by Westerners in the previous century were now used and imitated, which made the world of contemporary painting a colourful and strange place. This was even more true when it came to avant-garde literature. It seemed that anyone who was not part of the avant-garde was now out of date, excluded from consideration. No matter how naive such ideas were, they were, after all, a rebellion against long-term control of creative thought. When a big river breaks its banks, who can know which is good or bad? And who knows what might not finally come out in the wash?

When fashion plays the leading role, tradition will accordingly be marginalised, neglected and abandoned. Who will think about the contemporary significance of traditional art? Who will explore the contemporary orientation of traditional art? Local artistic expressions can only continue in a mummified, lifeless form.

During this period, Xiao Shen was interested in encouraging avant-garde art. Every time there was a seminar on avant-garde literature or painting, there he would be. The avant-garde was all about being shocking, startling those who came across it. Critics had fallen into the same trap, with sterile arguments about who was further in advance of the pack. During this period, Luo Fu and his colleagues at the art college had begun to turn their interest to ever more extreme installation art and performance art. Chu Yuntian would still occasionally meet Luo Fu for a chat, but he felt that they were increasingly lacking in any common ground. He and Luo Fu really were not going the same way.

During this period, Yu Changshui became interested in Tibetan art. He often travelled to Tibet, visiting every corner of the seven counties of Ngari Sakü. He was very enthusiastic about Tibetan painting techniques and their use of colour. Even at first glance, you could see a strong Tibetan influence in his most recent paintings. He was determined to overcome the problems of harmonising the mineral pigments and gold used in Tibetan paintings with the ink washes of Chinese art.

"These are two different cultures," Chu Yuntian said. "This is not a problem you can solve technically. In art, there are technical problems, but the bigger issue is the philosophy, literature, culture and aesthetics behind it. If you don't understand these background issues, it can't be solved just by technique. Can you turn English and Chinese into one language?"

Yu Changshui understood that his argument was logical, but at the same time he felt it was all airy-fairy and remote – not the kind of attitude with which you fix real-life problems.

One day, Yi Liaoran called and explained that he was going to publish a collection of his paintings, so he requested Chu Yuntian write the preface for him. Chu Yuntian immediately replied: "I'll have it ready for you in three days."

He agreed so quickly because they had always been friends who spoke the truth to one another, and also because he felt that Yi Liaoran was going somewhere, which made him worth writing about.

Three days later, he had it written out and felt very satisfied. In a space of just three thousand words, he fully described the skill with the brush, the charm, the nature, the breadth of mind, the sentiment and style, the unusual techniques he employed and the amazing talents of this remarkable man from Huizhou. He called Yi Liaoran's landscape paintings "wild landscapes". No one had described them like that before.

Yuntian wrote:

> Ever since the Tang dynasty, whether it is in the work of Jing Hao and Guan Tong, or the paintings of Liu Songnian, Li Tang, Ma Yuan and Xia Gui, we see landscapes that have been the subject of human intervention. Their mountains, rivers, stones and trees all have artificial elements. Just like the flowers and trees in public parks, they are nature shaped by man. This is not true of Yi Liaoran. His mountains, rivers and lakes are all natural. Wild landscapes are free; wild trees

and wild grasses grow at will. When painting, he has the confidence to follow his brush and do whatever he wants, letting nature take its course.

Yuntian also wrote in the piece:

All this stems from the painter's worship of nature! Who else still paints like this?

Having got this far, he couldn't help writing a poem as his conclusion:

With brush like a willow bending in the wind and ink like deep valley mists.
In a moment thousands of miles are encompassed, with mountains and cloudy whisps.

When Yi Liaoran read what Yuntian had to say, he was so moved that he called and said loudly: "You are absolutely right in calling them wild landscapes! You really do understand me, Yuntian!" Then he asked: "If I'm a wild landscape, what are you?"

Flustered, Yuntian didn't think and said: "I'm a humanistic landscape."

"Now you've said it," Yi Liaoran bellowed. "Humanistic landscapes are literati landscapes. You are different from other painters. There is literature in your paintings!"

Their conversation, and the inadvertent articulation of this concept, made Chu Yuntian start to think about the essence of his painting. Were his paintings genuine literati paintings? There were no literati paintings like his in the whole of history.

Two years later, the head of Japan's Asahi news agency visited Chongqing, which happened to be the same time as an exhibition of Chu Yuntian's work opened in the city. Mr Nakae liked the paintings very much, and he invited Yuntian to exhibit in Tokyo. The Japanese always strive for quality, and they wanted to print a catalogue with really high-quality reproductions for his exhibition. When the Asahi news agency showed the proofs to Ikuo Hirayama, president of the Japan-China Friendship Association and a great painter in his own right, he greatly admired the pictures and decided that he wanted to write a preface for the collection. Ikuo Hirayama was well-versed in Chinese culture. In his preface, he said that Chu Yuntian must have studied Song paintings, which secretly surprised Yuntian. He was amazed that someone else could actually see the foundation of his art and the tradition behind it from his brushwork. To Yuntian's further surprise, Ikuo Hirayama bluntly called his work 'modern literati paintings'. This was not something anyone had ever said before.

Here, he first defined Yuntian's work as literati painting and then said that it was not a traditional literati painting, but 'modern' literati painting. This put Yuntian's art in a context that demanded thought and analysis. Now, there were no longer the requisite academic circles in China, so no one could put forward such a concept. This reminded him of the discussion he had had on the phone with Yi Liaoran that day about 'humanistic landscapes'. It should be said that Ikuo Hirayama's theory was more academic. He decided he would like to have a chat with him and hear more of his opinions.

One day during the exhibition in Tokyo, Ikuo Hirayama invited Chu Yuntian to meet him at the Tokyo University of the Arts. Ikuo Hirayama was the president of this famous Japanese art school. Just that day he had received the medal of honour from the Japanese emperor, and he looked energetic and cheerful. White flecks shone in his grey hair, while the remaining black hair was also glossy. Ikuo Hirayama was tall for a Japanese man. He had a ruddy complexion and a constant smile, and his handshake was firm. Yuntian was deeply impressed by the towering trees in the university grounds and the solemn and noble Gandharan statue of the Buddha he had in his office. He liked the quiet and reserved atmosphere of the university. He knew that Ikuo Hirayama loved Dunhuang and had been to the Mogao Grottoes time and again, donating a lot of money for the protection of the site.

Ikuo Hirayama was a scholarly artist and not in the least interested in polite platitudes. He cut through Chinese history in a few words. Both scholars and artists would discuss the most important issues in his recent thought. To begin with, he didn't mention Yuntian's painting exhibition at all, since he went off on a tangent talking about Chinese history and culture. He bluntly said that although Chinese culture developed very early and reached a remarkable peak, it had since stagnated.

He said that there was a very strange phenomenon in Chinese history, in that the Tang, Song, Ming and Qing dynasties all lasted for three hundred years. He didn't understand why this should be the case. There were many emperors in each dynasty. After each emperor ascended the throne, he was busy changing the calendar, minting new coinage, reforming the government and appointing key officials at court. However, if a society does not make progress, it is equivalent to standing still. He believed that China had wasted too much time and needed to get out of this strange historical cycle. He said he placed his hopes on the country's current reforms. With China's magnificent civilisation to build on, once they took off, no one could catch them up.

He spoke sincerely and gave honest criticism.

Yuntian agreed with him, but he also had his own topics of concern. Knowing that their time was limited, he changed the subject and asked directly: "Why did you call my work modern literati painting?"

"Don't you think there is a literati quality to your paintings?"

"But my pieces are completely different from traditional literati painting."

"Times have changed," Ikuo Hirayama said, "and so have paintings. But there are literati qualities to your paintings. I know you are also a writer. Chinese art has always emphasised the literary qualities of painting, and literati values. That is quite different from the tradition of Western art."

"I agree," Yuntian said. "Chinese people don't just look at paintings, they read and evaluate them. In fact, Japanese and Chinese art is the same in this regard. Your paintings, and Kaii Higashiyama's, also have a literary element to them."

He said with a smile: "In the time of Sesshū Tōyō, Japanese painters studied Chinese Song-era paintings. Later, that fell to one side, along with the rest of Chinese literati painting. After the Meiji Restoration, we were influenced by the West and explored modernism. Without any contemporary relevance, art loses its vitality."

"But we have a bigger problem," Yuntian said.

"What's that?"

"Traditional painters had a deep poetic cultivation and they paid attention to the allusions implicit in their work. But now people are too Westernised, the professional division of labour is too absolute, there are fewer and fewer Chinese painters, and the tradition of literati painting has been broken. The literary qualities of painting are less and less valued."

"The modern era will certainly produce a new generation of literati," Ikuo Hirayama said. "You are one yourself. Don't your works bear all the hallmarks of modern literati paintings?"

Although they had only touched on a range of subjects and did not go deeply into anything, Chu Yuntian gained a lot from this short conversation; that is, he began to consciously establish his own theories about 'modern literati painting'.

After his return from Tokyo, Yuntian wrote a series of articles, expounding his views on the history of literati painting, exploring the essence and characteristics of the genre, and discussing his theories about contemporary literati painting. He believed that the literary characteristics of modern-day literati painting lay in its connection with prose, not poetry. Because prose is freer from stylistic constraints, it is more in tune with the way contemporary people think. He placed these articles in order and gave them to Cao Ying to print as a book. In order to emphasise that this was in some measure a call to arms, the title of his book was *The Literati Painting Manifesto*.

He thought that this might have an impact on the art world and cause some discussion, but his ideas were too academic. When the book was printed, it had no effect at all – he might as well have thrown it straight into the sea. The only mention was a short thousand-character review in *Art Daily*, saying that it was "the first book on the subject of literati painting since Chen Shizeng's *The Value of Literati Painting*". But it then went on to say: "Chen Shizeng's essay, written during the Republican era, was a lament for the demise of literati painting."

It seemed that no one was paying the least attention to literati painting, let alone pondering what modern literati painting might be. Such a topic, remote from the noisy world of fashion and avant-garde art, was as easily drowned out as the buzz of a small mosquito. So he fell into the habit of expecting his art and thinking to be disregarded.

He was not afraid. Those who think deeply are not afraid of loneliness. Real thought comes from resolute solitude, in the time before its value is generally recognised.

There was also a conversation about the relationship between Chinese and Western cultures which turned out to be of great significance to Yuntian.

Again, it took place abroad, in the Museum of Modern Art in Vienna. He was there to see a retrospective exhibition for the late Austrian painter Max Weiler. He liked Weiler's abstract works and admired the way in which he had devoted himself to art, turning his back on commercialism throughout his long life. Yuntian and Weiler never met, but he had become a very close friend of his wife, though they had not encountered one another until after the artist's death. Mrs Weiler was the promoter of her late husband's paintings.

Weiler, a modern Western painter, attracted Yuntian's attention because he was fascinated by ancient Chinese painting. He often introduced some of the charm of Chinese art into his own abstract works. This made his paintings unique.

To commemorate her beloved husband who had died some years before, Mrs Weiler had arranged this exhibition specially. The paintings on display all contained a kind of spiritual harmony with ancient Chinese painting. From these completely abstract modern works, Chu Yuntian was surprised to make out a clear artistic relationship with such long-ago artists as Guo Xi, Ma Yuan and Xu Daoning from the Northern and Southern Song dynasties.

He looked at Weiler's paintings and thought of himself.

This exhibition did not just include the artist's work. In some places around the hall, there were Ming-style official hats, chairs, display stands for flowers and tables; on the tabletops, there might be a scholar's rock or an antique white porcelain vase. The display was simple and elegant. Obviously, this was to hint at the unique cross-cultural connections to be found in Weiler's paintings.

After he had seen the exhibition, Mrs Weiler invited Chu Yuntian to chat in the museum café. Also present was a gentleman with messy hair and a free and easy demeanour, whose name was Kopp.

Mrs Weiler introduced Kopp to Chu Yuntian. She explained that he was the curator of the exhibition and that he had organised several major exhibitions in Europe. He had also been many times to Beijing and Shanghai.

During their conversation, Yuntian and Kopp soon found some topics of common interest. For example, traditional Chinese ink painting is representational, but Max Weiler's work was abstract. How did he integrate these two quite disparate things into a unique whole?

Kopp pointed out to him that Weiler was born in the Tyrol and so would have been aware from birth of the mountain peaks and deep valleys. He was born with the kind of character that only mountain folk have, so it was easy for him to find commonalities with the great rocks, forests and clouds, as well as the tranquil and lofty atmosphere depicted by the great masters of landscape painting in ancient China. Weiler didn't care about the details. What he learned from Chinese paintings of a thousand years ago was a calm, generous and flexible spirit, joined with a supreme respect for nature. Kopp believed that these were the characteristics that made Max Weiler fall in love with Chinese landscape painting. He found no such thing in Western landscape painting.

Max Weiler used his abstract forms to merge with the spirit he found in Chinese art.

Yuntian remarked: "Some people say that Chinese painting in the Song dynasty was highly realistic, but it became freehand after the Yuan dynasty. In fact, the realism you find in the Song dynasty is quite different from Western realistic paintings. Chinese ink painting has always been subjective and idealistic. Chinese painters believe that 'when painting you should seek out complementary forms and look on them with affection'. This is the fundamental reason why

Weiler was able to naturally integrate ancient Chinese art into his own abstracts."

They each listened carefully to what the other had to say and appreciated one another's point of view. When you have this kind of conversation, you can cut right to the heart of the matter of many different topics.

"It's a pity that your avant-garde artists don't cherish these aspects themselves," Kopp said.

"Why?" Yuntian asked. "I thought you were most enthusiastic about Chinese avant-garde art! Do you think our avant-garde art has gone wrong in some way?"

"It's very simple. Your avant-garde art is not for you, but for us. That's why I often get asked to curate exhibitions in China, because I know Western taste. And because they want…" Kopp lifted his hand and drummed his fingers against his temple, as if looking for a word. Finally, he said: "…to go global."

"That is somewhat stupid," Yuntian said with a smile.

Kopp shrugged and said: "Yes, it's ridiculous. We don't want to see you do the same things as us. We would prefer to see things that are different from ours."

"Maybe some of us think… you represent modernity."

Kopp smiled and said: "We should all have our own modernity. The key is to figure out what that is and who we are."

While talking with this knowledgeable curator, Yuntian had an idea growing ever stronger at the back of his mind: he was going to study the cultural essence and aesthetics of Chinese painting.

Mrs Weiler smiled at them and said: "You got so excited when talking I was starting to wonder just how much caffeine you'd had."

CHAPTER 9

On the thirtieth day of the twelfth lunar month, according to Chinese custom, families should stay at home to celebrate New Year. But early that morning, Chu Yuntian and his family had loaded themselves into a van heading for Beijing, along with Xiao Shen and Yu Changshui. Some two years earlier, Yuntian had negotiated with the Academy of Social Sciences to transfer Xiao Shen to the Academy of Painting, to edit a journal called *The Artist*. Xiao Shen wanted to make art criticism the driving force in the journal, and Chu Yuntian admired his enterprising spirit. He made sure to drag him along to any important events.

Two days earlier, Luo Fu and Hao Jun had come to Yuntian's house and invited his family to Beijing to see his "amazing new work". Luo Fu said his latest pieces would not only give his reputation wings but also shock the Chinese art world. Yuntian asked him what he had been doing. Like any magician, he refused to disclose any information in advance and asked them to be present at the scene to feel the moment of shock for themselves.

Yuntian asked Luo Fu: "Why did you choose to open your exhibition on New Year's Eve? Everyone is busy preparing for the holidays. Isn't it difficult for people?"

Luo Fu said with a smile: "We wanted to attack that tradition. That in itself is a piece of performance art."

"That isn't art," Yuntian countered. "That's a barbaric imposition on your friends."

Despite this disagreement, they felt forced to go, especially Sui Yi. She was not in the least interested in avant-garde art, but it was difficult to refuse. They decided to go to Beijing early in the morning, see the exhibition and come back after lunch, which would not affect them being at home for dinner on New Year's Eve and watching the gala on TV.

The exhibition was held on the floor of a large, abandoned factory in the suburbs of Beijing. Now the factory had been transformed into an exhibition hall. Some small houses attached to the grounds were rented by artists engaged in contemporary art as studios or workshops. This idea was copied from Soho in New York and had become very fashionable, so contemporary art exhibitions of various famous names were often held there. They parked their car nearby, only to find there were already hordes of people inside and outside the exhibition hall. When they walked over, Sui Yi pointed to the roof of the tall exhibition hall and said: "Someone is about to jump!"

There was indeed a man standing on the roof, naked except for a pair of white shorts. He seemed to be in a state of hesitation, making up his mind as to whether to jump to his death. Xiao Shen said easily: "He's not going to commit suicide. That's just another piece of performance art."

"On a cold day like this!" Yiran said. "He's not wearing much – isn't he freezing?"

"Some people cut themselves with knives and then plant grass in their wounds. Some people hammer nails into the backs of their hands, and some dig a hole, jump into it naked and then ask their assistants to pour buckets of cockroaches on top of them. That is performance art. They are devoting themselves to their art." Xiao Shen smiled sarcastically.

"They are doing this for art?" Sui Yi queried. "Does art need to be extreme? Is it necessary to be quite so outré?"

"Yes! It's the only way to get noticed," Xiao Shen said.

"Is art only about getting attention?" Sui Yi smiled. "From a psychological perspective, self-harm is the clinical manifestation of patients with psychiatric problems."

They all laughed.

As they were talking, a woman dressed in bright clothes advanced towards them. At first glance, she seemed to be wearing two flowered scarves: it was Hao Jun! She cried enthusiastically: "Here you all are, and Yiran is here as well. Great! You'll love this, I am quite sure of it. Luo Fu is in the exhibition hall. He asked me to come and get you. We're just about to start. Follow me!"

She really was a very capable woman.

The opening ceremony was at the gate to the exhibition hall. The scene was one of chaos. Hao Jun grabbed Chu Yuntian's arm and pulled him to the front to introduce him to several seemingly important people. Chu Yuntian was quite famous in the world of Chinese art, but he didn't know these people at all. There were some ordinary faces, some peculiar ones, some looked arrogant, some looked cold, and there were two or three foreigners, which reminded Yuntian of the man he had met in Vienna – Kopp. Yuntian shook hands with them and stood off to one side. A man came up with a microphone in his hand. He was dressed most strangely in a fluffy coat, his hair was done in cornrows swept back behind his head, and there were many vertical wrinkles carved down his large face. It was rare to see a Chinese person like that – he looked more like a Native American. He spoke only one line in a pure Beijing accent: "There are so many great works waiting for us that anything I could say here would be superfluous. Let us begin!"

The exhibition opened like this, which was another novelty.

Yuntian and the others followed the crowd as they trooped in. Before going more than a few steps, they were brought up short. A row of about seven people came walking towards them, entirely encased in white. When they looked more carefully, it turned out that they had all been wrapped in bandages from head to foot, and blood was seeping out from inside, as if they were hospital patients who had suffered serious injury. They walked straight forward, looking fierce and terrible. Sui Yi had once worked in a hospital and was accordingly sensitive to the sight of people wrapped up in bandages, so she instinctively took a step back. Yiran hid behind her.

Yuntian smiled at them and said: "There's nothing to be afraid of. It's just performance art."

Moving forward, they beheld even more peculiar and shocking things.

Hao Jun didn't ask them to look at other people's works. Pulling them away, she shouted: "Come on! Come on! It's right ahead. Luo Fu's work is the focus of the whole exhibition, and it is right in the middle of the hall." After charging through the crowds for a while, she suddenly said: "Here we are! Look!"

She smiled at everyone in triumph, as though the Bermuda Triangle had manifested itself in front of them. But all that Yuntian could see was a huge square box more than ten metres in each direction, painted grey, with two doors to the east and west. That was all. What was so special about this?

What was special was inside the box. The real weirdness was also inside the box.

They stepped inside and encountered two people, a man and a woman. The man was dressed in black, the woman in white. Both were painters. The man in black was holding a black brush and a black paint pot. He was standing on an A-frame ladder to paint, and the ladder was also black. The woman was over on the other side, and her brush, paint pot and ladder were all white, the same as her clothes. They were black and white, in clear contrast with each other.

The way they worked was very strange.

While the man in black had painted all four walls in the box black, the woman in white climbed up the white ladder and changed the four wall panels back to white with her paint. After a while, when the woman in white had just painted the box white, the man in black stepped on the ladder again and painted it back to black. They kept changing back and forth, black and white, white and black. This was the sum of Luo Fu's installation.

This piece was called 'History'.

When they came out of Luo Fu's strange box, Hao Jun looked at everyone's faces, as if waiting for their excited and surprised acclamations. Excitement and surprise can't be faked, but they politely congratulated Hao Jun one after another. Sui Yi asked why she hadn't seen Luo Fu when Yiran pointed out that the man standing on the ladder with a black brush was him. Everyone was surprised, but Hao Jun said she was quite right, and praised her for her sharp eyes. Sui Yi asked Yiran: "Did Uncle Luo see you?"

"Oh yes," Yiran said, "but he ignored me."

Xiao Shen said with a smile: "He can't talk to you. At the exhibition site, he is part of his installation."

"Yes," Hao Jun said, "he's amazing. These days, as soon as he gets inside the box, he doesn't pay attention to anyone, not even the woman with the white paint. It's like he's possessed." She boasted a bit about Luo Fu and then said: "He asked me to accompany you to the restaurant ahead of him. He'll join us sometime after twelve."

They went to a very spacious restaurant, and soon after they sat down Luo Fu came running, still dressed in black. He was glad to see his friends from Tianjin. Looking at his expression, he was expecting praise and admiration from them. Yuntian always cared greatly about the feelings of others, so he said: "I have never seen anything like it. You expressed your view of history through ridicule."

Luo Fu was thrilled. He wrapped his arm around Yuntian and said: "You've always supported me, man."

Xiao Shen had no idea how to keep his mouth shut on such occasions. "Isn't your work a little too obvious and cartoonish?"

Chu Yuntian often went to art events with Xiao Shen and knew very well that he was a frank and ruthless critic, but Luo Fu thought that he was engaged in very important work. Yuntian was worried that Xiao Shen's sharp criticism would make him unhappy. He was trying to think of some way to make the moment pass, when Yiran suddenly said to Luo Fu: "If you mix black with white, it's grey. You painted the outside of your work grey. Do you mean to say that history is always grey in the end?"

Yiran's words surprised everyone, including Yuntian and Sui Yi.

Luo Fu swept Yiran up in his arms and shouted: "Here is our greatest critic, so much better than your uncle Xiao Shen!"

His words were a humorous counterattack to Xiao Shen, who didn't care.

Everyone happily ate, drank and chatted. Then, amid the

hubbub, came the sound of an ambulance. After a while, someone came and whispered in Hao Jun's ear. Her expression changed a little, and she said to Yuntian and Sui Yi: "It seems best if you go now. Just now the artist on the roof with the performance piece entitled 'Jumping' had a moment of inattention, and really did fall – he may have died. The ambulance is here, and I understand that someone has called the police. Once the police arrive, you won't be able to leave."

Chu Yuntian understood that they were going to be busy and so he should leave immediately. They got up quickly. When they walked out of the restaurant, a party of three or four others came in. From their dress and hairstyle, they looked to be extreme avant-garde artists flaunting their personalities. Luo Fu stopped them and told Yuntian that they were all internationally renowned contemporary artists. He introduced Chu Yuntian to them and mentioned his position in the Artists Association. He wasn't expecting them to behave as if they'd never heard of him; the middle-aged man with a big earring in his left ear looked at him with disgust, while the others stalked away with icy expressions, without so much as a turn of their heads. It made Yuntian feel very uncomfortable. He didn't say a word.

The area outside the exhibition hall was now being treated as the scene of an accident. The man who had jumped from the roof was being loaded into an ambulance. From the gaps in the crowd, you could vaguely make out a patch of blood on the ground, which was appalling. Sui Yi reached out to hide Yiran's face because she did not want her to see this. Just at that moment, a police car drove up with flashing lights. They hurried out to the car park, got into their van, waved to Luo Fu and Hao Jun through the window, and made their way through the crowd and onto the road.

As they sped down the motorway back to Tianjin, everyone was silent at first. Xiao Shen didn't know how to evaluate such a dreadful mess. Yuntian was also silent and seemed to be unhappy about the arrogant and unreasonable people he had bumped into at the door of the restaurant. Sui Yi suddenly said: "That was about as disgusting as eating a bug." Women prefer to speak of their feelings.

Sui Yi's words drew out what Yuntian wanted to say from his heart. "I don't understand how this anti-art thing can be so hot."

"We have the right conditions for this kind of thing," Xiao Shen said. "Do you think we just have our five thousand years of high civilisation? That we just have the quintessential expressions of Chinese art? That's what *you* have in *your* head. Everyone else is busy worshipping money, putting cash above all other considerations. They are ignorant, with a terrible inferiority complex and a veneer of Westernisation. All they care about is – How can we be famous? How can we make Westerners admire us? How can we make money? How can we win by surprise? They aren't really trying to achieve anything, and there is absolutely nothing they wouldn't do for cold hard cash. That's what you saw today." He paused and then continued: "When I was looking at the exhibition just now, I was reflecting that in recent years, I have been a fanatical promoter of innovation, modernism, avant-garde and contemporary art. I have pushed for this with all my strength! But from the looks of things, we have gone astray – maybe even reached a dead end. I think I have made a mistake, I have been promoting something completely stupid. I'm asking myself where exactly does the problem lie? That is a question we must ask ourselves seriously."

As Xiao Shen talked about his ideas, Yuntian was also worried and said: "What we saw today made me feel very pessimistic. Because I noticed that, except for the people in the inner circle, none of the crowd in that hall was really there to see the art. They were all just hoping for some excitement."

"You can't stop this trend," Xiao Shen argued. "Historically, this is also a kind of rebellion, and as such it is necessary. As long as you're not pessimistic about yourself."

The last sentence carried some weight with Yuntian.

When a raging torrent sweeps everything in its path, it all depends on whether you can stand, whether you are like a boulder with enough weight behind it to stay as stable as Mount Tai, whether you have long, thick roots thrust deep into your own land, whether you have grasped the foundations of civilisation from ancient to modern times. If not, you will be whirled away by the flood, drowned in it and become one of the many unfortunate victims of the times. You cannot swim against the tide, but there is no need to follow it blindly. If you find pleasure in it, move up and down with it, and think yourself a trendsetter of the times, imagining that you have reached some pinnacle of fame and fortune through your own efforts when in fact you have been lifted by the rising tide, you will be making a terrible mistake! When this fashion passes, you will come to understand that everything was but an illusion and a game. In the end, you will find yourself beached by the current and become worthless flotsam and jetsam.

If you are determined to stand firm, you must learn to live at peace with yourself, to calm yourself so that you can really meditate on art. Man's power can only be found in himself.

CHAPTER 10

Chu Yuntian had no idea that just one year later he would get to know a painter of astonishing genius. It was just the same when he met Yi Liaoran in Jiangzhou, in Shanxi Province. However, the artist he met this time was more sober, purer, more thorough, more conscious in artistic spirit, and of even greater significance to him.

For some time, while continuing to ponder his art, he also carried on publishing in-depth theoretical discussions on Chinese philosophy, culture, art and aesthetics along the lines of *The Literati Painting Manifesto*. As a painter, there were very few people with such broad and profound knowledge of both Chinese and foreign cultural traditions who could work on such a purely theoretical research topic. Painting is physical, and theory is metaphysical. One is about image and the other about logic, and it is hard to find anyone who can master the two. However, Chu Yuntian was also a writer, and he wrote well, in a style that was clear and easy to comprehend, so it came to be that his essays did have some impact. A publishing house in Henan Province had the sense to ask him to produce a collected edition of his articles, with illustrations. Even the title of the book had already been decided: *The Nature of Chinese Painting*. It was all very smart looking, with some literary value. The publishing house invited him to go to Luoyang to consult on the presentation and illustrations for the book, suggesting that he take the opportunity to go peony-viewing as well. This was the end of April, which was the time when the old capital and its beautiful flowers would be looking at their very best and most poetic.

He arrived in Luoyang, and during a break in proceedings in his meetings at the publishing house, a man was waiting for him out in the corridor. On enquiry, he turned out to be the art editor for the publishing house. His name was Zheng Fei. He was short and strong, with a stubby beard, a little bald patch on the middle of his head, and a long fringe of hair hanging down below it, which looked slightly strange, but he turned out to be both simple and enthusiastic. He said that one of his friends was working on a big painting, really big and fine. He wanted to explain just how wonderful the painting was, but he just didn't know how to put it into words, and he got in such a stew that he was just gesturing with his hands, while his eyes glittered with a strange light. It was as if he were trying to explain something too wonderful to be put into words – he kept stammering and stuttering and simply could not express himself properly; in the end, he got so stressed that he just said: "If you don't see this, you'll regret it for the rest of your life!" Then he added: "If you have time, I'll take you to see it. Any time is OK, I have a car!"

Chu Yuntian asked the people from the publishing house about this, and they agreed: "The painting is amazing. But the artist is someone nobody has ever heard of."

It didn't matter a jot to Chu Yuntian whether he'd heard of the man or not. What mattered was how well he could paint. He asked his editor to inform Zheng Fei that he'd like to visit the painter the next morning.

The following day, Zheng Fei drove his car to pick up Yuntian. The car looked like a self-build; the body was like an old rectangular iron box, and the paintwork was lumpy and blistered – in fact, the whole car seemed to be cratered and scraped. The inside of the car was a mess, with rock-hard seats on which were piled cushions, coats, backpacks, empty water bottles and children's teddy bears, while the footwells featured a mulch of fruit peel and nut shells. Along the way, Zheng Fei constantly scolded his car and apologised to Yuntian. Yuntian said with a smile: "Your car looks like the kind of thing that an old farmer has built for himself. Give it another hundred years, and it will be in a museum."

Zheng Fei's car proved almost impossible to drive, stopping and starting at random. He couldn't decide if he didn't know how to use the clutch properly or if there was some problem with the engine. Whenever the car stopped, Zheng Fei apologised and said they would be there soon. He wanted to explain about the artist to Yuntian while they were in the car, but he struggled to make himself understood at the best of times. His poor car and dreadful driving skills made him anxious and even more incoherent.

What Yuntian understood from his mumbling preamble was that the painter's name was Gao Yuqi. He was about the same age as Yuntian. He had graduated from the local art academy and worked as an art editor in a magazine. He painted figures so well that even some great painters from Beijing had come to admire him. However, things are very unfair, and it transpired that artists in Beijing have a place on the national stage, while those from the rest of the country are required to content themselves with remaining obscure regional painters. He lived in the ancient capital of Luoyang, which had long been relegated to a backwater, hundreds of miles away from a cultural centre like Beijing. He never participated in any national art exhibition, nor won a single award, nor did his name ever appear in any list of honourees. He also refused to put his pictures up for sale, so his works had no market price. Who would know just how fine his paintings really were?

He firmly believed that he was the greatest of figure painters. But what does it matter, even if you think you are the emperor? You still have to go out to buy breakfast on the street, visit the public lavatory and then take the bus home. It does not matter how confident, arrogant or resentful you are. In the eyes of ordinary people, you are just an ant walking around like all the other ants.

Fortunately for him, an entrepreneur fell in love with his work. This man had studied art when he was in college and had a very fine eye. He said he "saw the future of Chinese painting" in Gao Yuqi. It was a stroke of luck for a poor artist to find a discerning rich patron. When Gao Yuqi confided his dream to the entrepreneur, he rented him a huge house as a studio. It was his dream to create a vast painting, two and a half metres high and one hundred metres long. The subject matter was kept secret, but it would take five to seven years to paint. The entrepreneur asked him to go through the formalities which would ensure he kept his job open at the magazine where he worked, while all the expenses were borne by him. After the painting was completed, he promised to build a museum that would function as a permanent home for this one work. It would be hard for any painter to receive such a commitment for a single work of art, though of course, since this was a private arrangement, there was always some element of risk.

However, for the sake of the painting he had so long wanted to paint, Gao Yuqi was determined to run any risk. The magazine agreed to keep his position open for him, but that was just a resignation by another name. Who could say whether the magazine would still need him if he wanted to return after seven years? Nevertheless, he began work on this huge, idealistic project armed only with a brush. When he took this step, he was determined to stake everything on this one spin of the wheel, even if it might cost him his own life.

The entrepreneur was entirely sincere in his support. He had rented him an empty workshop at a factory as his studio. Since his home was far from the factory in the heart of the city, the entrepreneur arranged for a car to pick him up every day. He also provided him with a stipend to cover his expenses at home and here in the studio.

He had been at work this way for three and a half years.

"Here we are," Zheng Fei said, and the car stopped abruptly as if it had fallen into a pit.

They were in a large garment processing factory, which consisted of many workshops and a large courtyard. Many finished goods, containers and trucks were parked in the yard. They went in through a passage between two buildings and came out into another courtyard. On all four sides, there were large and simple buildings constructed to the same specifications.

Yuntian followed Zheng Fei into one of the workshops, with a straight, wide corridor running down the middle and two rows of doors on either side. When they came to the middle door on the left,

Zheng Fei shouted: "Yuqi, here we are." As soon as the door opened, there appeared a middle-aged man, though he looked much younger than his age. He was not tall, but pale-skinned, modest and quiet. He was dressed in plain blue trousers and a blue coat. Yuntian thought this must be Gao Yuqi's assistant or someone of that ilk. Unexpectedly, the man stretched out his hand and said: "Thank you for coming. I'm Gao Yuqi."

How could he be Gao Yuqi? Yuntian asked himself. Why did he look so young?

Zheng Fei seemed to know what questions were swirling in Yuntian's mind. He said: "Yuqi looks more than ten years younger than his actual age. But just you wait… his paintings are amazing!"

While he said this, Chu Yuntian felt himself surrounded by a world of ink. Before he could take a closer look, he realised that a vast painting nearly one hundred metres long spanned the four walls of this spacious workshop, with him in the centre. He couldn't make out what he was painting. He just felt the wind and the rain, grandeur, boldness and momentum swallowing him up at once. There was no need to look closely, no need to understand what was going on – without the slightest preparation, he was overwhelmed, shocked and conquered in the blink of an eye. He had seen too many paintings, ancient and modern, Chinese and Western, but he had never had such a feeling before. Chu Yuntian was unable to speak for a moment.

He stepped forward and gradually made out the forms of hundreds of farmers rushing forward in the picture. What was this about?

With Yuntian's sensitivity to society and the world around him, and Gao Yuqi's truthfulness and accuracy in portraiture, he soon realised that the man was painting migrant workers! He had depicted the thousands of migrant workers who had left the countryside to work in urban construction during the past two decades. This was part of an unprecedented historical transformation, as people who had been rural dwellers for the last five thousand years moved towards a modern urbanised society. He had painted the greatest theme of the modern era, marking the most important social issue today!

If Luo Zhongli's 'Father' and Luo Fu's 'Five Thousand Years' represented the awe-inspiring tradition of farming from generation to generation, then what this man was depicting was a new and magnificent image of people who had once been farmers!

Gao Yuqi explained to him the general idea and structure of his masterpiece. It was amazing. The painting was divided into three parts. The migrant workers forging ahead were mainly from the younger generation. They were the ones who dared to rush forward, the main group of migrant workers – a new generation emerging from the loess plateau. Yuqi told him something from his own experience that explained the origins of this painting. Back in the late 1980s, as the migrants returned to the city after New Year, he saw a group of young farmers crossing the road, some carrying bedding rolls and some with luggage. A few had perhaps come to the city for the first time; there were those full of curiosity and hope, those with confusion in their eyes, while others were in a happy mood, laughing and talking. Gao Yuqi said: "Their new life was just beginning – it was such an emotional moment for me! Some people say that they come to work in the big city to fill their stomachs and earn money to support their families. But we shouldn't forget that they've built all the modern high-rise blocks, highways, sports fields, plazas, bridges and houses in our cities. Without them, there would be no modern cities in China today. What wonderful people they are! They've created the world we live in! I decided to paint a huge picture for them, something to commemorate them. I didn't want to focus on just one person, since we are talking about an entire generation!"

Every word he spoke showed his passion for his art and moved Yuntian deeply.

Gao Yuqi then explained that the middle part of the painting mostly depicted middle-aged farmers, who have been left to take care of every aspect of the sowing and reaping in their country villages. The final part showed the older generation of farmers who had stayed out in the countryside, often looking after children and the homes of younger migrants. These three parts combined to depict the entirety of what life was actually like for contemporary workers.

In today's vibrant and ever-changing society, who can accurately grasp the unique characteristics of the times, the backbone of our lives, the silent soul of our times? Of course, it can only be real artists.

The studio contained a large wooden table, on which there were inkstones, water basins, countless pots of colour large and small, as well as lunch boxes, rice bowls, thermoses, half-eaten baskets of fruit and many water bottles, both empty and full.

At the other end of the big wooden table, there were a large number of reference picture books, sketchbooks, drawings of individual characters and preparatory drafts of various parts.

These are the instruments and props of the artist's life.

Looking at his massive collection of sketches, Yuntian was equally impressed by his hardworking, solid sense of realism, and his technical ability. Because of these skills, he had been able to paint countless characters without any similarities to each other. Each person showed their age, personality and mood – even subtle psychological states were captured. He must have worked himself to the bone, depicting so many different individuals, each one of which seemed to leap from the paper.

How broad and profound must his sympathy be for the people of this vast and complex era!

Yuntian noted that his method of shaping images by texturing and haloing was unique, and he had never before seen such boldness in splashing great pools of ink.

He also noticed that there were many large sheets of paper with paintings covering the ground in the middle of the studio. Some were only partially drawn on, while others were completely covered. Gao Yuqi said: "Sometimes when I am dissatisfied with a certain figure or section of my painting, I immediately remove it and start again. I will never let anything I regret stay in my painting."

"You said this painting would take five years or more to complete," Yuntian remarked, "but over such a long period, your technique, methods and character modelling will change, and your understanding of your painting will continue to deepen. That means it will become inconsistent. What are you going to do about that?"

"That's a very good question," Gao Yuqi said. "I've thought about it myself. I will solve it through a process of constant revision.

Maybe after the whole painting is completed, I might revise it for another six months, so it will be consistent."

Yuntian was surprised. What a magnificent idea it was, but what a huge amount of work! Was he going to exhaust himself for his art?

He couldn't help asking him: "Do you need any assistance?"

"I've been keeping an eye on you," Gao Yuqi said, "looking at your paintings and reading your articles. Right now, you have the purest and most independent views on art. I would like to hear your opinion of my painting."

Yuntian spoke from the heart: "I think that when this picture is finished, it will be the greatest work of Chinese figure painting in the twentieth century, both in terms of artistic conception and creativity." After thinking for a moment, he went on: "I hope you can always maintain a sense of integrity in your art, while you also remain focused on every detail. Your talent should give you confidence enough. Believe me, I am not just being polite."

It seemed that a weight fell from Gao Yuqi's shoulders. He was so moved that tears sparkled in the corners of his eyes. "Thank you," he said. "I'll finish it. Frankly, I've been at the end of my tether the last few days. I really needed you to tell me this!"

Yuntian understood that the reason why Gao Yuqi invited him to see his work was that he was trying to gain confidence from the praise of people he could trust. He needed that spiritual support. Spiritual things need spiritual understanding and encouragement. Being treated as a confidant by this painter of rare genius also moved Yuntian. He said: "Once your painting is completed, I will hold a major exhibition for you in the National Art Museum of China!" He wanted to infuse his gifted new friend with his own unswerving belief in his talents.

Before he left this remote and magical studio and got back in the car, the two hugged excitedly a couple of times.

On the way back, Zheng Fei was overcome by the excitement and drove his car wildly. He not only drove the wrong way twice, but he also turned into a dead end. He seemed to be carried away with delight. Yuntian felt that Zheng Fei was quite adorable for this. He too was a painter, but he selflessly praised one of his artist friends. This was completely different from the arrogant folk he'd encountered at the contemporary art exhibition in Beijing that New

Year's Eve. He remembered the saying: A real artist loves the art in himself, not himself in art.

During those two days in Luoyang, he'd looked at the ancient capital outside the window, which had sacrificed its defining characteristics to modernisation, and he'd sighed over it. Now he felt a renewed confidence. Perhaps it meant that the spirit of history and civilisation in this place had not died, nor yet been dispersed. Although on the surface it might seem to have disappeared, leaving no trace behind, somewhere unexpectedly out in the wilderness it would quietly send out a vigorous branch, with strange flowers blossoming forth with an undiminished vitality.

Sitting in Luo Fu's new Land Rover, listening to him proudly declare that he would soon be taking his performance art piece, 'History', to the Biennale in Venice, and that Hao Jun had already gone on ahead to make preliminary arrangements for him, Yuntian was not happy. He thought back to a month ago in Luoyang when Zheng Fei drove him in his old homemade car to visit Gao Yuqi, a genius that nobody had ever heard of. How absurd and unfair the world can be!

"Are you only working on performance art nowadays and not painting any more?" he asked Luo Fu.

"You know, performance art doesn't sell for money," Luo Fu explained. "Hao Jun is always asking me to put paintings up for auction, and I don't have anything to send them. I would need to paint something, but to be honest I don't feel much now when I pick up a brush…"

Yuntian was shocked; a painter's brush should be where his most sensitive nerve endings can be found. If you pick up your brush and don't feel a thing, is not that the same as a person losing all sense of self? In the normal way of things, he didn't have much contact with Luo Fu; he didn't know how much his once talented friend had now changed.

Today, they were both going on a special trip to see Luo Qian, which was something that had not happened for many years.

The idea had started out so well. That day, when Yiran was playing *A Maiden's Prayer* on the piano, Sui Yi remembered a scene described to her by Yuntian back in the 1970s, when he, Luo Qian and Luo Fu had listened to Yannian playing this very song in an empty building on Sichuan Road. Although she was not present that day, Yuntian had described the scene so vividly that she remembered it all this time. The past was distant and clear, sad and sweet, which made her feel suddenly nostalgic. When you feel nostalgic, you are sure to miss your old friends. She asked Yuntian how long it had been since he last saw Luo Qian. Yuntian thought about it and said he couldn't really remember. That made him feel a little guilty. Sui Yi said: "You and Luo Fu should go and see him. It wouldn't be right to wait for him to come and see you. If Luo Fu doesn't want to go, you should go by yourself."

In this way, Yuntian had dragged Luo Fu off to see their long-lost friend.

When their car turned onto Hengyang Road, the scene that met their eyes was not at all what they had expected. Not only had Luo Qian's courtyard been demolished, but all the old houses had gone – a huge space had been cleared. In that open space, there were just ruins, with a wall or a corner of a house sticking up here and there, old trees leaning to one side; the rest was just rubble. They stopped at the side of the road and walked over. Luo Fu's eyes were sharp, and he said: "Luo Qian is still there. Isn't that his house?"

A greyish-yellow, shabby and very simple hut stood alone in the middle of the great open space, and the surrounding trees had all been felled. But it was still Luo Qian's house. Their wonderful secret little salon, the warm cabin glowing with light on cold, wet nights, now looked so small, humble, pitiful and helpless. From a distance, it looked like a shoe that someone had tossed to the ground. Why did his house remain when all the others had gone? Was he still there? They ran over, only to stop dead in their tracks. A large circle was painted on the walls and doors, with the cruel word 'demolish' written inside it. Several long wooden strips were nailed across the double doors, sealing them. Luo Qian no longer lived here. He had gone. But where? Why didn't he let them know?

They looked around and found an old man who was employed to guard the construction site. "He was the very last to go," the old man said. "He moved out three months ago."

They asked him where he had gone. The old man guarding the

construction site was a little hesitant. Luo Fu quickly pulled out a good cigarette and gave it to him. When the old man had been assured that they were old friends of Luo Qian, he took out a note and said: "Here is his address and telephone number. He asked me to keep an eye on the house for him and let him know when they knock it down because he wanted to come back and collect the bricks. If you take down his address and telephone number, I'll keep the note he left for me."

They wrote down Luo Qian's contact details, returned the note, thanked the old man, got back in the car and drove off to the new address – Violet Garden off Xiqing Road. Luo Fu said: "Luo Qian always was an amazing guy. He must have held on to the very end and forced a luxury house out of the developer!"

Xiqing Road leads out to the suburb of Yangliuqing. They were now outside the city proper, so there were more fields than buildings by the sides of the road. As they kept going, searching for their friend, they finally found a piece of wood roughly nailed to a tree trunk by the side of the road. The words 'Violet Garden' were written there, but two of the Chinese characters had been misspelled. Luo Fu laughed heartily at that and said this must be a housing estate being developed by the local peasantry. Yuntian didn't like him laughing at a friend like that.

This housing estate was quite simple, but still had qualities that set it apart. Although the buildings were rough and the layout a little confusing, they were all spacious bungalows with grey roofs, white walls and large windows filled with sparkling glass, and there were many trees. The soil of this place must have been fertile – the leaves were all green and shiny, and the grass was lush. Luo Qian lived at Number 19. They found the number, and seeing his new house half hidden among the trees, Chu Yuntian remembered his old hut and thought Luo Qian must like the feeling of being concealed here. As a result, he had the warm sensation of returning to the past.

Luo Fu took a gift from the boot of his car and shouted to Luo Qian to come out of the house. The door opened and he emerged. Seeing their unexpected arrival, Luo Qian seemed somewhat confused and laughed along with Luo Fu. As he welcomed them, he asked: "How did you find me? Which one of you is Holmes and which is Watson?"

Yuntian immediately sensed a change in Luo Qian. He seldom joked before, nor would you often have seen him with a smile on his face.

"We went to find the last holdout," Luo Fu said, "and then we tracked you down from there. Of course, Holmes is me."

"What do you mean by calling me a holdout?" Luo Qian said. "They were trying to cram me into a high-rise. I simply can't live with hordes of other people, so I didn't want to go. The collusion between developers and local officials is something fierce. They used everything they had against me. For a while, they were even threatening to lock me up, but I wouldn't move. Eventually, they found this place for me. It is out in the suburbs, so the price was low. They thought I wouldn't come, but they didn't know this was exactly the kind of place I wanted." Luo Qian took them through the garden under the trees, entered the house and said: "See what you think…"

Luo Fu thought he'd become a farmer, but Yuntian felt that he had entered a little paradise. The house had three main rooms, and in front and behind there were large green areas and clumps of trees. It was difficult to see the neighbours and others wouldn't be able to see him. Luo Qian said that he had an agreement with the estate to allow him to build a low wall in front of and behind the house. He was just waiting for the bricks to arrive once his old house had been demolished. Yuntian thought: What's the difference between this place and Luo Fu's mansion? Is it just the luxury? Luo Qian hates vulgarity. But he must be feeling very happy right now.

Yuntian now noticed something else – an absence of paintings on the walls. Was this just because the house was new, and they hadn't been hung yet? The furniture was no longer the tables and chairs made from planks of wood hammered together, so it was not as rough as it used to be. Where was the olive-green wine jar used for flower arrangement back in his old place? No trace of the past could be seen. All the furniture in the house was the normal, regular kind. He smelled the scent of varnish and new wood. He asked Luo Qian if he had made it himself. Luo Qian smiled, but before he could reply, a door opened and a woman came in from outside, carrying a bag of vegetables. She was in her forties, quite tall and a little fat, with a plain face. At first glance, she was a simple and easygoing person. Luo Qian was a little embarrassed and then introduced them to his wife, Xia Rilian. The woman took it all in her stride, inviting them to make themselves at home while she went and got them some tea.

He was married? Oh, that's a good thing – he had finally emerged from his long period of solitude. What about his art? Just now when they had been looking around, they'd seen the bedroom, and then one other door was half-closed – he caught a slight whiff of oil paint. He wanted to see what Luo Qian was working on now, but he'd reached out and closed the door. Obviously, he didn't want them to look; or perhaps he didn't want Luo Fu to see. He knew that Luo Qian could be difficult and did not like to ask.

While they were chatting, there was a sense of strangeness. All three were aware of it.

This was due to the alienation among people who have not met for a long time, so at that moment they couldn't find a common topic of conversation. A hidden gulf seemed to have opened up between them, and there was also the complex psychological barrier created by their different social positions. If you talk without saying anything, you are just making conversation for the sake of it. Yuntian kept coming up with new topics, but nothing could arouse any kind of common interest. They were a bit like people from different countries who could not communicate in any language.

Chu Yuntian said to Luo Qian: "You could buy a stereo. There is so much more good music to listen to now than we used to have." He thought this might be something the three of them could discuss.

"If you are going to get one, you should buy Sansui, it is so much better than Philips," Luo Fu said.

He wasn't talking about the music they had once enjoyed so much, but about brands. Luo Qian was not interested in this subject at all.

Chu Yuntian changed the topic of their conversation again. He remarked that Luo Qian's wife's name, Summer Lotus, was very beautiful and picturesque. He said Luo Qian should dig a pond in their garden and plant water lilies, like in Monet's garden.

Luo Fu was brandishing a cigarette, and now he fanned the smoke in front of his face away with one hand and said: "Why are you still talking about Monet? He is completely out of date. In Paris, only tourists care about Monet."

"Didn't the silk scarf you brought back from the United States for Sui Yi have a design from one of Monet's water lily paintings?" Luo Qian asked. However, this time, Luo Qian wasn't criticising him angrily, he was laughing.

Chu Yuntian felt that there was no longer the slightest understanding between them and so there was nothing to talk about. He got up, took out two cans from his pocket and said: "This is a present from Sui Yi. Nothing valuable, but you always liked to eat this."

Luo Qian took them in his hands and saw that it was Sichuanese Fuling pickled mustard. He seemed to have been given a shock; it suddenly made him nostalgic and emotional. In fact, this should have been how the whole visit went – certainly, that was what Sui Yi expected. Luo Qian patted Yuntian on the shoulder and said with a sigh: "Wish her all the best from me."

Luo Qian escorted them to their car and waved them on their way.

Yuntian was silent for a long time. When they were about to get back to the city, he said to Luo Fu: "None of us spoke about it at all today."

"Spoke about what?"

"Painting," Yuntian said. "In the past, it was our favourite topic."

"We've all gone out separate ways," Luo Fu said lightly. "There's nothing to say."

Yuntian didn't reply, because Luo Fu wasn't wrong. But he suddenly felt desolation in his heart, and a very cold saying came to his mind: People have to get together, but when the time comes, they must part.

But he didn't say anything.

They had originally been as three natural streams, running wild through the mountains. They had traversed trees and rocks, climbing slopes and jumping cliffs, running as hard as they could.

They met in a deep valley. At the moment of meeting, they were full of passion. Their bright waves had embraced each other and their splashing waters had enriched one another. They used their own inspiration to stimulate the vitality in the others' lives. They relied on each other, trusted each other, inspired and promoted each other. They had turned their previous loneliness into a magical abundance, only to force their way out of the deep valley until they leapt over great mountains.

But once they had made their way to this boundless plain, they started to change. Alienation and separation were perhaps only to be expected. So, you find your way into another huge black river with its billowing waves; he debouches into a quiet blue lake, while I wander across the bare earth, drawn in by the bone-dry dust until gradually burned to oblivion by the merciless rays of the sun.

Yesterday was wonderful, unforgettable, moving and sad, but who has the power to call yesterday back to today?

PART THREE

下

IT IS THOSE WHOSE
SOULS ARE ILLUMINATED
BY BEAUTY THAT ARE REALLY RICH

CHAPTER 1

It is often a difficult process if you want to change your life, but easy enough for others. Why? Because everyone has a door, which means other people can come in. Therefore, some people keep their door heavily guarded, while others never give it a second thought. The former are mostly cautious, timid or have been hurt before; the latter have natures that are simple and straightforward.

Important people usually live carefully, so there are railings by the door and high thresholds. It is difficult to get close to them. Artists are not like that at all. They live by intuition. Most of them have only door frames, and some don't even have that. As long as they enjoy your company, you can easily enter their world.

Do you know how much influence this person who has just come in will have on you? Do you know if this person has any reason to get close to you, or has made clever plans in which you play a part?

Chu Yuntian first heard the name Bai Ye mentioned by another painter. He was praising a young artist called Bai Ye for her excellent painting and fine character; he said she was "so pure and so extraordinary". Yuntian had rarely heard anyone praise a woman in such terms. What kind of person could be described as "so pure and so extraordinary"? Yuntian had always valued the characters of individuals, especially when it came to women. Then the painter went on: "Bai Ye said she'd love to get to know you better than when she was your neighbour."

When and where did he live with such a remarkable neighbour? This gave him the idea that he'd like to meet her. One day, two men came from a publishing company in Shanghai to meet him. He remembered the name Bai Ye and asked them about her. The skinny, older one with glasses smiled and said: "Oh, yes, she's come back from abroad – a very fine painter. She's very beautiful and obviously well brought up. However, she's also hard as nails in her own way. Why, would you like to meet her?"

Yuntian waved away the suggestion. How could he say that he wanted to meet her, especially when talking about a young female painter? However, he was intrigued: why would the older man in glasses say she was "as hard as nails", and in what way? It was impossible for him to enquire further so he changed the subject. Another time, someone else remarked that a young artist called Bai Ye had a "refined temperament". It seemed that she must be a good person if that was the deepest impression she left behind. This made Yuntian develop certain illusions about this young artist that he had never even met. This is not surprising; painters always think in images.

A year later, Chu Yuntian had produced dozens of paintings about autumn, which he was very proud of. Of the four seasons of the year, he loved autumn best – it was the most abundant. From early autumn to late autumn, no matter whether you think of its fullness, brilliance, brightness and relaxation; or of its sparseness, depression, wandering and loneliness, it naturally creeps into one's emotions and moods and comes to embody all kinds of feelings about life. Yuntian's series of paintings were not big; most of them were painted on four-foot square paper. After the photos of these paintings were sent to Yu Changshui, someone from a gallery in Shanghai saw them and admired them very much. The man said that every one of those paintings was like a crisp piece of prose, so he wanted to hold an exhibition for Yuntian. The man was so eager that he phoned three times in one day. Yuntian couldn't help but agree.

There was only one condition – he did not want to sell. He had never sold a painting he was really proud of. A good painting is a pleasure bound by the moment of its creation, a work of chance, something that can never be painted again.

The exhibition was scheduled for the middle of October, by which time the hot weather in Shanghai would be over and the autumn would be cool and comfortable. The location of the gallery was also very good, on Huaihai Road. Yuntian wanted to go with Sui Yi since she hadn't been to Shanghai for many years. However, two days before his departure, the Artists Association informed him that his presence was required at a meeting in Beijing. As a result, he would have to fly to Beijing the day after the opening ceremony in Shanghai, so he decided to take Yu Changshui with him.

Your life is in the hands of the gods. If there had not been this meeting in Beijing, Sui Yi would have gone with Yuntian, and everything would have been different. Other things would have happened, and the ending would not be the same.

The gallery that was holding Yuntian's exhibition was not large, and their openings were seldom so well attended. But the opening of Yuntian's show was different. First of all, he was a famous artist and had many friends in Shanghai; second, he had many readers who wanted to meet him and ask him to sign copies of his books for them; and third, the title of his exhibition was taken from a piano piece played by Richard Clayderman, who was popular at that time – *Autumn Whispers*. The title was sufficiently intriguing that there were many people at the opening ceremony.

With Yu Changshui's help, he was able to force his way through the crowds. Towards noon, he escorted a couple of Shanghai painters out to the lobby to say a few words, shake hands and then wish each other goodbye. When he turned around, an extremely beautiful, bright-looking girl was standing in front of him. The 'brightness' was the first thing that struck him. The girl's expression was also unusual. She did not seem to feel constrained because they were strangers, or timid at the first sight of a great painter. Instead, she smiled at him, smiling as happily as if they were old acquaintances who had not met for many years, and bowed slightly.

Who could she be? She was dressed simply – a pair of jeans that had been washed so many times they were bleached, a light brown, loose pullover, that's all. She wore no make-up, so her thin red lips, clear white skin and long eyelashes all showed their natural colours. Her hair was pulled back in a ponytail and tied with a thin red velvet band. Who would dress so naturally? Or to put it another way, who would be so good at disguising themselves?

Yuntian stopped short. Was it the girl's natural, pure and noble beauty that made him pause, or because he did not know why she smiled at him so familiarly?

When she smiled, two faint dimples appeared on either side of her mouth, which added to her beauty.

He stood there, not knowing what to say.

She said to him: "I am Little Ye… your neighbour Little Ye!"

Yuntian couldn't imagine who she could be. He'd misheard her name and was quite sure he'd never known anyone called 'Little Hey'. The girl continued: "At the time of the 1976 earthquake, didn't you live on the top floor of the red-roofed building by the Qiangzi Canal?"

"Oh yes," Yuntian said. "But I'm very sorry. I don't remember having a neighbour at all…"

She smiled regretfully and said: "You've forgotten the little girl who used to live next door. So you'll have to get to know me as I am now." She held out a hand and introduced herself: "My name is Bai Ye!"

He took her hand. It was not big, but very smooth and soft. Not many people have attractive hands.

So this was Bai Ye! The Bai Ye that others had mentioned to him more than once! She was none other than the artist of 'refined temperament' that he wanted to meet. She was standing in front of him now. She really was extraordinary, with all the elegance and purity of a southern spring, but wrack his brains as he might, he simply couldn't identify her as a former neighbour. He was a little sorry, and he didn't know how to express this, so he felt embarrassed. Bai Ye could tell exactly what he was thinking. She was a chatty girl and just said cheerfully: "I'm happy just to look at your pictures this time. Next time, we can talk about when I used to live next door."

With that, she waved to him, turned and walked away lightly, as if a breeze was wafting her away. That was all she said before leaving.

However, she left a question mark in Chu Yuntian's head about his old neighbour, and he couldn't stop thinking about her. She also left an unusually beautiful and fresh impression in his mind, and he enjoyed thinking back on this very special feeling about a member of the opposite sex.

That afternoon, Chu Yuntian was very busy. The gallery manager pulled him aside to talk, repeatedly saying that there were several collectors here who really understood art and wanted to buy his paintings. He said that as per their original agreement, he didn't want to sell, but the gallery manager kept pestering him and finally he agreed to sell three pictures. In the evening, several friends from Shanghai art circles invited him to a dinner party, so he didn't return to his hotel until after nine o'clock. He had just washed his face and sat down to relax a bit when the front desk downstairs called and said that there were some friends here to visit him and they were waiting in the hall. He quickly changed out of his suit and went downstairs.

When he got to the hall, he didn't see anyone. Looking around, he saw someone sitting over in the coffee shop on the right-hand side, waving at him. He could see that it was Bai Ye. He was a little surprised but also happy, as if this was something he had secretly been hoping for.

He walked quickly over towards her, and Bai Ye stood up. She had changed into a dark green dress. It was a little cold that night, so she was wearing a thin black coat and her hair was still casually held back from her face. The sombre-coloured dress brightened her pale face.

Before he could speak, she asked: "I know I'm disturbing you by visiting you this late. But I'm not willing to let you forget all about 'Little Ye'. I can't help asking you, do you remember me?"

As Yuntian faltered, she smiled and said: "It was almost twenty years ago, not to mention a different epoch. It's not your fault, I'll help you remember."

She was very good at making herself feel like an old friend. Yuntian smiled and agreed.

"The house you lived in was one of a row of three, side by side. They have some such houses in Shanghai too, which I guess were also built by foreigners. You lived in the one on the far left, didn't you?" She picked up three small canisters of salt, pepper and what have you from the table and placed them in a row. She patted the one on the far left and then said, pointing to the one on the far right: "My family lived in this one. There was another one in between us."

"Oh, so you weren't in the same building," Yuntian said. "There was another one in the middle. No wonder I don't remember you."

"I remember you quite well. My mother always told me that the tall uncle from over the way was an artist. Once you painted the trees in your garden, and my mother took me to see it. You hugged me and kissed me."

Then she smiled again. This time, she looked a little shy. The details of her recollections gave Yuntian the feeling that he had known her for a long time. Thinking about it, he did seem to remember something of the kind. "Your mother was tall and very slim, yes?" he said. "I remember my wife saying that she was very beautiful. By the way, I remember, she also said her daughter – that is, you – was very cute."

"You see, it's all coming back to you." Bai Ye smiled, revealing deep dimples and bright white teeth. "I remember your wife was always so kind. How is she now?"

"Very good."

"And you had a daughter. Younger than me, so I guess she's at university now?"

"She's at the École Supérieure des Beaux-Arts in Bordeaux, but she's not there to study painting. She's interested in art history."

"That's one of the best fine arts institutes in France. I studied in France too, but I graduated from Versailles – and studied art history for a while as well. Nowadays most painters don't know anything about art history and don't bother to read books – it's a real shame."

"Why did you come to Shanghai?"

"My father works in finance, and Shanghai is better for him. We followed him," Bai Ye explained.

Originally, Yuntian had wanted to ask about her paintings. He hadn't seen any of her work yet. But Bai Ye was more interested in recalling the past, which led her to recall many happy memories about those three small buildings. She was reflecting on her childhood, while Yuntian had never forgotten those bitter and arduous years – this gave them a common past. Therefore, she was not a sudden intruder in his life, but an old friend stepping out of the past. But it was because she came out of the past, bringing with her so many memories, that she was able to make room in his present – she had already got her foot wedged in the door.

It was already eleven o'clock when Yu Changshui tracked them down in the coffee shop. When he caught sight of Bai Ye, they just nodded to each other. Did they know each other?

Yu Changshui told Chu Yuntian that they would have to be out of the hotel by seven tomorrow morning. The plane was due to leave at 10.30. Bai Ye knew that it was time for her to go. She took out two albums of paintings from a handbag and said they were her works. She smiled and asked Yuntian to have a look at them when he was on the plane.

If Yu Changshui had not been present, their goodbyes would certainly have gone quite differently.

After Chu Yuntian returned to his room, he had the feeling that something wonderful had been cut short before it had even begun. He felt a little disappointed.

He flew from Shanghai to Beijing for the meeting and then returned home. Sui Yi was waiting for him with a sumptuous dinner and iced beer. Later on, she sat down opposite him across the table and smiled as she watched him wolf the food down. After dinner, she listened proudly to his account of how 'Autumn Whispers' had gone. People had spoken admiringly of his theories on the literary nature of painting expounded at the opening ceremony of the exhibition. He gave her a lot of good news. He also liked to see the satisfied look on her face. It now dawned on him that he hadn't brought her any gifts, not even a box of her favourite sesame-seed Cloud Cakes. He had thought about it before setting off, making a mental note on the subject, but he still forgot. What a terrible thing! Even if he hadn't had time to buy it on the first day, he could have bought her a box in one of the shops at the airport. Why? What could he have been thinking?

Sui Yi asked questions about this and that, enquiring if he'd met anyone special. This was like pulling out a bung.

"Do you remember when we lived in the attic by the Qiangzi Canal, one of the neighbours had a daughter called Little Ye?" he asked.

Sui Yi thought about it for a moment. Yuntian was sure she didn't remember. Then she suddenly said: "I know! I remember her quite well! A dear little girl. Her mother was very good-looking, with a beautiful figure, and so nice – such a lovely woman."

"How do you remember all that?"

"I always remember good-looking people. They lived in the house on the far side of us. Sometimes she'd take Little Ye to play outside the house, and I'd see them there when I got off work. I think her mother used to work in a drama troupe, but I don't know if she was an actress or something behind the scenes... Did you meet Little Ye at your show? Does she not live in Tianjin?"

"Her family moved to Shanghai ages ago. She is a painter now," Yuntian said.

"Oh really? How interesting that she became a painter too. Is she very like her mother? Is she beautiful?" Sui Yi asked.

Somehow, Yuntian felt it was difficult to answer this question. He thought about it and said: "I don't think I ever saw her mother, but she's pretty enough. By the way, she studied art history in France too, but she's been in Paris."

"She'd be about the same age as Yiran. Oh, no, she'd be four or five years older. Have you seen her paintings? Are they any good?"

Yuntian couldn't wait to take the two thin picture books out of his travelling bag and hand them to Sui Yi. As she turned over the pages, looking up now and again to show her surprise, Yuntian said: "I didn't expect her paintings to be so good... She's really got something there."

"Such fine work, and such a unique style!" Sui Yi said that with an expression of warm approval on her face.

Yuntian felt very satisfied, as if someone were praising his daughter, or Sui Yi herself.

He kept those two volumes of paintings in his studio and looked at them from time to time. The signature Bai Ye on the title page reminded him of her beautiful face when he first met her.

That winter, the Academy of Arts invited Chu Yuntian to Ji'nan to select works for a new national exhibition. He was the head of the selection team in the category of traditional Chinese painting. Yu Changshui had gone to Shenzhen for something, and it so happened that Fei Liang was then working on a large painting destined for the conference room of a hotel in Ji'nan. The Academy of Arts phoned up Fei Liang to help Chu Yuntian out while he was in Ji'nan. When he arrived at the station, Fei Liang picked him up in his car and handed him a letter. Chu Yuntian sat in the car and opened the letter. The message was only a few lines long –

Dear Chu Yuntian:
  You will see my painting today, and I feel very lucky that this should be so! I am not asking for your help, but I would like to hear your advice. I will be in touch tomorrow night.

The signature was in a foreign language, but not in English. He wondered if it might not be French, because Yiran occasionally used a few words of French when writing home. Yuntian immediately realised that this must be a message from Bai Ye. She was very clever in not stressing her purpose, but there was a certain hope revealed by her letter. However, Yuntian was serious and objective about art, and when it came down to it, he would just look at the paintings when making his decision. "Who gave you this letter?" he asked Fei Liang.

"A member of Shanghai Artists Association – he's called Chen Fei, quite a young man..." Fei Liang replied. "He was delivering some paintings for consideration. I've never seen him before."

"Will he be staying in the same hotel?" Yuntian asked.

"No, no," Fei Liang assured him. "This time, you judges are all staying in one hotel, but the people sending their works for selection won't be allowed anywhere near you. The paintings are all going to be on show in the hotel, so you can evaluate them there. They don't want you going anywhere to ensure that the selection process is entirely confidential. You'll have two days for consideration, and it will all be over at noon the day after tomorrow. If you don't have any reason to stay longer in Ji'nan, I'll buy you a return ticket for that afternoon. I'm staying in the hotel where I'm working on the painting. If you need me, you can just give me a call."

"OK," Chu Yuntian said. "I'll phone you if I need anything."

Yuntian was worried that Bai Ye might be waiting for him in the hotel lobby like last time, or that she would come looking for him, but she didn't. It seemed that she was not the kind of person to seek fame and profit. Not only did he see no sign of her, there was not even so much as a phone call from her. Yuntian had never liked rapacious women. He thought that her temperament and taste were indeed unusual. Temperament is not just a matter of superficial demeanour but can be a sign of real character.

The works under consideration were all hung on screens erected in one of the hotel conference rooms. He and the judges looked at each one, discussed and commented on them. While commenting, they marked their score on the form they held in their hands. They were proceeding in order, when suddenly Bai Ye's painting came into view.

He wasn't looking for her painting, but it jumped out at him, and not only at him but also at all the other judges.

The judges were unanimous in their praise – just as Sui Yi had said, her paintings were very fine and in such a unique style.

In this painting, one metre twenty square, she used her own artistic language, in which there were no brushstrokes at all. At most, a little faint outline would melt into the surrounding layers of wash. She was obtaining a watercolour effect in fine brush painting, but no one had ever achieved this kind of wash before, whereby things seemed to be emerging from a mist, giving it a dreamy, illusory quality.

There were no brush marks, no heavy ink lines, just light ink, light colour and an insubstantial effect. She controlled the clarity of the image to just the point where it seemed hardly to be there at all, and the hazy beauty thus revealed made the artistic conception of her painting implicit and profound. Did she want to distance herself from you or lure you into the painting?

The title of her painting was 'Expectation'.

From a distance, it depicted a mountain village surrounded by flowers and trees growing lush and thick. From a closer look, it was a complex and harmonious intersection and integration of various colours. This was a highly original painting in its psychedelic feeling and distinctively modern character; but underlying it all was a strong foundation in traditional painting techniques and meticulous practice. The judges all expressed their admiration.

One judge said: "Although this painting is not an absolute masterpiece, it does open the door to a modern interpretation of traditional painting techniques." This was praise indeed.

"Since there aren't any brushstrokes at all, just washes, does the expressiveness become limited?"

"This is just what the artist wants. Pushing wash techniques to such an extreme – that's very creative."

"Besides, it shows a fine artistic conception and excellent taste."

"I appreciate the fuzziness of its language," a judge from Guangdong said.

"The fuzziness of the artist's language serves to arouse the imagination of the audience, which is not just a technical innovation," Chu Yuntian couldn't help saying. "This is a fine and original work of a kind rarely seen in the modern era." Somehow, at that moment, he couldn't help showing support for Bai Ye. That was something he had never done before.

In the field of painting, Chu Yuntian's words were considered authoritative. He always started from the art and only cared about the work itself. He was objective and fair, as well as possessing a measure of popularity, so everyone was convinced of the truth of his words. He said what he did, and the rest was a foregone conclusion. No one expected it, but in the final round of voting by the judges, Bai Ye got a very high score.

After the judging was over, Chu Yuntian was happy as he had rarely been before. Was this because Bai Ye made the cut? No, it was because a talented and lovely young artist was selected! He asked himself whether he had in fact interfered on her behalf and whether he had violated his artistic conscience. He decided that although he thought highly of her, it was based on her merits. Bai Ye was talented, imaginative, unique and tasteful, although her work was still a little thin because she was so young.

Thinness is not entirely an artistic thing, because it depends on having experienced life.

. . .

When he returned to the hotel in the afternoon, he received a call from Bai Ye.

"It's me, Little Ye!"

As soon as he heard those clear tones, he saw the deep dimples that appeared in her cheeks when she smiled. He felt very happy.

"Have you seen my painting? The photographs in the book I gave you last time are too small… You must see the originals," Bai Ye declared. Naturally, she was still unaware of the evaluation results.

"You are right. The scale of the original work is the scale of the painter's emotions when at work. Once reduced, it will lose much of the feeling of the original," Yuntian said. "I admire the fuzzy language you create with washes in fine brushwork. That is something very unique to you. A unique technique and unique aesthetics."

"You're amazing! In a few words, you've summed up everything I've been trying to understand for many years. Can I come and see you today? I'd like to talk to you some more." Bai Ye spoke warmly, with a hint of eagerness.

Yuntian also wanted to see her, but shortly some painters from the Shandong Academy of Arts and several officials from Ji'nan Cultural Department would be coming to see him. Bai Ye had produced one of the pieces that would be on display. If she came and people spotted her, it would look bad. He told her this, with some embarrassment.

"Quite honestly, I want to know what other people think of my painting," Bai Ye said.

Knowing that she cared about the fate of her work, Yuntian was afraid that she would be worried. His heart softened, and so he told her something he really shouldn't have said: "Everyone agreed with me. Don't worry." He paused and then added: "But don't tell anyone."

Bai Ye was overjoyed. "I won't say a word, you can rest assured," she declared. "The most important thing is that with your support, I have the courage to carry on painting."

After that, Bai Ye said she would not come to the hotel to see

Yuntian. In the evening, he got together with the Shandong painters for a small celebration. Shandong people are so fond of drinking that they won't stop until everyone is drunk. After Chu Yuntian returned to his room, he just tumbled down to sleep, not even taking off his clothes. The telephone woke him in the morning. He thought it would be Fei Liang, but then he heard Bai Ye speak. Her voice was different from before; it seemed a little lower and more drawling. He thought she wanted to come to see him off and he told her not to do so. But no matter what he said, she did not reply. Had she hung up on him? He said "hello" twice. Suddenly, a low and timid voice came down the line: "I won't come and see you off because I'm afraid people might see. I'm fine. I just wanted to hear your voice."

Then she hung up the phone. There was only a buzzing dialling tone.

This remark confused Chu Yuntian. He felt his heart suddenly beat faster. In particular, she had stopped using respectful language towards him, which made him feel that his relationship with this talented and beautiful girl was something quite special.

And everything she said in the end, in that abrupt and bold statement, meant a lot to him. He would think of it from time to time afterwards, but he couldn't quite figure out what she meant by it. It was like her painting – hazy and ambiguous.

CHAPTER 2

A few months later, on a cold spring day, the new national art exhibition opened in Beijing. The triennial national exhibition attracted painters from all over the country to gather in the capital like migratory birds. The opening ceremony was a sea of people, all talking at once in an endless hubbub. Chu Yuntian was feeling particularly energised before taking the stage to give his speech. He was wearing a long dark blue coat, and as usual he looked a little untidy and his hair a little messy, but he combined a certain solemnity with his relaxed demeanour, especially during his speech, which made the opening ceremony particularly magnetic and moving.

Photographers' flashlights exploded around him. Later, a reporter described Chu Yuntian as "looking like a raincloud full of lightning".

In addition to his influence, depth of thought and eloquence, the reason why the Artists Association invited him to make a speech was that he had set a rule for himself after becoming chairman: he would never send one of his works to any competitive national art exhibition, nor would he take any job – honorific or otherwise – in industry. He did exactly as he said. Everyone respected his character.

Today, Yuntian opened with the words: "Whether the art world is making progress depends on how many dazzling works are produced by talented young painters." He then added warily: "Of course, we should also not neglect new lights achieved by old painters."

His words made everyone laugh, especially the older artists present.

As he spoke, his eyes fixed upon a woman in a long, brick-red coat in the audience. It was the moment he said "dazzling works" that he recognised her: Bai Ye. This made him feel very excited and energetic, and what he said next was even more impassioned.

After receiving his invitation to attend the exhibition, Chu Yuntian guessed that Bai Ye would travel from Shanghai to Beijing because her work would be on display. Being selected for a national art exhibition is not only a witness of an artist's strength but also a sign that wider art circles are starting to pay attention to them.

Did she also want to take this opportunity to see him?

Ever since they said goodbye on the phone in Ji'nan, the meaningful words she left with him had been lingering on his mind, but since then she had not had any contact with him, whether by phone or letter. Why should he be so hung up about that sentence?

Chu Yuntian, who was by now middle-aged, was never again going to behave as he did over Yufei, nor would he fall into the trap of becoming deeply in love. Although he still had romantic feelings and felt his heart beat harder over the poetic and picturesque nature of life, it was more than twenty years since he had passed that peak. Especially since he had hurt Sui Yi so much – that was a scar that remained in his heart.

However, when this beautiful, talented and remarkable Bai Ye appeared and took the initiative to approach him, was he not repeating the same mistakes? At least he had not done so yet! At most, her overtures had just reactivated the romantic notions sleeping deep within. What this had led to was only some emotion, some happiness, some imaginings. Being flirted with by the opposite sex is a manifestation of personal charm, and anyone might be proud of it. But right now, he was still sober; he had no intention of letting himself fall again into difficulties from which he would be unable to extricate himself. Therefore, he would not make any effort to get in touch with her. What's more, what really interested him at that time was the issue of socially responsible art and his own paintings, particularly the latter.

This time Yuntian came to Beijing for two reasons: first, to attend the opening ceremony of the national art exhibition in the morning; and second, to see the preview of a large calligraphy and painting auction at the Continental Grand Hotel in the afternoon. Yu Changshui had described to him what grand occasions auctions of calligraphy and painting were several times. Because he had never so much as attended an auction, he knew little about them. Today, he wanted to take a look to see for himself what was going on in the crazy calligraphy and painting market. He had never been to such an event before, just as he had never been in a nightclub or concert hall.

At the exhibition, he was quickly making his rounds when he saw a group gathered some distance ahead. Through a gap in the crowd, he caught sight of a woman in red talking, and a second glance told him it was Bai Ye. A TV reporter was interviewing her in front of her painting 'Expectation'. Bai Ye seemed to have a sixth sense directed towards him since when he saw her, she also saw him. It was a little magical.

Bai Ye immediately ran through the crowd, took him by the arm and pulled him towards her painting. She told a photographer: "Please take a picture of me with Chu Yuntian. I am a huge admirer of his work."

Yuntian didn't want to do anything of the kind, but he couldn't refuse. Fortunately, they stood together naturally and easily, smiling into the strong light of a bank of cameras. That is how he ended up in a photo with this young woman.

At that moment, the TV reporter came up with his camera and wanted to ask Yuntian to talk about Bai Ye's painting. He shook his hand and declined. Bai Ye was very smart, and she knew that Chu Yuntian wanted to avoid this sort of thing. She wasn't the kind of person who would put others on the spot, nor did she want to drag celebrities into situations where they felt obliged to support her. She politely stopped the TV reporter and asked Yuntian to carry on and see the rest of the exhibition. In this way, she allowed him to perceive the elegance of her social manners.

. . .

In the afternoon, in accordance with their original plan, they went to the Continental Grand Hotel to see the works coming up for auction. There was no proper hall at the hotel, so various banqueting halls and conference rooms had been allocated to be exhibition space, and the works had been divided by date and subject. The people coming to view each exhibition area were so crowded in they were pressed up against one another. Chu Yuntian was seeing this for the first time, witnessing the popularity of auctions as a medium for sales, which was by no means how he had originally imagined it.

That morning, Yuntian saw a pure art exhibition in the museum. Now, he was looking at a purely commercial exhibition. With his sensitivity, it was obvious that these represented two quite different worlds. Looking at paintings in the museum, people are emotional and rational. There, they mainly look at the work itself. Here, they were also inspecting the title, signature and seals. In a museum, the public use their eyes; at an auction, they use their brains to calculate. And there is a price tag under each painting.

Yuntian asked Yu Changshui: "What's the biggest difference between the exhibition here and the exhibition at the museum this morning?"

Yu Changshui said with a simple and honest smile: "There are prices on these works."

"Does the price determine the value of the painting?"

"Of course not, but here they follow the laws of the market, which are different from ours. We talk about the quality, and they talk about price. That's all they want to know about."

"I guess that paintings commanding a high price ought to be pretty good," Yuntian said.

"Not necessarily," Yu Changshui declared. "Sometimes it's just the opposite. Paintings that sell well at high prices can be absolute rubbish."

"That's very interesting. When we get back home, if you have the time, I'd like to know more…"

Walking around the exhibition hall, Yuntian saw the paintings of many people whom he knew. He thought: Are these painters selling their works, too? He then spotted a piece by Yi Liaoran, entitled 'A Lone Pine on the Cliff at Huangshan', an eight-foot scroll. Stunned, he could not stop himself from saying: "Is he also sending work to auction?" Looking again, he saw the price was very high. He asked Yu Changshui: "Does Yi Liaoran often put his work up for auction?"

"His paintings frequently come up for sale. Some overseas collectors like his work, and the prices have been rising. However, it is not necessarily Yi Liaoran himself who sends his pictures to auction. Maybe he gave them to someone else and they are selling them for cash." Then Yu Changshui went on: "Your paintings occasionally are put on sale here, but you certainly didn't send them! It's the same principle. Last time, there were two of your four-foot square paintings, depicting the water towns south of the Yangtze River, and the hammer price was very good. However, the people who bought the paintings didn't know that you hadn't put them up for auction, and they may well have thought that you were getting the money."

"How am I to prove that it was nothing to do with me?" Yuntian wailed.

"Why should you want to prove anything of the kind?" Yu Changshui asked. "Painters need money too. Everyone wants to have their pictures accepted by these people for sale. I've got two pieces of my own in the exhibition hall over there – just small works."

"Do you have pictures in every auction here then?" Yuntian asked.

"I want to get married," Yu Changshui said, "and I'd like to buy a house, and in the future I'd like to have children. I've been sending pictures since last year, but they haven't sold very well."

"OK," Yuntian said. "Let's have a look at them."

They came to Yu Changshui's two small pictures. "They are still in your Tibetan manner," Yuntian said. "Why not use the freehand ink brushwork you're so good at? It's calm, atmospheric and delicious."

"The auction company said there is too much ink painting now, and buyers can't tell whether they are good or bad. Tibetan-style paintings have the advantage of strong characteristics. Several buyers from the south have been eyeing my paintings, and up until now, provided I send them here, they are sure to sell. It's just that the price is a little low – the estimate is just twenty thousand yuan per painting," Yu Changshui explained. "They said that the estimate should not be too high to begin with. Once you can command a certain price on the market, then collectors hope that your paintings will appreciate further in value, and that's when the price goes up – just the same as with shares."

Yuntian didn't speak. He didn't like these commercial home truths. Yu Changshui realised this, and he was afraid that Yuntian thought he didn't care about art any more and only about getting a better hammer price on his work. Suddenly Yuntian said: "You know, twenty thousand yuan for one painting is not at all bad. One painting can pay for a four square-metre room."

Yu Changshui was amazed, and they both burst out laughing.

Yuntian was always considerate in the way he did not allow his principles to impose on others.

As they were talking, someone came over and asked: "Which one of you is Mr Chu Yuntian?"

"That's me. What's up?"

"You are wanted on the phone," the man explained. "Please come with me."

Yuntian was puzzled: how could anyone be calling him? Who would know he was here? He followed the man into an office. When he picked up the phone and spoke, there was a clear laugh at the other end of the line. As soon as he heard that sound, he knew it was Bai Ye. The sound was as good as seeing her face. "Don't ask me how I found you," she said. "If I want to find someone, I will track them to the ends of the earth."

Yuntian didn't know what to say to her. Fortunately, she immediately carried on: "Let me tell you a secret first. I've joined the Artists Association and I'm going to be one of your foot soldiers. There's another secret that you'll find out about soon enough. Anyway, I'm getting closer and closer to you. Do you welcome that?"

Yuntian didn't know how to answer.

"I wish you a safe journey back!" Bai Ye said, and then she hung up.

She always stopped abruptly, never dragging on, making him feel relaxed in her presence and leaving him hanging, something like a riddle, calling on him to think, ponder and remember.

Yuntian put down the phone and turned to see Yu Changshui. "It was that painter from Shanghai, Bai Ye," he said, and he was now feeling even more curious. "How did she know I'm here?"

"Oh, her!" Yu Changshui remarked. "She came to find me at the opening ceremony this morning and said she wanted to see you this afternoon. I said you'd be here to see the paintings on show. She left without saying anything. What do you mean – did she track you down here? Is everything all right?"

"It's OK, there's nothing to worry about," Yuntian assured him.

They were about to leave when two people, one short and one tall, came up to them, laughing. The greasy, pudgy man leading them said to Yuntian: "Are you Mr Chu? I'm the vice president of the Jiahe Corporation. My surname is Ma. Two days ago, Mr Yu said that you would like to come and see our show. We are very happy, very glad to see you. It is an honour to meet a genius such as yourself, indeed it is…" As he spoke, a fat little hand passed over his business card. A large mutton-fat jade ring was shining on one finger.

President Ma invited Chu Yuntian and Yu Changshui to join him in a nearby reception room. After sitting down, he said: "Our exhibition here is completely different from your exhibition this morning, isn't it?"

"This is a commercial show," Yuntian remarked. "Of course it's different."

Yuntian's words carried a slight derogatory implication. But what President Ma said next was interesting. Still smiling, he riposted: "I was there at the art museum this morning too and listened to your speech. You're right. Your paintings are works of art, and mine are commodities. But works of art can only be circulated after they have been turned into commodities. Furthermore, your exhibitions are where painters become famous. But once that has happened, they all come to me. Why? Because they want to sell! With fame, their paintings are worth money. Who doesn't want to sell if that means they can get rich? Who doesn't want to make a good price? When you think about it from that point of view, we are part of the same stream."

Chu Yuntian smiled. He didn't like Mr Ma's fallacies, but he didn't want to argue with him. Mr Ma always understood people, and so he seemed to sense what Chu Yuntian was thinking. He then continued: "I know, what I said is a little vulgar. But no one can live without money. That's the truth of the matter! Think of Tang Sanjian, an old painter from Tianjin – you must know him. He used to be very upright and claimed that he would never deal with any auction house, but he came through the door three years ago to sell his paintings, and he cooperated with us very well. At first, his paintings didn't sell any better than some of the younger artists, but now they are getting just a fraction of what he does."

"Why?" Yuntian asked.

Mr Ma was so proud that he stretched out his arm and almost knocked the teacup on the table to the ground, making his tea spill. After a moment of panic, he continued with a smile: "That's the power of the auction house. Thirty per cent is down to the work of art, seventy per cent is how you sell it. Now, painters like Tang Sanjian mainly sell because they are 'old'. Old because he's part of a former generation, a past era. This is especially true of those who were famous before the Cultural Revolution. After the Cultural Revolution, their works became 'vintage' or even 'antiques', and so they are more valuable. He's a real treasure. Antiques become more valuable as they get older. Since the Cultural Revolution, he has painted nothing but plum blossoms. We called his plum blossom paintings 'Tang Plums' – it has a good ring to it. After that, his paintings were easy to sell. Some commentators say that Tang Sanjian ought to price his works by the number of flowers, at a cost of three thousand yuan per blossom." He laughed heartily.

"In that case, you should take up flower painting," Yuntian joked. "Trees covered in blossom."

"What? Who else paints plum trees?" Mr Ma said. Obviously, he didn't understand.

"Lots of people," Yuntian said. "Guan Shanyue is good at painting plum trees. Didn't Wang Mian of the Yuan dynasty also paint plum trees? 'There is a tree by my inkstone pool, Each of its flowers blooms inky-cool. There is no need to praise colours bright, Just enjoy the pure scent that fills the light.'"

"You are very knowledgeable," Mr Ma said. "One day, you should ask Mr Tang to paint another plum tree for us. I can guarantee a sky-high price."

Yuntian didn't respond but instead asked him: "I see you have a landscape by Yi Liaoran, a great painter from Huizhou. Does he also cooperate with you?"

"No," Mr Ma said, "his paintings are sent to us for auction by other people – he has never contacted us himself. Many collectors are on the lookout for his paintings. I hear he has a strange temper and his whereabouts are often uncertain. He stays in the mountains for several months each year. Huangshan is so huge – how could I possibly find him? I've heard that you are very close to him and have mounted an exhibition for him. Could I ask you to take a letter to him to say that we want to act as his agent? We are one of the three largest calligraphy and painting auction houses in China, so as long as he promises to give us exclusive rights of sale, we'll be sure to sell for the price of gold!"

After hearing these words, Yuntian felt a sense of disgust. He wanted to end this conversation about money as soon as possible, so he got up and left in a rush.

In the car on the way back, Yu Changshui said: "Mr Ma wants you to ask them to act as your agent. It must be very important for him."

"Why didn't he say something?" Yuntian asked.

"You really don't understand businessmen," Yu Changshui said. "He told you how he made Tang Sanjian a force to be reckoned with – that was all said for your sake. He didn't explain that directly, because he wants you to go to them. If you approach them, they will have the upper hand. If he asks you, they won't."

Yuntian knocked his head and said: "I don't have the brains or energy to deal with these people."

Yu Changshui saw that Chu Yuntian's arrogance was on the rise again and stopped talking.

There is a special comfort to driving at night. The newly built Beijing-Tianjin Expressway was flat and smooth, and the car raced like a spaceship through the night sky. Yuntian asked the chauffeur to turn on the cassette player. Listening to music in the car at night allowed him to feel its infinite beauty.

Now, enveloped by the vast, never-ending pleasures of music, Chu Yuntian's mind replayed for him all kinds of scenes that had happened during the day: the opening ceremony with its sea of people, the emotions he had given vent to during his speech and the paintings that he noticed. What followed was Yi Liaoran's 'A Lone Pine on the Cliff at Huangshan', the 'Tang Plums' of Tang Sanjian, the very different crowd at the auction and Mr Ma's words. Then a woman in brick-red jumped out of the crowd and took a photo with him, her elegant beauty and the pregnant words she'd spoken on the phone… At this time, a long and lingering violin melody aroused a beautiful, gentle feeling in his heart. Didn't she say there was another secret, and that she wanted to get closer to him – what was that about?

CHAPTER 3

After seeing the lively auction preview at the Continental Grand Hotel, Yuntian began to pay serious attention to the role of money in the art world.

Previously, he had often encountered evidence of the link, but he was not interested and ignored it. He pretended it didn't have anything to do with his beloved art and career; he shied away from any issue of money, put it aside and ignored it. But from this day on, he finally saw clearly that this was another world, a strong and unavoidable realm, and it had everything to do with himself.

In the past, he thought that he worked in the mountains and rivers, and this other world was like the ocean. At most, it was a place where some artists occasionally went fishing for food. Now it was different. He found that its waves were already rolling across the shore and drowning his land. Many artists had already become loyal subjects of that other realm.

To understand these things, he made friends with a man named Yu who specialised in art auctions. Mr Yu knew about ceramics, wood, modern calligraphy and painting. He was in his sixties, bald, with a pair of round glasses, and he liked to wear traditional Chinese-style jackets. Mr Yu was experienced, intelligent and honest. In the auction house, he was thought to be a reliable person who made a living thanks to his keen eye. On the day in question, Mr Yu was sitting on a rattan chair in Yuntian's garden and sipping a cup of bright green tea. What he said to Chu Yuntian was worth pondering.

"Although you and I have been dealing with art our entire lives, we are two completely different kinds of people. We can't talk about who is better and who is worse, because we each do our own things."

"You are a painter, and your work is done before the completion of a painting. We sell paintings, and our work is done after the painting is finished."

"What you care about is artistic value. We turn artistic value into commercial value."

"When you look at a painting, you don't care who the artist is. When we look at paintings, we also look at the artist. Someone who is not famous, no matter how good they are, they're not worth money. When the artist is famous, a bad painting can still be worth a lot of money.

"You call a painting a work, and we call it an auction lot. An auction lot is a commodity. You care about whether an artwork is good or bad. We think first – is this real or fake?

"If you look at a painter, you will see his skill in composition and technique. If we look at a painter, we will see his price. For us, whoever has the highest price will be the best.

"So in your studio, skill is something to be used in the painting. But our skills are unrelated to art."

Yuntian said with a smile: "Du Mu says in one of his poems: 'Skill is unrelated to the success of a poem.'"

"Don't laugh," Mr Yu said. "The key to selling paintings is the selling part. Why do painters now try to hype themselves up? They ask the media to publicise their work, they do buy-one-get-one-free offers, even buy-one-get-three free, they get into fights, raise the price on the spot and pretend to sell to fake purchasers. There are many methods. You could write a book about them. Why? It's all about raising their price."

Yuntian thought of Luo Fu's big show. "I know," he said, "and I've heard a lot of hype. But if the painting is bad, raising the price will just lead to a crash later."

"It's not our business whether it crashes or not at some point in the future. We just care how it sells right now," Mr Yu said. "And I hope you noticed that the word I used just now was 'price', not 'value'. The price is the market price. To put it bluntly, how much per square foot. The price is relatively stable, but it can also be manipulated."

"I don't understand," Yuntian said.

"Raising the price requires investment. Every time I hold an auction, I have to find a group of people who are willing to buy your paintings at a high price, and that gradually consolidates your market price."

"But how do you do that?"

"Didn't I just tell you? Buy one, get one free, or get two free, or even three, or just pretend to sell, then return the money and get the painting back. Of course, you have to pay a handling fee, but you can view that as an investment – your price will be set."

"But what do I want to have a set price for?" Yuntian asked.

"You don't understand!" Mr Yu exploded. "Let me put it this way – you sell one or two paintings occasionally, but they are sold privately. To our way of thinking, that's bad! Because your paintings don't have a fixed market price, that means they can't circulate any further. If you want to have a market price, you have to sell at auction. Everyone knows and recognises how much each painter's works sell for at auction. But no one knows how much your paintings are worth because if you don't participate in sales, you have no price. If you really need a certain sum of money and have to sell some paintings, how can you do so? Therefore, painters have to work hard to get a good market price, so afterwards they don't have to worry about a thing."

"I don't care about the market, nor do I wish to have my works overpriced." Every time the conversation turned to this topic, Yuntian became all the more determined to hold himself aloof.

Mr Yu smiled and said: "I'm just telling you a few home truths, and you should be paying attention. How many people now really know about art and love it? How many people in China today have paintings hung up at home? They make their pile, get their houses done over by an interior designer, and then they hang up a painting or two – it's all about looking arty. Only a few people who buy paintings at our auctions have a clue about the art. Who would spend a hundred and eighty thousand yuan on a work by a contemporary artist? The painter is still alive, and you're buying hot from his brush – that's pretty dumb, don't you think? Most people who buy paintings at auction are looking to turn a profit. We get two main kinds. The first kind are the sort who've made a lot of money, who hope that calligraphy and painting will go up in value – they buy paintings instead of stocks and shares. The second kind are businesspeople who want them as gifts – they buy paintings instead of jewellery. In their eyes, naturally, whoever commands the highest price is the best painter! Everything in the world is better the more valuable it is. Right? Now it's your turn to say something..."

"It used to be that those who painted well commanded the highest prices," Yuntian said, "but now it seems the reverse is true – whoever has the highest price is considered the best painter. It's a kind of fraud!"

"The market has its own laws," Mr Yu said. "Right now, we have a market economy, and cash is king! For painters, fame makes them money. If you become more famous, then your paintings will be worth more money."

"Then you don't have to put so much work into your paintings."

Mr Yu put the teacup down on the table and said: "I see you understand."

Was that Mr Yu feeling pleased with himself? Yuntian smiled bitterly. He thought to himself: What a terrible era this is.

In such an era, a large number of artists quietly transformed themselves in response to market forces. Chu Yuntian knew that some painters considered the 'Spring Auctions' and 'Autumn Sales' as their main arena. The market has its own rules – it doesn't conform to you; you must conform to it. For example, it prefers famous artists, in particular, artists popular with buyers. It also likes flexible, up-to-the-minute partners who agree on the importance of maximising profits. So Chu Yuntian saw many young, promising artists plunge into the market, flattering and fawning on any potential buyers, smoothing down the edges and corners of their characters, and pandering to the vulgar. Their original talent gradually disappeared, lost in the mix. From the fact that even Yu Changshui was sending pictures to auction, he could see the momentum of this kind of commodification of art. Yu Changshui explained that he was going to get married soon and was in a hurry to buy a house. That was only natural. But what about the 'Masters' who try their best to sell at a vast price? Each one was more arrogant than the last, they were all showing off their wealth, and they had become idols in the hearts of young painters struggling with market forces.

Chu Yuntian heard Xiao Shen say that even students at the Academy of Fine Arts were busy selling their paintings. They would begin selling paintings while they were only just learning to draw. To know how to sell, you must be proficient in all kinds of commercial tricks. One particular second-year student specialised in 'ugly' paintings. Ugly people, ugly things, ugly stones and ugly trees – they all sold well. Many students couldn't be bothered to learn from their teacher since they wanted to study with him and draw ugly pictures.

A free-market society is certainly a wonderful flower in full bloom.

One day, Fei Liang called Chu Yuntian to say that an Overseas Chinese woman artist would be holding a solo exhibition in the Art Museum at the cultural centre the day after tomorrow, and she wanted to invite him to attend. She'd asked Fei Liang to tell him that he must not refuse.

Chu Yuntian was rather surprised. Could this be Bai Ye? She was not an Overseas Chinese, but she had studied abroad. Besides, if Bai Ye was holding an exhibition here, why didn't he know about it before now? Or was she trying to surprise him? Last time she'd told him of a secret, and that she wanted to "get closer" to him. Bai Ye was always surprising – she liked to take people by storm. For example, every time she saw him, she would engage in a kind of sexy flirtatiousness, but after saying goodbye that was it. Was this due to him misunderstanding her, or was she deliberately using this ambiguous approach to bind him and get closer to him step by step? Or was this natural for her, to be so unpredictable? Anyway, nowadays girls all seemed to be on the hunt for mature, successful older men. She was very young – could it be that she was indeed also very manipulative?

A short while later, Fei Liang arrived and handed him a dark grey invitation. He realised he was wrong the moment he saw the style of the invitation letter: it was far too sombre and gloomy. This was not in the least Bai Ye's style. Looking at the opening lines, the title of the exhibition was 'The Ancient East', and the artist's name was in English; he had no idea who this might be. Then, he spotted a Chinese name in English – Tang Ni. He remembered that she had been a student of Mr Xu at the Xinhua Middle School – a talented artist who'd gone to work as an art editor for a Beijing publishing company, while also producing some fine black-and-white prints. Had she perhaps gone abroad, got married there and changed her nationality? Thinking back, it was more than twenty years since they'd met. In twenty years, anything can happen and everything can change. He decided to go and congratulate her and see what her paintings looked like now.

That evening, Yuntian told Sui Yi about it. She said that he should invite Luo Fu to go with him. He didn't say a word. Sui Yi understood the reason for that –

At the French International Biennale the year before last, Luo Fu brought a work called 'Painting on the Wall', which was performance art. At the scene, there was a dilapidated wall with a landscape painting hanging on it. In fact, the picture and frame were painted on the wall. Luo Fu played the role of the owner of the wall. Every other hour, he walked over with a palette and brush in his hand and changed the scenery in the picture frame to something else. He changed it over and over again to express his inner depression, longing and uneasiness.

This work was well received at the Biennale and won a prize.

The episode made Yuntian very angry. Obviously, this was based on what Luo Qian had done after he had been attacked during the Cultural Revolution – it had been an unforgettable and unspeakable trauma for his old friend. How could Luo Fu plagiarise it and use it in a work to show himself off overseas? How would Luo Qian feel if he knew? At that time, he wanted to go and shout at Luo Fu, but Xiao Shen stopped him. "Don't you see that his originality has dried up? Besides, performance art is now dead in China."

Xiao Shen was right. After that, Luo Fu never returned to the Biennale. There had been no news of him for more than a year. If his creative abilities really were exhausted, his life must be very sad. He was never a person who could think, and it's hard for a person without the capacity for reflection to get out of an artistic dead end.

Yuntian thought about it and called Luo Fu. As soon as Luo Fu heard that Tang Ni was holding an exhibition, he said he would pick up Yuntian and go with him.

Two days later, Luo Fu parked his car at the door of Yuntian's house, jumped out and rang the doorbell. Yuntian was startled when he opened the door. Luo Fu was so thin, his face was very dark, his hair was very dry and his shoulders quite bony. He seemed to have lost his former air of athletic health and fitness.

Luo Fu saw Yuntian's surprised expression, smiled and asked him: "Don't you recognise me?"

"Why are you so thin? You don't look at all well. Have you been sick?" Yuntian asked.

"I've been a little tired the last few months. It's nothing serious."

"I'm glad. Let's go."

Luo Fu dodged past Yuntian and said: "I have to say hello to Sui Yi. I haven't seen her for nearly a year. If I don't say hello when I come past, she'll complain about it later." He ran into the house laughing and calling for Sui Yi.

Sui Yi came down and was stunned at the sight of Luo Fu: "What on earth has happened to you?"

"Yuntian also said I am too thin just now, but I haven't really lost much weight. It's just that I work too long hours every day. Anyway, since I've said hello, Sui Yi, I'll be off now to the exhibition with Yuntian. I'll come to see you one day, and you can make me something delicious to eat…" Luo Fu turned and ran out.

"OK," Sui Yi said. "Bring Hao Jun, and I'll cook Western food for you."

Luo Fu waved, rushed out of the door and got into the car with Yuntian.

Since they hadn't seen each other for a long time, they talked in a very friendly and companionable way in the car.

"People do the most extraordinary things nowadays," Yuntian

remarked. "I don't know where they will end up in a few years. I hear that Tang Ni has become an American citizen."

"One day someone called me up and said she was going to hold a painting exhibition here. When I asked around, it turns out her husband is a Hollywood film director. That's pretty amazing!" Then he added: "You'll never believe it when you see her paintings. She's working the same way as you!"

"What, like traditional Chinese painting?"

"Saying 'traditional Chinese painting' is too old-fashioned. Now it is called 'ink wash.' Ink wash has oriental characteristics, but follows international trends in art." Then Luo Fu added: "If she produced oil paintings or woodblock prints abroad, who would be interested? She has to use ink wash to get attention!"

"Why is painting all about getting attention?" Yuntian asked with a smile. "You're not supposed to be a circus performer." As he spoke, he recalled something and said: "I remember that when we last saw Tang Ni at Mr Xu's house, Luo Qian was there. Did you ask him to come too?"

"You always like to think back on the good old days," Luo Fu said, "but he doesn't. Last time we went to his house, I asked him for his phone number on the way out. He said he hadn't put in a phone yet. In fact, I saw a phone standing on a corner cabinet, and I didn't like to say so. If he doesn't want to keep in contact with us any more, let him. It's boring trying to force a friendship with people!"

Yuntian didn't say anything. The car had already arrived at the cultural centre.

When they drew up to the Art Museum, in the distance they could see Fei Liang waving his hands. As they got out of the car, Fei Liang said to Yuntian: "Tang Ni has been so stressed because you didn't turn up. The opening ceremony couldn't be delayed any more. It's just finished."

Luo Fu teased Yuntian: "She didn't invite you to see her work, she wanted the chairman of the Artists Association to give her some face. You've messed things up for her."

"Don't be silly," Yuntian said. "Why would I be here if not to look at the pictures." Then they entered the hall.

Tang Ni came up to greet them. "I'm so sorry," Chu Yuntian said. "We got held up by a traffic jam."

"All these ceremonies are a waste of time," Tang Ni said briskly. "How about you go straight to look at the paintings." As she said this, she smiled at him.

From this brief exchange, Chu Yuntian felt that Tang Ni was now a completely different person from the one he met twenty years ago.

Her appearance had not changed much; she still somehow lacked femininity, but she was quieter and her speech had become more gentle. She was wearing a pair of black jeans and a loose grey-brown coat with the placid air of a middle-aged person. Tang Ni now would never behave as she had in the past – taking an apple out of her pocket and biting into it when she felt hungry. As he saw when walking into the exhibition hall, her paintings were still powerful and lively. What she had produced were experimental 'modern ink' paintings of the kind popular at home and abroad. The paintings were large, semi-abstract and featured lots of broad ink strokes and all kinds of accidental effects on rice paper. They were clearly shaped by Westerners' expectations of Chinese culture: deep, grand, tortuous, obscure and mysterious. Some Chinese characters would appear in her paintings. However, these words were disassembled, unreadable, fabricated or out of context. These made-up Chinese characters, intended to poke fun at the classical writing tradition, had almost become a standard trope in experimental ink painting by modern artists, symbolising the absurdity of traditional Chinese culture.

Accordingly, Tang Ni's exhibition was entitled 'The Ancient East'.

Chu Yuntian once wrote in an article: "This is a way of distorting our own culture to pander to Westerners' orientalist views. However, it is precisely this kind of childishness that has been most readily accepted by the West, which is sad. From this, we can also see how wide the gap is between Chinese and Western cultures, and how deep is the misreading of history!"

Today, these paintings were nothing new to Chu Yuntian. They were far less novel and shocking than her prints that he'd seen at Mr Xu's house twenty years before.

As Chu Yuntian looked at the paintings, he asked her: "Are these paintings for Chinese people or Westerners?"

Tang Ni thought his question highly apposite. "To be honest, I live in America, so of course my buyers are Westerners."

"Do they like this kind of thing?"

When Tang Ni heard that, she threw her head back, and her short hair seemed to form a halo. This gesture reminded Chu Yuntian of the frank and cheerful Tang Ni of yesteryear. "They don't just like it, they love it! My paintings sell very well. Some major companies order them from me to hang in the lobby or reception rooms of their headquarters."

Chu Yuntian turned to Fei Liang and said with a smile: "Did you hear that? Your big paintings ought to be even more popular in the United States." Then he turned his head and asked Tang Ni: "Do American painters care much about selling their work?"

Tang Ni seemed to find this a childish question: "Selling paintings is the top priority for all painters."

"Why?"

"This is the age of globalisation! Isn't it the same here?"

"Yuntian is the exception," Luo Fu broke in with a joke. "He's an alien who doesn't eat or drink!"

Luo Fu was obviously very interested in the success of Tang Ni's paintings, and he asked all manner of questions. They also talked about the stock market. Luo Fu then invited her to join them for lunch at a Taiwanese restaurant opposite the cultural centre. Tang Ni was happy to accept.

Chu Yuntian decided that if he went, all he would hear about at lunch would be cheerful chit-chat about their experiences in selling their paintings. He made an excuse and took a taxi home.

Tang Ni's account of selling her work made Chu Yuntian think, much more than her paintings themselves did. He could see from Tang Ni's paintings that all the features in her work were intended to be selling points. Chu Yuntian decided he wanted to talk to Xiao Shen when he realised that Xiao Shen had gone to Zhengzhou for a meeting so he asked him to take the time to go to Luoyang to see Gao Yuqi on his behalf. Chu Yuntian hadn't heard from Gao Yuqi in ages, and he wondered if the progress of creation had slowed down. This was just a feeling he had, but Xiao Shen would find out when he saw Gao Yuqi. He also asked Xiao Shen to take Gao Yuqi ten bottles of Xuanzong ink from the Japanese company Boku-Undo. This kind of ink was not only very black but also quite similar to Cao Sugong's seventeenth-century 'Glossy Smoke' inksticks. The colour was very strong, and various greyscales become exceedingly rich after being mixed with water.

Chu Yuntian also had another purpose in mind. He wanted Xiao Shen to see this rare but unknown genius with his own eyes. Xiao Shen would be delighted to meet someone like Gao Yuqi!

CHAPTER 4

As soon as Xiao Shen set foot on the train from Luoyang to Tianjin, he took out his mobile and called Chu Yuntian. He couldn't help but feel the seismic effects caused by the overwhelming experience of Gao Yuqi's masterpiece, 'Migrant Workers', and the aftershocks just kept on coming. Gao Yuqi, a quiet and introverted painter, showed amazing talent, great spirit and remarkable technical skills, all of which made Xiao Shen's excitement difficult to control. He seemed to have just stepped down from a majestic mountain, and he was feeling at once overwhelmed and invigorated.

In this mercenary world, who can open the way for you to a new and better realm?

"I have called you five times in a row," Xiao Shen told Yuntian. "Am I disturbing you? My fellow passengers are starting to get annoyed. They've made me call you from the gangway connection between this and the next carriage."

Yuntian was quick to reassure him: "No, no, I like to listen to you. Your feelings right after the event are the most direct, the most real and the most vivid."

Xiao Shen laughed and said: "My mobile will soon be out of battery."

Yuntian had an indescribable feeling of comfort in his heart. He had asked Xiao Shen to go, hoping he would feel the same as himself. He had not expected that his experience would be even more vivid!

Xiao Shen also sent him a very important message that Gao Yuqi had recently developed an even more magical technique with brush and ink. This was giving him great confidence. For more than six months now, he'd been occupied by reworking most of the completed paintings, labouring day and night! This huge project was being overhauled in pursuit of supreme artistic beauty, for he had made another great discovery to which he was prepared to sublimate himself!

No wonder I thought his progress was slow, Yuntian thought to himself. I see!

He seemed to see a genius working like crazy, alone in the empty and forgotten workshop in the Central Plains. He felt ashamed that he had never experienced such extreme creativity.

The next afternoon, Xiao Shen came to see him. Yuntian told him about his feeling of self-reproach. "None of us are on the same level as this man. He has totally removed himself from the commercialisation of contemporary culture – a hermit, far away from the hustle and bustle of this world. We can't avoid vulgarity, but at least we haven't removed beauty from its throne in our hearts."

Well said. Yuntian thought that this was a motto he could live up to himself.

He asked Xiao Shen what kind of revolutionary painting technique had made Gao Yuqi decide to rework such a vast picture with hundreds of individual figures. Xiao Shen took out a paper bag from his backpack and gave it to him. He said: "Yuqi wanted you to have these. Take a look…"

He pulled a stack of seven-inch glossies out of the paper bag. At first sight, Yuntian was amazed. He felt a new, powerful and strong sensation, like the momentum of the Yangtze River when it has been racing for thousands of miles. He was impressed by the rich and rhythmic black-and-white contrast, and the shades of grey – especially in the profound delineation of the characters' personalities, the free vertical and horizontal brushstrokes and the dripping ink which showed that he had entered into possession of his own independent kingdom. Pointing to some details in the photos, Yuntian said: "I like this kind of brushwork. It appears careless, but here – you see!

This large patch of ink seems to show nothing, it seems pointless, but it serves to throw into relief the portrait there. And look here! These large sections of clothing and trouser legs are done freehand, the ink dripping down, like the 'drip glaze' that you find on Jun wares. He doesn't care, he's happy to let it be…" He suddenly raised his head and shouted: "Sui Yi – you need to come and see this!"

At any such moment, he naturally called on her to share the experience.

Yuntian said thoughtfully: "He has made a giant leap forward here. It's really worth his while to start over! Just think of Surikov's 'The Morning of the Streltsy Execution' – he painted that for several years, and then just when he was about to finish, he suddenly had a better idea on the composition, destroyed the original work and resolutely started all over again. This is what a real artist should do!"

"I want to go to Luoyang and see it," Sui Yi said.

"But right now we shouldn't disturb him – let him concentrate on his painting," Yuntian said. "He's probably a year and a half away from completion, right? We can't let anyone else know. Otherwise, the dealers will be after him."

"Now that you mention it," Xiao Shen said, "I feel really ashamed."

"How's that?"

"This time, I said something I shouldn't have to Gao Yuqi."

"What did you say?"

"I asked him who the painting would belong to. Would it be his or the entrepreneur's?"

"What did he say?"

"He said, I just want to give birth to my baby!"

"That's great." Yuntian smiled at Xiao Shen. "What a vulgar question to ask!"

Xiao Shen smiled, a little embarrassed.

Then, addressing both Xiao Shen and Sui Yi, Yuntian said: "I want to talk to you about something else."

"What?"

"I saw Luo Fu recently. He seems to be in a bad way – he's got so very thin. When I happened to pat him on the shoulder, it just seemed to give. In the old days, his shoulder was hard – it would have been like patting a rock. Now he's all skin and bone. I am quite worried about him."

"I felt the same when he came round the other day," Sui Yi said. "In the evening, I called Hao Jun. She says that he has not been working on anything at all – he doesn't paint any more and just relaxes. I was rather surprised – relaxing doesn't make people thin."

"I noticed that he's not happy even when he's laughing," Yuntian said. "But he was certainly paying attention when talking to Tang Ni about selling paintings."

Xiao Shen had kept silent all this time. Then, unable to hold back, he said: "I know that you haven't really been talking to him since his piece 'Painting on the Wall' at the Biennale in France, but I do still have some contact with him. He is under a lot of pressure, particularly because of Yu Miao. That pair were the mainstays of the oil painting department at the art college, and they were also the most influential painters in oils in the entire country. Yu Miao used to help him a lot. Back in the seventies, every time they were ordered to produce a painting, Luo Fu did the main composition, and Yu Miao helped him with the fine details of the figures. To tell the truth, Yu Miao was much better than him in the realistic depiction of details, but those are just trivialities. Luo Fu's advantage was his conception, sense of momentum and a good overall grasp of composition. One was in charge of the bigger picture, the other of the details. The two cooperated to make the best of each other. Yu Miao's a good guy and listened to him in everything. They always had a good relationship. Now in the auction market, Yu Miao's exquisite skill has become a major selling point. He doesn't have to cooperate with Luo Fu any more and so he's dumped him. You may not know much about what's happened at auction, I guess…"

"Actually, I have heard about this," Yuntian said. "He does paintings somewhat like Tong Zifei, but looking like those old Shanghai advertisements featuring beautiful pin-up girls. But where Tong Zifei only paints pretty women in costumes from the late Qing dynasty, he only paints women in cheongsams from the thirties."

"But his hyperrealism is very fashionable now. In recent years, Yu Miao's paintings have become even more true to life than a photograph would be, and they sell very well. Each painting costs as much as a BMW. And what about Luo Fu? He has put all his efforts into keeping up with the latest fashions. Abstract paintings, installation art and performance art have between them eroded all his previous skills. Now he wants to go back to painting so he can sell, but he can barely hold a brush. He's been panicking, so how can he possibly relax?"

"What's the rush?" Yuntian asked. "It takes a while to paint something marketable. It's not just a matter of skill, you also need to find your selling points."

"Luo Fu is under an awful lot of pressure…" said Xiao Shen, now lowering his voice, "from Hao Jun."

"Why should she be pressurising him?"

"She's panicking worse than Luo Fu is." Xiao Shen smiled. "She needs money more than him. But she can't paint for him. She can only put him under ever-increasing pressure."

"What can she be doing to him? They surely can't be quarrelling?"

"It's worse than that!" Xiao Shen said. "Anyway, let's not talk about it. People in the art school often use Hao Jun's own words to disparage him, saying that he's run out of talent. Anyway, I don't know whether it's true or not, but I've heard that he and Hao Jun have been on the brink of divorce more than once."

Yuntian and Sui Yi were too surprised to say a word. After a long silence, Yuntian said thoughtfully: "This is quite different from the world of Gao Yuqi that we were just talking about. We are lucky to have someone like Yuqi, standing apart from fame and wealth. He has made me see that the sacred flame of art is still burning, and idealism has not been entirely wiped out by consumerism."

Two months later, as soon as Yuntian entered the elevator at the painting academy, he bumped straight into Fei Liang. Fei Liang said to him: "I was about to call you, but here you are."

"What is it?"

"A bunch of painters from the Shanghai Academy of Art have come for a meeting. They said they would love to see you. Three out of the five people they've sent know you already," Fei Liang explained.

"Fine, I'll see them now."

Yuntian pushed open the door of the reception hall. When the people inside saw him, they all stood up and greeted him. Two were famous painters in Shanghai, and he knew them well. The leader of the delegation was the vice president of the Shanghai Academy of Art, a specialist in Shanghai-style freehand flower and bird painting. He remembered his name as Lü Chi, meaning 'Green Pool', mainly because it was so unusual. He was also easy to remember because he wore a brownish beard, and nowadays not so many people had a beard. They introduced themselves and handed over their business cards. Suddenly, the Shanghainese visitors looked at each other as if they had forgotten something. Then everyone turned to stare into the main room, where someone was looking at the flowers.

Yuntian's academy included a flower painter who liked to grow his own subjects. There were many plants and flowers in the main room.

The flower fancier was a woman. Only her back could be seen. As if she had heard her companions greet her, she turned around. The green leaves and flowers set off a beautiful face – it was Bai Ye!

When she saw them, she quickly walked over as if drifting in the breeze and greeted Chu Yuntian in a very friendly way. She seemed to want to give her companions the impression that she was very close to him.

Everybody sat down. "The painting, 'Expectation', that Bai Ye had in the national art exhibition has caused a real stir," Lü Chi said to Yuntian. "We would like to thank you for your support. Bai Ye has now signed a three-year contract with our academy. She will be working for us full-time as a member of our institution. In the future, we hope you will provide more advice so that she can continue to participate in forthcoming exhibitions and win awards."

All the other painters smiled and agreed, joining in the chorus of thanks.

Chu Yuntian felt a little puzzled. How did they know that he'd played a role in the way Bai Ye's work was selected for the exhibition? Although his comments on her work were very important in the review process, it had certainly not been his decision alone, but the result of the judges' vote. Was this some kind of self-promotion on her part? Or was this man just being polite to him because he was the main judge?

"Many new talents emerged from this latest national painting exhibition," Chu Yuntian said. He wanted to subsume Bai Ye in the crowd of other young painters, but his eyes happened to fall on Bai Ye's face, which always moved him. He could not help saying: "Of course, your Bai Ye is an outstanding artist. She owes that to the training and support she's received in Shanghai." He turned to Bai Ye and asked: "Have you officially signed a contract with the academy? When I was young, back in the seventies, no one supported me like that!"

He made everything natural with a little joke. Jokes are a kind of wisdom for people who can tell them.

At this time, Yuntian asked Fei Liang to invite the liaison office and academic department, Xiao Shen, editor-in-chief of the magazine *The Artist*, and several other painters to discuss how to carry out future exchanges between their respective academies in Tianjin and Shanghai. Xiao Shen suggested that a forum should be established to hold a symposium every other year, which could be a cutting-edge topic of interest to everyone in the painting world, or a thematic academic discussion on the works of an individual artist. Everyone agreed to that. Then Lü Chi proposed their first topic: "Next spring, we plan to hold a seminar on Bai Ye's work. This will be the first meeting for our forum. How about we co-sponsor it? And, of course, Chu Yuntian will preside!"

Bai Ye stretched out two white hands, like two little white doves, and waved the suggestion away vigorously. "That wouldn't be right," she said.

Was this a hook baited for Chu Yuntian, or a trap?

After a lively and cheerful conversation, the guests from Shanghai headed back to their hotel. Yuntian still had more to do. When he escorted the visitors to the lift, Bai Ye followed him. It seemed that she had something private to say to him, but since there were others around, she had no opportunity to actually say it.

Yuntian sent them on their way, finished his work, and on the way home his mobile phone rang. He answered. A voice breathed at him: "I want to see you tomorrow."

It was Bai Ye. "How do you know my number?" he demanded.

She hung up.

He thought about what Bai Ye had said over the phone. It made him feel stressed.

The next day, he learned from Fei Liang that the previous night, the academy had arranged for their visitors from Shanghai to tour the Haihe River. This morning, the plan was to go to the Temple of the Queen of Heaven and the Drum Tower. At noon, they would eat lunch in the former Italian Concession, and in the afternoon they would take a carriage tour around the Five Avenues district. In this way, they would see the unique characteristics of old Tianjin: half-Chinese and half-foreign. They'd be flying back to Shanghai that evening and would not have time to meet him again. However, at about two o'clock in the afternoon, Fei Liang called to say that they were walking through the Five Avenues district and heard he lived nearby, in a classic old British-style house. They were very interested in visiting Chu Yuntian and seeing life in the former foreign concessions in Tianjin.

Yuntian didn't know that the two Shanghainese editors who had visited him at home in the Five Avenues had told Bai Ye all about it when they returned. All these seemingly accidental little things were delicately arranged by her.

He could not refuse, and immediately told Sui Yi: "Little Ye will be coming here soon."

"Who?" For a moment, Sui Yi didn't understand.

"That artist I met last time in Shanghai. She used to be our neighbour when we lived by the Qiangzi Canal. When I told you, you said you remembered her. She is now a painter under contract at the Shanghai Academy of Art. They came to Tianjin yesterday."

"Did you see her?"

"Yesterday, when I went to pick up books and letters from the academy, I met all of them. They came with a vice president of their academy, to establish a cooperative agreement with us."

"Why didn't you tell me?"

"I was busy and forgot."

"Did you ask her to come?"

"No. Today, the academy invited them to tour the Five Avenues.

Fei Liang just called and said they heard that I lived nearby and wanted to see the house."

Sui Yi thought for a moment and then said: "Let them come. I'll ask Little Xia to clean up the living room. It's a real mess."

Little Xia was the helper they'd hired the past year. She was in her twenties and from Tongling in Anhui Province – a kind and hardworking girl.

Bai Ye and the others walked through the ivy-covered gate to Yuntian's house, down the stone cobbled path and then entered the garden. Soon, they were enveloped by the deep and quiet atmosphere of this old house. The sense of time and age also contained a kind of dignity, which was quietly emitted by the unique details of each element in the building: the mottled walls and the smell of leaves shaded from the sun. History is accumulated; it is rich and profound. It scorns the glittering lightness of wealth alone. This kind of atmosphere, all unconsciously, forced the visitors to choose their words carefully.

Yuntian and Sui Yi came out of the front door. As people who grew up in this house, they had taken their tone from it.

Without waiting for anyone to introduce her, Bai Ye ran up to them. Instead of talking to Yuntian, she addressed Sui Yi affectionately: "Auntie, I'm Little Ye! I've come to visit you."

Sui Yi was taken aback. The first thing that surprised her was the beauty of the girl. "Are you Little Ye? You look so much like your mother, but even more beautiful than her! Your mother used to be so good-looking."

Bai Ye seized hold of Sui Yi's hands and said: "You look as lovely as you did then, Auntie, and you're still so young!"

"How could that possibly be? My daughter is over twenty."

"I know. She's studying art history in Bordeaux. I studied art history in France as well, so I guess we are kind of sisters."

As a group, they chatted easily as they walked along and entered the living room via the garden terrace. Over the years, the living room had been transformed by Yuntian and Sui Yi. They had not pursued luxury, but paid attention to the depth and aura of this old British house. Whether it was the style of furniture, the colour of each piece and knickknack, all were carefully chosen. Yuntian was proud of the various marble and bronze sculptures he'd brought back from Europe, particularly an early nineteenth-century Italian stone bust of Mozart. There was also a pair of singing angels, sculpted in wood and then painted in gesso and gilded, which were said to come from a church in Dresden abandoned two hundred years ago. These Western sculptures had all the more piquancy when juxtaposed with the blue-and-white Ming dynasty porcelain and ancient ceramics. He had even replicated the stone fireplace destroyed during the Cultural Revolution, and you could genuinely kindle a fire in it. Sui Yi was most proud of the vases and other such pieces that dotted the house. Every single one of them had been 'discovered' thanks to her keen eye for beauty.

The guests were busy looking around, but Sui Yi insisted they sit down and have some tea.

"I didn't expect to see such fine Western-style houses in Tianjin," Lü Chi said. "We have them in Shanghai too. Your house is a bit like Ba Jin's on Wukang Road."

"I know Ba Jin's former residence is bigger than this," Yuntian said, "and it has a front garden. Our house is more enclosed and lacks a garden in front."

"Tianjin and Shanghai are not exactly the same," Sui Yi pointed out. "In the past, there were nine foreign concessions here, and each was autonomous. The houses were built in their own national styles. Now they look very historical."

"Which concession would the Five Avenues have belonged to?" Lü Chi enquired.

"The Five Avenues were an extension of the British concession," Sui Yi explained. "The buildings here are different from those in other concessions because the earliest residents were wealthy families who moved to Tianjin from all over the country. To put it in modern terms, they were immigrants. They came here and built houses, and they could have whatever they liked. From the back windows of our house, you can see the huge white mansion that was put up by the Sun family of Shouzhou in Anhui Province. The property extends from here to Dali Road, Changde Road and Yunnan Road, so you can imagine how big it must be. There is a swimming pool in the grounds, in the Moorish style. The founder of the Sun family was Sun Jia'nai, the tutor to Emperor Guangxu and founder of Peking University. After Liberation, the house was taken over by the state. When Chairman Mao came to Tianjin in the fifties, he stayed there. There are other houses like it in the Five Avenues area. Many important people in the Republican era had mansions here."

"Which is exactly why your academy arranged for us to come here for a tour," Lü Chi said.

While she was talking, Bai Ye caught sight of the sketch of their old house over by the Qiangzi Canal. She exclaimed and pointed it out to her companion: "Those three red pitched-roof houses are where Chu Yuntian and I used to live. They lived on the top floor of the house on the left. I lived here – on the first floor of that building there. This painting makes me feel so nostalgic!"

"I had no idea that your friendship went back so far," Lü Chi said. "No wonder Mr Chu gave you so much support in the selection process for the national exhibition."

Bai Ye looked very proud. Sui Yi was irritated, though she gave no sign of it. She hadn't known that Bai Ye had one of her works selected for the national art exhibition, let alone that Yuntian had given her "so much support". Why was this the first she heard about it?

Yuntian felt that Lü Chi's words had inadvertently exposed something that could look bad for him. He quickly broke in and said: "I didn't show her any support. Her work was much admired by all the judges."

By saying so, he confirmed that he had evaluated her work. Why didn't he say so when he came back from Ji'nan? Why didn't he mention it when he came back from the national art exhibition in Beijing?

Sui Yi held a question mark in her mind, so she was not as enthusiastic as she had been about the visit from Bai Ye and the Shanghainese painters.

When they left, Yuntian and Sui Yi saw them to the door. Bai Ye hugged Sui Yi, and Sui Yi patted her as she said goodbye to everybody.

This subtle change in her attitude was soon perceived by Bai Ye, an intelligent and shrewd woman, and she immediately inferred that Sui Yi had discovered that Yuntian had concealed his contact with her. Why did he hide it? That was the question.

Of course, Bai Ye was very proud of this concealment. Keeping quiet about her meant that she was a secret, which showed that she had a personal understanding with him. That was exactly what she wanted.

CHAPTER 5

A sense of foreboding had pierced Sui Yi's heart, silently activating a long-forgotten memory: Yufei.

The incident had deeply hurt her, almost overturned the boat she had shared with Yuntian for so many years. But it was all done and dusted. Ever since that day when Yufei and her husband Xu Dayou, the gallery manager, came to visit, that particular element of the past was dead. Once the final full stop has gone down, the event moves into history.

But now that one had gone, was another coming?

It couldn't be true. Although there was something she didn't know going on between Yuntian and Bai Ye, it might not be the deliberate concealment of something bad. Maybe it was nothing, and because it was nothing, Yuntian hadn't bothered to tell her. Sui Yi thought the matter over carefully.

Sui Yi was a good person. She had no evil thoughts, so naturally she would not suspect others of things she was incapable of herself. She and Yuntian had grown up together; they knew each other well, and she trusted Yuntian almost too much. He had hurt her so deeply over Yufei. At that time, she felt pity for him when she saw his repentance. Would he repeat this mistake? In the end, the memory of the wounds sustained at that time was too deep, which naturally made her instinctively alert, and gave rise to extra sensitivities where this kind of thing was concerned.

Fortunately, Bai Ye was different from Yufei. She was far away in Shanghai, so it would be hard for them to meet. Besides, she was not yet important in the world of art; no one would mention her. In fact, Yuntian didn't speak of her for a long time after that day. If he didn't talk about her, why would Sui Yi raise the subject? She was not the kind of woman to think it clever to keep harping on an uncomfortable topic.

Yuntian saw the matter quite differently.

He had deliberately kept his relationship with Bai Ye a secret from Sui Yi. First, he was afraid that after what happened with Yufei, she would be sensitive and suspicious. Second, Bai Ye, as a girl with an extraordinary temperament, really had moved him. But now he was starting to feel uncomfortable about her. The two of them were somehow at odds. She didn't genuinely care for him as Yufei had, and she seemed strangely dependent on him. Although he was aware of how she had taken the initiative, approaching him step by step, he could not be sure of her feelings. He had never encountered such a way of showing affection before and didn't understand it.

However, he was now totally different from the man he had been twenty years before. After experiencing so much together, both happy and sad, he and Sui Yi had become ever closer. Over the years, more than a few women had fallen in love with him, and he often received courtship letters and photos. That was something he could take lightly and didn't mind telling Sui Yi about. But this time, perhaps because Bai Ye was so unusual, she had provoked a groundswell in his 'romantic' nature, and he avoided saying anything about her to Sui Yi. Of course, even now, it was not as if he and the girl had anything to conceal. It should be said that he was not intentionally keeping anything quiet but was kind of hiding himself away psychologically. However, is hiding oneself away a cause of trouble?

Would he really fall into such a trap?

An obstacle had arisen between himself and Bai Ye. Was this the generation gap?

First of all, Bai Ye and Yufei were not members of the same

generation. The biggest difference between the two generations lay in the word 'utilitarianism'. Yufei's generation had experienced social equality, and nobody had much time to think about matters such as worldly success or material gains, nor did they expect to find these things in their emotional lives. In Bai Ye's time, Chinese society had become Vanity Fair. Everyone was looking out for number one, and it was hard to keep their feelings untainted. Once love is tied up with fame and wealth, it is hard to avoid falsehood, and even turn your affections into a tool to pursue profit. Of course, every generation contains all kinds of people. The biggest difference in the world is the difference between people. But what kind of person was Bai Ye?

There was always a tiny voice in Yuntian's heart – before he ever met Bai Ye, the thin and bespectacled old Shanghai editor who came to visit him commented on her: "She's hard as nails in her own way."

What did that mean? Was it because she was determined to paint in her own style? Or was her personality hard? Was she "as hard as nails" to other people? Or was this attempting to put her down because she was so very able?

It is so difficult to judge a person. Moreover, jealousy or other emotions are too often mixed in.

After Bai Ye left Tianjin and returned to Shanghai, there was no news from her, just like after their previous leave-takings. What was she doing? Did she miss him? It was puzzling. If she was really as fond of him as she said, she ought to take the initiative to contact him. Yuntian hadn't received any messages, phone calls or letters from her, not even New Year's greetings. But if they met again, she would be even more active and bold, approaching him yet closer. This time, she'd asked Fei Liang for his mobile phone number, so he was expecting a text message. For a long period of time, every time he heard the SMS alert, he would wonder whether it came from her or not. He even looked forward to it. But every time it was not her, which disappointed him.

Finally, one day, he received a text message from her, in her usual hurried tone:

> We will finally meet in the middle of October this year. Don't say you can't come.

The same day, Fei Liang called and said: "Shanghai has been in touch to say that next month, the seminar about Bai Ye's work will be held at the Shanghai Convention Centre. Our academy is one of the organisers. Please be sure to attend."

When Yuntian came home, he told Sui Yi about it and said: "I'd like you to come too this time."

Sui Yi was very happy. He hadn't hidden something involving Bai Ye from her, and he wanted to take her with him. However, she hesitated a little. She said: "If it were a painting exhibition, I could go to see it, but this is a seminar. It's not appropriate for me to attend."

Yuntian said firmly: "No, no, you haven't been to Shanghai for a long time. It's only three days. Let's find someone to go with you and see the sights. We'll pay for our own tickets."

Sui Yi agreed with a smile and then arranged everything for their short trip. Yuntian asked Xiao Shen to go with him. Maybe some of the papers at the seminar could be used in the magazine *The Artist*. Fei Liang also went along, but he was busy organising the whole event. Yuntian asked Fei Liang to communicate with the Shanghai Academy of Art and Bai Ye herself, and everything was soon set up.

Bai Ye must have known that he was going, but she didn't call or send a message to express her happiness. She was a bit of a puzzle. Was this because Sui Yi had agreed to come too?

On the day before Yuntian and his wife's trip to Shanghai, Sui Yi came down with a cold and was running a temperature so she could not travel. Instead, Yuntian had to go with Xiao Shen and Fei Liang. Yuntian decided to shorten his trip to Shanghai. He would arrive and settle down the day before and then attend the seminar the next day. The seminar was due to last two days, but he would only attend the first day. After his speech, he would fly back the same evening. Sui Yi was sick at home, and he wanted to return as soon as possible. The next afternoon, they took the plane to Shanghai. On arriving at Hongqiao Airport, he thought that Bai Ye might be there to greet him with a smile, but he couldn't see her anywhere. The bearded Lü Chi was waiting for them, at the head of a small delegation. They came up to welcome them, shook hands and made polite remarks. "There is still a lot of work to be done to set up the seminar hall so Bai Ye is busy," Lü Chi explained. "She said she would come over when she's finished."

The people in Shanghai had arranged for Chu Yuntian, Xiao Shen and Fei Liang to stay in two different hotels. Lü Chi whispered to Chu Yuntian: "This was Bai Ye's doing. Yours is a five-star hotel."

The car arrived at the hotel and his luggage was taken away. Lü Chi had arranged for a banquet at the hotel to welcome Chu Yuntian, but Bai Ye still hadn't arrived. Lü Chi was a little unhappy and said to a colleague: "Could you ask her to come quickly? Chu Yuntian is here on her behalf – she can't just not show up. I called her mobile, but she's turned it off."

But from start to finish, there was no sign of Bai Ye. The door to the private banqueting hall would move, and Yuntian thought this time it must be her, but she simply never appeared. Even he felt this was peculiar. Something unexpected must have turned up. When Fei Liang called, her phone was turned off. After dinner, he went back to his room. Yuntian ended up just sitting there, waiting for her – it was the only thing he could do. He had no idea when she would come, so this kind of waiting gradually turned into a kind of anticipation.

After ten o'clock, someone suddenly knocked at the door, very softly. He recognised her knock. He could not say whether he was excited or a little nervous. He wore a loose shirt with his sleeves rolled up. As soon as he opened the door, he was taken aback. A large bunch of snow-white, fluffy and fragrant gypsophila appeared before him. The person holding the flowers was hidden behind them. The flowers were right there pressed against his chest. Those star-like blossoms on their delicate stems, spray upon spray of flowers brushing against his face, brought him a moment of incredible beauty. He had to take two steps back. The flower-bearer came in and clicked the door shut with a shoulder on the door, still hiding behind the big bunch of gypsophila. "Bai Ye, is that you?" Yuntian asked softly.

A voice came from behind the flowers: it was indeed her. In light, soft, deliberate and sexy tones she said: "Can you tell me what you want to say across these flowers?"

Her voice, her breath, her seductiveness reached him through the bouquet.

This was so romantic! Yuntian was out of control. He said something he had never previously given thought to: "I love you!"

Suddenly, the flowers were thrown aside. She hurled herself against his chest and kissed him, kissed him passionately. The same was true of him. During that exciting kiss, he felt hot all over, no longer conscious of the rules he set for himself in more sober moments. He was so carried away that he couldn't control himself any more, he wasn't thinking, and quite honestly anything could have happened next.

"Why are you pinching my ear so hard?" she whispered. "It hurts."

This sentence, however inadvertent, stopped him and brought him back to reality.

He gently pushed her away and sat down on the chair at some distance, trying to suppress the heat waves rolling over him. He grabbed a glass of water on the table and drank it, as if to quench the fire in his heart. However, Bai Ye seemed to recover from her fit of passion even faster than he did. Without saying a word, she stooped down and started picking up the scattered gypsophila. She was deliberately doing this very slowly.

By the time the whole bunch was back in her hand again, they had already passed this momentary embarrassment.

She spotted a vase on the cabinet, took it, inserted the flowers she was holding, put it on the table and then tidied up her coat. Her face was quite back to normal. This time she said nothing but smiled and nodded at him, as if nothing needed to be said. Then she went out, closed the door and was gone.

Everything happened so quickly. It was as fast as lightning, but what had happened during the storm? He dared not think. His primary feeling was one of regret, terrible regret. He had done wrong! Wrong again!

But he didn't understand how it had all happened. He liked her temperament, intelligence, talent, ability, understanding and amazing beauty. She apparently admired and worshipped him. He had also helped her, but that was all. At most, they had good feelings for each other. They hadn't had a single in-depth conversation, shared their thoughts on anything, or spoken of their emotions. Now that he thought about it calmly, they had not even really expressed their love or any deep affection. There had been no soul-stirring engagements, no deep affection such as he had enjoyed with Yufei, as they stepped hand-in-hand ever deeper into the gulf. Why was it so easy this time? How could he have crossed the line in just a few steps?

There was no doubt that she took the initiative between them. What did she do that for? Was she like other girls in yearning for a solidly established man, someone in mid-career?

If so, he needed to draw a line right now in front of his feet, but then again he had already crossed it. What should he do now? Obviously, he must not go any further. Could he do that? Could he control himself? Isn't what happened exactly what he was hoping for?

That night in the hotel, he failed to get to sleep. At one moment, he remembered the romantic scene just now; then he called home to ask Sui Yi if her fever had gone down; then he blamed himself; and after that, he stared in fascination at the magical bunch of star-like flowers on the table.

He was in a mess.

At the seminar the next day, Chu Yuntian gave a long speech entitled 'Fuzzy Beauty and Misty Poetry'. This was a speech for which he had done his homework well in advance. From the value of fuzzy philosophy, fuzzy poetry, fuzzy aesthetics and fuzzy beauty, he talked about the pioneering contribution of Bai Ye to contemporary painting. He positioned her paintings at a high level of academic significance, and then analysed the characteristics of her work in this context. This served to elevate Bai Ye's paintings to a new plane. Chu Yuntian's words were eloquent and convincing, and everyone seemed to be persuaded; Bai Ye herself was elated. But she was very clever, so during the seminar, she was sitting in a corner of the room, invisible to Chu Yuntian. She was afraid that he would be distracted by seeing her, especially after their intense scene the previous night.

After Yuntian finished speaking in the morning, he would return by plane that afternoon. The whole time, he kept calling Sui Yi. It seemed that only by caring about Sui Yi could he 'atone' for his actions. In this way, he knew that her fever had subsided, and her cold symptoms were getting better. He wanted to go to the airport ahead of time and buy some Shanghainese snacks for her. He hadn't forgotten his last visit to Shanghai when he didn't get Sui Yi any small gifts. However, Lü Chi said with a smile: "Don't bother. Bai Ye has already bought it for you."

At the airport, Bai Ye hurried up to him, her arms filled with endless little packages. "None of this is as nice as I would have liked," she said to Yuntian, "but at least Auntie can snack on them while watching TV."

Chu Yuntian returned to his former friendliness.

When he passed the gate, he turned back and waved to the people there to see him off. He saw Bai Ye standing there smiling. Instead of waving, she raised her right hand to touch her ear. This was the same ear he had pinched so violently when they kissed passionately last night.

At this time, Fei Liang, who was walking beside him, handed Chu Yuntian a large but light paper bag. Yuntian didn't know what it could be. Fei Liang said: "Bai Ye asked me to give it to you. She said it was a bunch of flowers."

Yuntian looked into the paper bag, and his heart lurched. It was full of gypsophila! They were the same flowers that had been scattered on the ground last night in that moment of strange passion! After gypsophila is dried, they will naturally be preserved. Did she want to make him a kind of permanent memorial?

During the flight, at an altitude of ten thousand metres, Yuntian was troubled by two contradictory states of mind. One was his sense of having let Sui Yi down; yet again he had to bottle something up to keep it a secret from his kind and good wife. He felt unbearably guilty. The other problem was Bai Ye's behaviour towards him – was this just another kind of love? He knew nothing about how the next generation conceptualised or demonstrated their affection. If she really had fallen in love with him, would that scene last night just be the glorious beginning of yet another relationship, as with Yufei? Fortunately, however, they were thousands of miles apart in Tianjin and Shanghai. His only choice was to leave this charming bud that had just burst through the ground in this distant place, never to return.

When Yuntian came home, Sui Yi was already on the mend, and she was sitting in the living room wrapped in a blanket and watching a TV series. He felt her smooth forehead with his hand. "I don't think I'm running a fever any more," she said with a smile.

"No, you're just the same temperature as my palm," Yuntian assured her.

No matter when Yuntian came back, it always brought her a burst of happiness. And every time he came home, he would feel the sense of stability and warmth that only home can provide. He gave her the presents from Bai Ye. She asked him anxiously: "Did the seminar go well? Was it successful?"

"It was OK," Yuntian said. "There were lots of people in attendance. I spoke in the morning and came back the same afternoon. The meeting will last two whole days. Xiao Shen stayed because he's speaking tomorrow. We'll find out how it all went once he comes back." For psychological reasons, he spoke of the seminar in a light, unserious tone.

Sui Yi took all her favourite Shanghai snacks out of their wrappings, and then asked: "How is Little Ye? Did she look happy? Was she dressed beautifully?"

"Of course she was happy," Yuntian said. "But she was so busy, being responsible for everything being done well. She didn't even make it to the airport."

"What is in that paper bag?" Sui Yi asked.

Yuntian's heart lurched, and he quickly said: "They put these in my hotel room. I thought they looked lovely, so I brought them back."

Sui Yi asked Little Xia to open the bag. She cried: "Oh, gypsophila, my favourite! I've always loved its softness, purity and freedom. Little Xia, could you bring the black vase from the studio? Gypsophila always looks best in a dark-coloured vase."

Little Xia brought the black vase, put water in it, inserted the flowers, and placed them on the small wooden table to one side of the living room. They were white and fluffy, and against the dark background, the thin stalks supporting the flowers disappeared, so that it appeared as if countless blossoms were floating in the air. Sui Yi smiled at the effect.

The two chatted easily. Yesterday's page had been turned. He hoped that it was gone forever, but who knew whether someone would someday want to flip back to it? Would it be Bai Ye, Yuntian or Sui Yi herself?

No one knows what tomorrow may hold.

A few days later, Xiao Shen came back from Shanghai. According to him, Chu Yuntian's speech had great repercussions, especially the elaboration of 'fuzzy beauty' from the perspective of philosophy, aesthetics and literature, which had made people think of the value of Bai Ye's work in a new way. Of course, some people thought that she should not be held in such high esteem. She was very young, after all, and she had neither the quantity nor the quality of work to justify these overblown evaluations. Xiao Shen said: "I also put forward some questions for Bai Ye to think about."

"Oh? Tell me more," Chu Yuntian said.

"I said that 'fuzzy beauty' is indeed a new concept, but it is a huge topic. I said to Bai Ye, now that this falls to you, you must think: Can you carry on with it? Right now, you are the only one using this concept and method. But that alone is not enough. How far can you get with it all by yourself?"

"What did Bai Ye say to that?"

"She didn't say anything. I don't think she's thought about it deeply. Girls often paint pictures in accordance with how they feel."

Sui Yi was tidying up the books on the table on the other side of the room. She interjected: "Why do you make things difficult for others? She's still only in her twenties. How can she have your depth?"

"Are you worried I wasn't cosseting her?" Xiao Shen said with a smile. "But an artist has to deal with all kinds of problems in his or her life."

"You asked a good question, forcing her to think," Yuntian said.

"Sooner or later, she's going to hit a dead end, so the sooner she starts thinking, the more prepared she'll be." Then he went on: "It was a good seminar. I heard Bai Ye went to a lot of trouble over it."

"She worked hard," Xiao Shen said, "but she had a lot of people helping."

"It seems that the team spirit of their academy is very strong. It would be good if our academy felt the same," Yuntian said.

"What do you mean 'the academy'?" Xiao Shen replied. "I heard she had lots of volunteers. There seemed to be an endless supply."

"How could she get so many volunteers? Nobody ever volunteers to help me!" Yuntian said.

"She's pretty. Lots of admirers!" Then Xiao Shen added: "She can really put them to work!"

"She's really beautiful. Beautiful people will have many willing to help them," Sui Yi said.

At this point, they all laughed. Yuntian realised that he knew nothing about this gorgeous woman's life.

CHAPTER 6

For two thousand years, people have been living an unchanging, traditional lifestyle, but then in the last twenty or thirty years they were suddenly introduced to a kaleidoscopic society. It is unclear whether the transformation made everyone change, or whether everyone's change accelerated the rapid and enormous shifts in lifestyle. This was an era when all kinds of desires might become reality. As a result, cities were growing rapidly, and material possessions were expanding exponentially. Material desires made people drool; and as a result, money worship became a popular 'religion' that bewitched people even further.

Who can imagine the flowers in the 1980s and the fruits in the 1990s in the art world – where each and every painting could now be purchased at so much money per square foot? In the history of art, there have been instances where an artist could enjoy success in their own lifetimes; this was true of Picasso and Rodin, and a Chinese example would be someone such as Qi Baishi. However most painters, including figures like Bada Shanren and Van Gogh, were poor. If the public really understood painting, loved art and talent, why is it that no one paid any attention to them while they were alive? Now there was a boom going on, and as long as you were willing to do whatever it took, as long as you worked hard and were inventive, your paintings would be transmuted into fine clothes, fine food, wealth and glory. As a result, the foot soldiers of the art world had gone crazy in this consumer age.

The market, however, had proved unpredictable. It could turn everything you touched into gold, make you rich beyond your wildest dreams, or it could treat you as cold as ice, cutting you off from any opportunity, so that you wouldn't see the slightest profit. It was mysterious, strange and dangerously unpredictable. It was the same as would be the case for an actor: he may not become famous even though he had film star looks and was good at his job. But he might become a star if he was eccentric or peculiar in some way. Only when you have become a star will you have fans, advertising revenue, endorsement fees, appearance money and so on rolling in an endless tide of wealth. However, to become a star, one must be familiar with the twists and turns of the market and possess almost superhuman wisdom. This indeed forced artists of every kind to show their mettle.

For the past five years, Tang Sanjian, who painted plum blossoms, ranked first in Tianjin in terms of the price he could command. Chu Yuntian thought that his plum blossom paintings were actually very good, clean and crystalline – old gnarly branches contrasted with bright, shining petals. He could also develop the composition; some were packed with lush trees, others showed just a few branches, horizontal or angled. It did not matter whether he was working on a huge piece or something the size of a fan – the flowers would be beautifully done. Red plum, black plum, green plum, white plum and plain plum; there was nothing he could not do. His paintings were in high demand, so naturally he could name his price. In recent years, he had made a brilliant move by increasing the price of his paintings by fifty thousand yuan per square foot every New Year's Day. If you didn't buy this year, the price would be higher the next. He produced a lot of paintings, and many collectors owned at least one of them. Everyone was looking forward to the value appreciating. As a result, the price of his paintings soared like fireworks on New Year's Eve.

Chu Yuntian knew of one person who was doing even better than Tang Sanjian, and that was Qu Fangge, who put a pot of wine on the painting table and painted while he drank. Qu Fangge didn't like the state of the market in Tianjin. He said that he'd leave this little patch for Tang Sanjian to play in; his battlefield was mainly in Beijing and Hong Kong. To begin with, his works were sought after by collectors from Taiwan and Singapore. At that time, the painting and calligraphy market on the mainland was just getting on its feet. These rich overseas collectors established a high benchmark price for his paintings. With the influx of money from the mainland into the overheated art market, the price of his work at auction went sky-high. The price placed on his work can be a stimulant for the artist, but gradually he comes to see only himself.

On one occasion, Chu Yuntian went to a TV station to record an interview, just as Qu Fangge came out of the studio. Qu Fangge walked straight ahead, his eyes turned up to the sky, followed by what appeared to be an entourage of three or four people – such was his pomp. Chu Yuntian happened to run into him head-on. Somehow, he didn't seem to see Yuntian and walked away looking as grand as ever. At that moment, Chu Yuntian was reminded of the scene some ten years earlier when he met several arrogant contemporary artists at the entrance to a restaurant when he went to see Luo Fu at the contemporary art exhibition. The market and money can change a person in this way.

"Right now, he's hot!" Yu Changshui said. "Last month in Hong Kong, his 'Eight Eccentrics of Yangzhou' sold for seventy million!"

"What painting could possibly be worth so much?" Chu Yuntian asked.

"His 'Eight Eccentrics' really is a masterpiece," Yu Changshui said, "but he can be too extreme in his opinions. Now he's saying there's no artist worthy of the name between him and Chen Laolian in the late Ming dynasty! According to him, Chen Laolian was one of the few painters there's ever been who's better than he is, and then Wu Daozi back in the Tang is better than Chen Laolian."

Chu Yuntian laughed and said: "Isn't that crazy? So for more than a thousand years, there are only three artists worthy of the name in the whole history of Chinese painting? Besides, it's not like he gets the final say! I think he has confused the price of his paintings with their artistic value. The price of paintings is a kind of drug."

"But now the world has changed," Yu Changshui said. "No

matter how good your paintings are, if the price is low, no one cares about you."

"The price changes. During the Great Depression, no one wanted art! The price of paintings is by no means a standard of artistic value."

"But where are these standards? Who decides them? Everyone has their own standard as to whether a work of art has value."

"You can understand it by studying the history of art."

He was not expecting what Yu Changshui said next: "The history of art is the past, and the auction market is our new reality. Now, which artists are better or worse depends on how much money they can command at auction."

Hearing this, Yuntian wondered if this talented young man who spent all day every day in his company had perhaps been kidnapped and brainwashed at some point. He mentioned this to Xiao Shen. He said with a smile: "You don't have to look very far for this 'brainwashing' – just look at our academy! The only thing that lot care about is money. Changshui already has a vested interest in believing the market is always right. What make of car does he drive now? He is buying an apartment in Shenzhen with his girlfriend."

"Will he go to Shenzhen to get married and leave us?" Chu Yuntian asked. He seemed a little worried. "Shenzhen is even more money-oriented than here–"

"You worry too much," Xiao Shen said. "There's only one Gao Yuqi, but it's good to have one like him. You shouldn't push your idealism onto others, but it's good to have someone like you as well."

Chu Yuntian had been very busy for many years. His early great achievements had given him the basic qualifications to go his own way, but now he felt a little lonely. Loneliness is invisible; it sets you apart – you feel that you can't really get hold of anything around you. In this era of commercialisation, if you want to make a profit, you have to get hold of a lot of things and a lot of people. Having turned a profit, you will find a lot of hands stretched out to grab at you. Then you will never be lonely: you're hot! But if you have nothing to offer, and you are useless to others, who will care about you? Who will be your confidant? Solitude will be all that you know.

If you choose loneliness, you must face it calmly. It's not easy to get used to being lonely.

Recently, Chu Yuntian often found himself thinking back to the 1970s and missing the little salon of the former Three Musketeers. But Sui Yi was the only person he could talk to about those days, giving voice to some of his regrets. However, one day, a chance incident left him with no means to express his nostalgia.

That day, he drove to a big bookshop to have a look at their new stock and bought a couple of things to read. On the way back, to avoid a traffic jam, he turned into the maze of little roads off Diantai Avenue. There, he spotted a small art gallery that had a narrow shopfront but was very smart looking. The name of the gallery was most unusual: the Backstreet Gallery. It was quite clever not to pretend to be sophisticated or elegant, but to let people feel that it was OK just to push open the door and go in. Yuntian stopped in front of the gallery, opened the door and went in. A long, narrow room was filled with oil paintings, large and small, and in different styles and themes. At first glance, it was clear that they were all the work of unknown artists, using this gallery to sell, and the prices were very cheap. He saw one particularly small oil painting that depicted the reflection of some ships in the water. The light and shadow, colour blocking and brushstrokes were all very good. They were only asking two hundred yuan for it. He asked the gallery person: "Are you really selling this painting for two hundred yuan?"

"Yes indeed," he replied. He was a middle-aged man standing with his broad back to him.

"Can you take it down for me?" he asked.

"Take it down yourself, if you'd like to have a look," the man said. He still didn't look around and Chu Yuntian didn't know what he was doing.

"OK, I'll take it," Yuntian said. "Please wrap it for me."

Now the man had to turn around. When he did so, Yuntian saw a smiling face with small eyes. He could never have imagined that it would be Luo Qian! He never expected Luo Qian to do such a thing: open a gallery and sell paintings!

Yuntian couldn't help saying: "What on earth are you doing here?"

Luo Qian's answer surprised him: "Why shouldn't I be here?"

Yuntian had no idea what to say next. "Do you remember when we went to Mr Xu's place, there was a dark-skinned, bulging-eyed, conceited man who was rude to everyone else?" Luo Qian asked.

Yuntian thought for a while and then said: "I seem to remember someone of the kind. On the day we went to meet Tang Ni, he just sat there motionless. I heard he was one of Mr Xu's former students. His paintings were very good."

"He painted this. He asked me to sell it for him."

"Why is it so cheap?"

"I don't really know. Maybe because he isn't famous. The cheaper it is, the fewer people will buy it. Isn't there an old saying to that effect? 'The more you want to sell, the less they want to buy.' The market has its rules. As soon as you go into business, you have to obey its rules."

"Unless you stay away from the market."

"It is OK to stay away from the market, provided you've got the money. If you want to survive or live better than before, you have to obey the market in the end."

With these words, Luo Qian explained why he opened a gallery. Yuntian had been a friend for many years and knew too much about his philosophy of survival, so he was extremely surprised. Luo Qian, a man of proud and arrogant spirit, had actually bowed his rock-hard head to reality and the doctrine of utilitarianism!

To Yuntian's surprise, Luo Qian led him to the other end of the gallery, where there was a small door. The door opened onto a small, dark hut. Luo Qian turned on the light, illuminating the six paintings on the wall, both portrait and landscape forms. They were all still lives, flowers in a vase, fruits, glasses of water and some pottery objects. The painting was very beautiful, elegant and quiet. The colour and strokes were exquisite, but these were all commercial paintings, the kind of decorative pieces you might have hanging in the living room. But these paintings were by no means the work of an ordinary artist – they were produced by someone with real talent and application. When Yuntian looked more closely, he realised that these commercial pieces were all the work of one man: Luo Qian! He was only too familiar with Luo Qian's brushwork and temperament. Although the theme, tone and connotation of his paintings were different from the past, it was still Luo Qian's work. What puzzled Yuntian was that he should have opened a gallery to make a living. What about these paintings? How could someone like him have subverted himself to paint pictures like these? What could have made him abandon his original artistic tenets to knock out works like this for quick sale? Had the Luo Qian of today joined the army of commercial painters such as Tang Sanjian, Qu Fangge, Yu Miao and Luo Fu?

Yuntian felt a chill. He didn't want to know what was going on. He didn't say that he realised these were Luo Qian's paintings. He just said that the pictures in this room were better than those in the gallery beyond, and then he left.

After leaving the Backstreet Gallery, he regretted having turned down that particular street. He wished he hadn't seen all this. Now, reality told him that the respect-worthy, highly principled Luo Qian no longer existed. He was a little unwilling to so easily lose a friend with such a long history, deep affection and supreme spirit.

When you have a lifelong friend, even if he leaves, you have not necessarily lost him; even if you are at opposite ends of the earth, the friendship may still survive. But if he changes, changes his beliefs, pursuits and personality, and alters the very things you used to depend on in your friendship, then you have truly lost him.

It was a bad day for Chu Yuntian.

When he got home, before he could even tell Sui Yi about how upset he was, she had bad news for him. An hour before, Hao Jun had called and said that Luo Fu had three paintings up for auction at Jiahe, Beijing next week. Hao Jun had found several wealthy buyers for Luo Fu's work and was also planning some counterbids to push up the price of the paintings. However, somehow or other Yu Miao had found out about this. He immediately sent Jiahe one of his hyperrealistic pieces, painted in an extremely fine, lifelike style, of beautiful women dressed in Republican-era costumes – those things sold like hotcakes. The title was 'Happy Days'. It depicted a group of fashionable women gracefully walking along the street, looking as if they were just about to step out of the painting. In the current market, it would be highly sought after. The buyers Hao Jun had found for Luo Fu happened to also be collectors of Yu Miao's works. However, as soon as Yu Miao's piece came up for sale, these collectors would be sure to simply abandon Luo Fu and compete for the other painting. This whole thing put Luo Fu in a really tricky situation. If Luo Fu withdrew his paintings and did not participate in the auction, it would show that he accepted Yu Miao's superiority. If he didn't withdraw, his works would still not sell. It was obvious that Yu Miao was doing this on purpose to annoy him!

"How can Yu Miao do such a thing? Why would he deliberately want to hurt Luo Fu?" Yuntian asked.

"Hao Jun said that this is already a fight to the death. Luo Fu has been trying to beat Yu Miao on price. The three pictures he sent for auction this time were all a terrible effort to paint. He can't afford to fail," Sui Yi said. "Luo Fu was so angry that he yelled, threw things and tried to hit people. He hasn't eaten or drunk anything for two days, can't sleep at night, and won't talk to anyone. Hao Jun is afraid that something is dreadfully wrong with him, and she was hoping to be able to talk to you."

"But I know nothing about selling paintings…" Yuntian thought for a moment and said: "Why don't you tell Hao Jun to talk to the buyers again?"

"Oh, she's done that. The buyers say they will help. But they buy and sell paintings for money. Can you really trust them?"

Neither of them knew how to proceed, so they were silent. After a while, Yuntian suddenly stood up and said: "I have an idea."

"Are you going to talk to Luo Fu?" Sui Yi asked.

"No point – he's stubborn as an ox." Yuntian said what he thought. "I'll talk to Yu Miao and suggest that he withdraws his picture. I'll ask him to help Luo Fu this one time, for my sake if nothing else."

Sui Yi laughed and said: "That's a good idea. How did you think of it?"

Chu Yuntian had never been to Yu Miao's house, so he asked a contact to find out the address and went round immediately. He didn't dare to contact him by telephone first, for fear that Yu Miao might guess the intention behind his visit and say that he was not at home.

Yuntian found Yu Miao's house in a beautiful residential area with trees and lakes in the east part of the city. Among the simple and solid red-brick buildings, Yu Miao's house was the largest of all, and the garden was also extensive. Some huge trees had been planted there, all of them ancient trees transplanted from the mountains. With enough money, even the most outré idea can be realised.

At first sight, Yuntian almost didn't recognise Yu Miao. He had put on weight, liked to dominate the conversation and gestured with his hands – apparently now that he was rich, even his personality had changed. His living room was far more lavish than Luo Fu's waterside villa in terms of its grand style, exquisite decoration and valuable furnishings. But in addition to the splendour, there was also a sense that he was making a parade of his newfound wealth, which made Yuntian uncomfortable. It is natural to love beauty, but showing off is an imposition on others, and not everyone can distinguish the difference clearly.

Yu Miao invited Yuntian to sit down and have some tea. Before Yuntian could speak, Yu Miao began: "Although we have known each other for many years, we haven't ever been close friends. I'm delighted you've come to see me here today at my house. However, there must be a reason for your visit... let me think..."

When he put it like that, it was difficult for Yuntian to explain the reason for his visit. Unexpectedly, Yu Miao turned out to be both straightforward and clever. "Are you here about the auction next week?" he asked. "Is this about Luo Fu?"

Yuntian had the impression Yu Miao was a narrow-minded, serious person, who was unlikely to listen to what anyone else had to say. He hadn't expected that he would turn out to be a quite different person today, speaking out confidently. Although he had something of the coarseness of the nouveau riche, he was still quite straightforward. Yuntian took over and said: "It's like this. I know you used to be good friends. In the past, the two of you worked together on many big paintings... you needed each other..."

Yu Miao laughed, and with a wave of his hand, he said: "There's no point trying that tack. Luo Fu turned his back on me many years ago. After he painted 'Five Thousand Years' he told me that I was only good enough to give him a hand. We've been enemies ever since." Speaking of this, he seemed to be getting angry. But he calmed down and said in a different tone: "I've always had a lot of respect for you, both as a person and as an artist. You deserve that. Since you are here, tell me, what is it you want me to do?"

Yuntian could see that he meant what he said. Now that the conversation had reached this point, he also spoke bluntly: "I want you to give way, just this one time. Your paintings are in high demand everywhere."

Yu Miao was overjoyed. "I see you understand," he said. "If I take this painting to Hong Kong, the selling price will be at least double! You have done everything for your friend, and I respect you for that. Today, I will do as you say…" Yu Miao waved his arms wildly and shouted: "I'll withdraw it from the auction! I'll call Jiahe in a minute and tell them so."

Yuntian felt as though a terrible burden had suddenly been lifted. He said excitedly: "That's really very kind of you!"

However, Yu Miao then said: "Tell Luo Fu that I'm only doing this once, and it's only for your sake!"

This remark made Yuntian realise just how bad the relationship between Luo Fu and Yu Miao had become. Especially in a time when profit was king, this was another kind of fight to the death.

When he got home, he told Sui Yi the result. She burst into tears; then she smiled and said repeatedly: "Great! That's wonderful." She called Hao Jun.

After a while, Luo Fu called back. The only thing Yuntian heard was Luo Fu shouting: "Yuntian…" and then there was silence. When Yuntian called out to him, he heard a deep choking sound over the line. When Yuntian called him again, there was no answer except for an engaged tone.

That night, Yuntian told Sui Yi about meeting Luo Qian earlier that day in the Backstreet Gallery near Diantai Avenue. She too was shocked. When she saw that Yuntian was gloomy, her words were a consolation to him. "His situation has changed from those days," she said. "He was single, and so it was easy to uphold his principles. Now he's got his wife, and for all I know they have children too – he's got responsibilities for all of them. If he doesn't sell his pictures, how can he care for them? You can't use yesterday's principles to measure today, nor should you force your ideas on others. In everyone's life, there will be things they look back on with regret."

"It's terrible. Life can transform even someone like him," Yuntian said sadly. "Even his artistic outlook has changed."

"Did you talk to him much?" Sui Yi asked. She was trying to get him to switch topic.

"He didn't say anything, and he didn't ask me about anything either. I asked him something about art, and he just smiled and shook his head. He didn't want to talk to me. It seemed as though it was something from the past."

Sui Yi stopped talking and listened to Yuntian's emotional voice.

"Today, I have lost two friends. They used to both be full of ideals and talents. When they should have spread their wings, they both gave up. One was determined to up his prices by whatever means, and the other has proved a slave to the principle of survival of the fittest. They were not lost in the wilderness but prostituted their art for money. Money has proved irresistible. This reality is too cruel, and I am afraid I too will soon be lost."

Sui Yi still didn't speak, because Yuntian had just said everything that was in her heart.

One day, Yu Changshui came to visit. He had just returned from the auction by the Jiahe Corporation of Beijing. He was looking extremely cheerful. The two paintings he sent for sale this year had gone for a good price. It was said that his Tibetan-style paintings had found a relatively stable group of collectors. Although his works were not very highly priced, it was more important that he have a fixed group of devoted collectors. Just as with planting flowers and trees, only when they find the right soil can they take root and grow. He planned to exchange his house in Shenzhen for a bigger one.

He said that although the prices of Luo Fu's three paintings were not high, at least they had been sold rather than failing to reach their reserve. Yu Changshui didn't know that Yuntian had gone to Yu Miao to get him to withdraw from the auction. He told Yuntian mysteriously: "There was originally supposed to be a painting by Yu

Miao up for sale, which was exquisite – he'd put a lot of work into it. Many collectors expressed an interest in that painting, but for some reason, Yu Miao suddenly withdrew it. If Yu Miao hadn't pulled it out, Luo Fu would have been in real trouble – nobody would have bought his pictures. Yu Miao's withdrawal saved Luo Fu. His paintings are just getting worse and worse now. His creativity and spirit have been destroyed, and his technical ability seems to have followed suit..." As he spoke, he handed Yuntian the auction catalogue.

Yuntian flicked through the pages and saw Yu Miao's painting 'Happy Days'; it was really exquisite and lifelike, and the reserve price was very high. However, in Yuntian's eyes, Yu Miao's paintings were just decorator's pieces, and he was not interested. Luo Fu's three paintings were also reproduced in the catalogue, and indeed they showed him to have run out of talent. From the realism of 'Five Thousand Years', he had suddenly leapt into abstract art and then devoted himself to performance art and installation art. Now he had been forced by Hao Jun to produce some commercial decorative pieces. He had lost sight of what he was trying to achieve, his artistic taste had been ruined, and he no longer seemed to know what he was doing. He had exhausted all his former energy and vibrancy in the hustle and bustle of Vanity Fair, in the pursuit of fame and wealth. Like a blasted oak, he could no longer produce bright green leaves. Art is a purely personal matter, and no one can save anyone else.

Yuntian turned to the last part of the catalogue, and a picture came before his eyes... hazy, gentle, unfocused, familiar: it was Bai Ye! The title was 'Memory of Spring'. He couldn't help but say: "Does she send her work for auction too?"

Fortunately, Sui Yi was not at home at this time.

"Absolutely," Yu Changshui said. "She came to Beijing to attend the auction." He smiled and said four meaningful words: "She's on the money."

"What do you mean by that?" Yuntian asked.

"Very active and up to every trick in the book! She's only had her work in a couple of sales and already some collectors are actually interested," Changshui said.

At this time, Yuntian was still looking at the reproduction of Bai

Ye's painting. He noticed a sentence in the introduction about her: "The famous painter, Chu Yuntian, vice chairman of the Art Association and director of the Art Committee, has declared: 'The fuzzy beauty of Bai Ye is a creative aesthetic language, comparable to that found in misty poetry.'"

Standing beside him, Yu Changshui asked: "Did you write that for her?"

"Of course not," Yuntian said. "This is something I talked about in my speech at the Shanghai seminar, but it is not even a direct quote."

"I told you she was right on the money!" Yu Changshui said. "She's even pressed you into service to advertise her."

Yuntian replied with a smile: "Then I will have to ask her for an endorsement fee." At the same time, he was not entirely pleased.

CHAPTER 7

Chu Yuntian had gradually come to feel that Bai Ye was a beautiful but elusive spirit.

Since that unexpected night in Shanghai, after their romantic kiss amid the falling flowers, he thought he would fall in love again, returning to the abyss that he had plumbed with Yufei more than twenty years before. He felt their emotions becoming intertwined, ever more tightly interlocked; however, he also felt guilt and regret too much to extricate himself. But over time, he found that this was not the case. Bai Ye didn't pursue him; she didn't even call him. But she would occasionally send him a text message:

> A 'fuzzy' hello.
>
> Forgetting the past means betrayal.
>
> My ear is hurting again.
>
> ...

These short messages were not at all like the little poems that Yufei had written out on paper slips to insert between the pages of a book. There was no burning emotion, no yearning of the heart. These messages, which would occasionally appear after a long period of silence, seemed only to maintain their unusual relationship. It was nothing like true love, where you wish never to be apart. Yufei was like a kitten, longing to snuggle up in his arms every day in a poetic and picturesque way. Bai Ye was like a beautiful bird, jumping around him, occasionally soaring into the air and then flying away. She didn't depend on him. Thinking about it, he realised that there was no deep feeling between them, that this was not like love. Love often happens regardless of the other side, so love comprises an element of independence and wishful thinking. As a result, loving is a happier experience than being loved. However, if there was no such emotion between him and Bai Ye, how could it have happened last time? How could there have been such an amorous kiss? If they hadn't both tried to restrain themselves at that moment, anything could have happened. She didn't look like a woman who engaged in promiscuous behaviour. So, what kind of person was she? Was it not as she had once said to Yu Changshui: "I love Chu Yuntian so much!"

If that was the case, he felt this kind of relationship also had something to offer. It would be relatively relaxed; they would not drag each other down. At most, it was a little secret between the two of them. He liked this woman of such extraordinary temperament and beauty, and was willing to maintain a special, ambiguous relationship with her.

Sometimes, he couldn't help sending messages back to her, but most of them were about art. For example, he would say: "Pay attention to the degree of fuzziness, and don't be so vague as to be puzzling."

She replied to his text message, but she still kept harping on the personal string:

> Are you talking about how I treat you?

Did the naughty, humorous, direct and flirtatious approach she took derive from the freedom of young women today? Did it mean anything at all? They came from two different generations after all. If two generations are brought together in an equal relationship, miscalculations may occur.

On one occasion, an exhibition of paintings by young artists from China and Japan was to be held in Beijing, and the Art Committee invited Chu Yuntian to serve as the director of the jury. Yu Changshui had paintings up for selection, so it was impossible for him to attend; instead, he took Fei Liang with him. This time, some of the judges were painters invited from local associations and academies of art. Among them, he spotted Lü Chi of the Shanghai Academy of Art. Because they knew each other, and because the Tianjin and Shanghai Academies of Art were in regular contact, they greeted each other very cordially.

"Bai Ye sent in another of her paintings," Lü Chi said, "and it is very good. She said that you should pay attention to the spatial sense of her picture. She was very proud of the composition of this particular work. It really is very good." After that, he pulled Yuntian aside and whispered in his ear: "I've already said hello to several judges. You now need to do your bit!" Then he said with a smile: "This time, several paintings by your Yu Changshui are also coming up for judgement. He called me and asked me for help. I've already mentioned this to several of the judges I know personally."

Yuntian was disgusted to hear this kind of personal canvassing. However, due to their friendship and Yu Changshui's involvement, it was hard for him to speak out against it, so he had to laugh. But at the same time, Yuntian felt that the vice president of the Shanghai Academy of Art was putting in a lot of work on Bai Ye's behalf. Was this not a sign that she was indeed "right on the money"?

When he was judging the works submitted, he noticed Bai Ye's painting. The square format, quite large, and the light colour, hazy and elegant, were very distinctive in her personal style. The topic was unique and the artistic conception quite ethereal. Against a broad yet indistinct background, a large bunch of flowers emerged, snow-white, fluffy, gentle, like stars in the sky, floating quietly in the air like fragrant smoke. The spatial sense of this painting was really well handled. It showed a great distance from front to back and had a strong sense of three-dimensional space. Looking again, he was quite taken aback. The flowers depicted were gypsophila! Wasn't this a symbol of their romantic impulse? Why did she paint this particular type? This bunch of gypsophila was the only witness to their passion and memento of their romance! Was the picture meant for him?

He looked at the title of the painting: 'True Love'!

His heart leapt. Yes, she had painted it for him, for them!

But the other judges did not understand why it was called 'True Love'. Among those present, he was the only one who knew the story behind the painting, and he felt his own presence in her art.

He listened to everyone praising the painting. It showed fine artistic conception, three-dimensional space, as well as beautiful colour and taste. Lü Chi asked Yuntian: "What do you think of Bai Ye's painting?" He was forcing Yuntian to make a statement.

Yuntian couldn't help saying: "It's a very touching piece – a masterpiece."

Everyone agreed that it was 'a masterpiece'. This sentence did express his true opinion. It was indeed a very fine painting with wonderful artistic conception and aura. But they didn't understand why Yuntian said it was 'touching'.

The painting was selected for the exhibition. Yu Changshui's paintings were also chosen.

After the meeting, Lü Chi asked him to have dinner to thank him. He declined. He said he had something to go back to. In fact, he didn't want Sui Yi to stay alone in their old and dark house.

On the way back, a text message appeared on Yuntian's mobile phone, with only a few words:

> Did you find it touching?

She got the news so quickly. She was amazing in that way!

He really had been moved. He could see real emotion in this painting. That bunch of gypsophila were like fireworks from the heart, glittering and shining through space, floating freely. He knew where her inspiration came from and why she had entitled her painting 'True Love'. Had she known that he would see the picture? Was this her confession to him?

For the first time, he took the initiative to confide in her by text message. He only wrote one word:

> Yes!

She didn't reply. They were silent and enjoyed that silence. But that may just have been his own feeling. He asked the driver to turn on the radio, which happened to be playing a Mozart Rondo performed by Vladimir Horowitz. As the car moved through the twilight, the music brought home the feelings in his heart at this time and the memories aroused by love.

On arriving home, he chatted with Sui Yi about the judging. When he mentioned Bai Ye's name, Sui Yi asked: "Did you see her?"

"How could she possibly be there? Everyone who participated in the evaluation would have to avoid her. She's in Shanghai. I didn't let Yu Changshui come with me either. Lü Chi came from Shanghai because he was also a judge."

Yuntian felt that Sui Yi had become sensitive about Bai Ye, but he didn't know why. They had not mentioned her for a long time in their conversation. Why had she suddenly become so interested? She was sensitive on the subject, but he was even more so.

A few days earlier, a painter from Shandong had invited him to visit Houshiwu at Mount Tai. When he was young, he travelled to Mount Tai with some painting friends to sketch from life. He went down the valley from the back of the South Tianmen gate. Only then did he discover that the back of Mount Tai was even lovelier than the front. The majestic scenery brought with it a kind of wildness, with jutting rocks and ancient twisted pines, which had a vast and unbridled beauty. He saw a collapsed ancient temple, which was most impressive. When the ancient temple collapsed, the roof was actually intact even after it fell to the ground. The four walls were gone. The whole roof was just lying there, like a huge dark grey hat thrown on the ground. There was also a bell taller than a man, with an inscription on its side. After the bell tower collapsed, it had been left where it fell. He had no idea how long this ancient temple had been deserted. Half of the bell was hidden by wild grasses, taller than a man. He picked up a tree branch and struck the bell hard. The cacophony startled the numerous black crows that lived in the ruins of the ancient temple. But he did not dare to go any further, because it just got wilder, weirder and even more deserted.

Now it was different. More and more tourists visited Mount Tai, and the influx prompted local painters to start visiting too. They were familiar with the route and wouldn't get lost.

Today, Yuntian drove the car and set out early in the morning. Just after the turn-off for Dezhou, he received a terrible phone call. It was from Hao Jun. He thought that there might be a problem with selling paintings again or some kind of quarrel between them. But this call was for him, and she never normally called him directly. This showed that something bad must have happened. As soon as she heard his voice, she began almost shouting for help. "You have to come… you have to save Luo Fu!" she screamed hoarsely.

Yuntian's mind went black. What on earth was wrong? Was he dead? Was he sick? Or mad? Or was he suicidal? "What's the matter?" he asked. "Where is Luo Fu?"

"No! You don't understand! He's gone!" Having shouted these words, she hung up.

Yuntian didn't understand what she was talking about, but he was sure something dreadful must have happened. He couldn't get through to Hao Jun when he called back, so instead he phoned Sui Yi, getting through to her on the third attempt. "I've been trying to call you!" Sui Yi exclaimed. "Luo Fu's gone missing!"

"What!" Yuntian cried. "Since when?"

"Hao Jun said that he's been behaving strangely for the past two months. He didn't sleep at night. He often went out onto their dock and sat there alone. He disappeared early this morning," she explained.

"What about his car? I mean, is his car still there? If the car isn't there, he must have taken it," Yuntian said in a state of near panic.

"The car isn't there, but his mobile phone is now off. Hao Jun says she's already called the police!" Sui Yi said.

"There's no need to panic. Try to get hold of Hao Jun and tell her I'm turning around right now – I'll be there as soon as possible. Let me know if you have any news," Yuntian said.

He found the nearest exit, left the motorway, turned around, got back on the motorway, and then headed back at top speed. All manner of possibilities flitted through his mind. He thought of Yu Changshui telling him a month ago that Luo Fu seemed to be depressed, not speaking any more or eating, his mouth so dry that he was constantly drinking water, not sleeping at night so he was getting terribly thin, his face all wrinkled. It was more than six months since he'd last set foot in the art college; he was no longer capable of teaching because he couldn't put brush to canvas any more. Yuntian knew that depression was painful and torturous, and worried that Luo Fu would seek relief by committing suicide. He prayed secretly that as long as Luo Fu didn't go to extremes on this occasion, he would spend time keeping him company, helping his old friend to regain confidence and get out of the slough in which he found himself. However, half an hour later, he received an even more frightening call from Sui Yi. She told him that the police had found where Luo Fu had gone. His car was parked on Bei'an Bridge. The door was open, but the car was empty. The police thought that he'd jumped off the bridge and fallen into the river!

Yuntian's hands and feet went ice-cold. He tried to calm himself down and asked Sui Yi: "Have the police found a body?"

"No," Sui Yi said feebly. "I'm afraid, Yuntian!"

"Don't be afraid. Try not to worry. They are just guessing. It doesn't mean that he's definitely jumped. I'll be in Tianjin in two hours. I won't stop off at home – I'll go straight to join the search for Luo Fu. I'll keep in touch!"

"I see. You must not drive too fast," Sui Yi told him.

On the way back, Chu Yuntian kept receiving calls. They all told him that Luo Fu appeared to have thrown himself into the river, but that was all they knew; there seemed to be no further information. When he arrived in Tianjin and had just turned off the motorway, Xiao Shen called and asked him: "Whereabouts are you?"

"Back in Tianjin. What's happened?"

"They've just found him, somewhere near Jingang Bridge. I want you to listen to me. Don't be too upset. You're driving and it's not safe–"

"I'll be careful. Tell me the truth. How is he?"

Xiao Shen was silent for a moment, and when he spoke, his voice was very low: "He's dead."

Yuntian slammed on the brakes, and the car behind almost hit him; it was a very near thing. The driver was so angry that he honked hard, rolled down the window and shouted at him, and then pulled out past his car. He sat in the driver's seat sobbing and crying. His car was stationary right there in the middle of the road, and the cars behind him were forced to slow down, until one by one they could pull round him and move on…

His mobile kept resounding with Xiao Shen yelling: "Yuntian! Yuntian! Do you hear me? Yuntian!"

Chu Yuntian got to Jingang Bridge as fast as he could. He saw a crowd had already formed on the banks of the Haihe River. Police cars were flashing warning lights, and some red cordons had been pulled across the broad area alongside the river. The atmosphere was very tense. Yuntian stopped his car and ran over. Through the gaps in the crowd, he could see two men loading a stretcher onto an ambulance. At that moment, he realised that because the body was soaked in water, the middle of the stretcher was heavily bowed, revealing the shocking sight of a heap of wet, black curls protruding out from under the cloth sheet, while a bare forearm hung down from the side. It was Luo Fu. No matter what he did in the future, it would mean nothing to him. Yuntian stood there, weeping helplessly.

Xiao Shen noticed him and rushed over. Yuntian hooked his arm round Xiao Shen's shoulder; he seemed to have lost all his strength and could not so much as stand. Xiao Shen kept patting him on the back, as if to give him strength. He said: "You need to be strong. I'm afraid this is the best thing that could have happened to him. If he'd lived, his burdens would have been too much for him." Then he said: "He was under so much pressure – from the market, from public opinion, and from Hao Jun. This was his only way out."

Some tragedies are inevitable. They are the result of the gradual accumulation and superposition of different malignant causes.

The various staff members from the art college gradually dispersed, along with the idle onlookers. Yuntian, Xiao Shen, Yu Changshui, the director of the college and some of the painters were left, but not Yu Miao. Two middle-aged men with familiar faces walked over sadly. When they introduced themselves, Yuntian realised that they were two of Luo Fu's cousins – actually his biological brothers. Yuntian had met the two of them when holding the funeral for Luo Fu's adoptive parents after the earthquake more than twenty years before. He didn't expect to meet them again on the occasion of another death; it made everything all the more tragic and sad. They shook hands but had nothing to say to each other since they were wiping away their tears with the backs of their hands. "Where's Hao Jun?" Yuntian asked.

"She's gone back home in her car," one of the cousins said. "She was making such a fuss here that it was impossible to get anything done."

Yuntian could hear their dissatisfaction with Hao Jun.

They discussed how to proceed with Luo Fu's funeral.

Xiao Shen said to Yu Changshui: "Yuntian went off to Shandong this morning and then had to come rushing back – he can't have had anything to eat. You get some food and bring it to the car. I'll drive him home."

When Yuntian got back into his car, he felt his legs could no longer support his weight.

Luo Fu's memorial service was held at the College of Art. Many people came to mourn and pay their respects, including painters from Beijing and other cities, as well as any number of former students. Luo Fu was a straightforward and honest person. Friends came from near and far to see him off. Some of his former students remained very grateful for all he had done for them. They too travelled from their various home cities and knelt together in front of the coffin for three minutes. Apparently, Tian Yufei was one of them.

On this day, Chu Yuntian didn't seem to see anyone. Many people came to shake hands with him, but he didn't know who they were. Three colours predominated: white, black and yellow; paper flowers, real flowers and elegiac couplets seemed to go fluttering past. He didn't even look to see how the hall was arranged. He took Sui Yi and bowed three deep bows in front of Luo Fu's coffin. As a lifelong friend, it was very important to him to say goodbye properly. Sui Yi was already crying bitterly. She almost fell over several times, bumping into Yuntian as her body slumped forward. He took her arm and walked over to Hao Jun and Luo Fu's cousins to shake hands, but he couldn't speak. He felt that his whole body was full of rolling dark clouds, filled with lightning and thunder. He knew what had taken Luo Fu away; it was the most powerful thing in this commercialised era. There was no way to resist it, no way to fight; you had to obey. But obedience was the greater tragedy.

Yuntian and Sui Yi left and were just about to get in their car and go home when Yu Changshui ran over and said to Yuntian: "Luo Fu's cousins asked me to tell you to please wait a minute. When it's all over, they'd like to go to his house."

"What's the matter?" Yuntian asked in surprise.

"They want to talk about Luo Fu's will," Yu Changshui said, drawing closer.

"What do they want me for? What can I do?"

"They said you were Luo Fu's greatest friend, and they trust you to be fair. Everyone will accept what you say."

There was anger on Yuntian's face. "Luo Fu's body is still unburied and they're already arguing about the will!" He said to Yu Changshui: "You can tell them that I've never cared about my own property, let alone other people's. The only reason I'm here is because of my lifelong friendship with Luo Fu."

With that, he helped Sui Yi into the car.

For many days, Yuntian stayed at home, silent and depressed. He and Sui Yi didn't say a word about Luo Fu, but they both thought about him a great deal. They were simply not willing to aggravate the pain in each other's hearts, and they each digested their own sadness. Really deep pain is like the onset of a severe winter; you cannot escape. You must wait for its fierce coldness to pass, as day follows day.

Then on one occasion, Yu Changshui remarked that a strange thing happened on the day of Luo Fu's memorial service. At the end of the day, a stranger walked into the empty hall and stood in silence in front of the coffin. The man was quite tall, with a flat head and a strong body, dressed in black, his eyes expressionless and blank. He stood still for a long time. The staff went up and whispered to him that the ceremony was over, but he didn't seem to hear them. None of Luo Fu's relatives and friends had ever seen him before, so he could not have been someone very close. Why did he stay there for so long? After about seven or eight minutes, he turned around and went away alone. He left without shaking hands with any of Luo Fu's relatives. Who could he be?

Sui Yi and Yuntian both knew it must be Luo Qian. Sui Yi also guessed that Yuntian must have asked someone to send him an obituary. Apart from Yuntian, no one in the art world knew anything about him. But neither she nor Yuntian spoke of the matter. It's better to keep what you know in your heart.

These days, their minds were filled with thoughts of the past. Past joys, smiling faces, their energetic bodies, cheerfully undergoing hardships, holding hands to keep warm, the small salon frequented by the Three Musketeers, helping each other through the turmoil of the earthquake, and of course the righteous hand he extended when their marriage was in trouble.

In Yuntian's mind, there was a deeper layer to his thoughts: Luo Fu was a talented artist, who'd triumphed in socialist realist commissions in the 1970s, then in the 1980s he'd painted 'Five Thousand Years', only to get caught up in contemporary art in the 1990s, and interior decorators' pieces in the new century. How could this have happened to him? Why did Qu Fangge and Yu Miao succeed, while he fell from grace? In fact, Yuntian knew the reason quite well. He regretted failing to give his friend more attention and warnings at various critical junctures in his life and career. How long had it been since he last really talked to him? Had he not long dismissed Luo Fu from his circle of true confidants? He had indeed bought his paintings on the quiet, but he didn't tell Luo Fu what he had done and why. Did he alienate him spiritually, or did he alienate himself?

Yuntian understood that there was no one to blame. In this era when cash was king, how many people could set aside mundane considerations and be as independent as Gao Yuqi?

He had watched a talented artist fall into the Slough of Despond, gradually losing his soul and finally destroying himself. How many other talented artists were still following this path? Who could stop them? Considering these thoughts, he let out a long sigh in his secluded garden, under the shade of the tall fir tree.

CHAPTER 8

There are only two reasons for cracks in a good thing: first, there were cracks in the past that have been repaired, but now they have opened up again. Second, the original was fine, but then a small crack appeared unbeknownst to everyone, and then it just grew larger and larger. Why did it split in the beginning? Who knows? No one was paying attention. But when it really starts to gape wide, it will be difficult to heal.

A year later, as the shadow of Luo Fu's suicide slowly receded, the rift in Yuntian's family started to appear.

The first clues dated back to the day of Lü Chi and Bai Ye's visit. During their conversation, they inadvertently mentioned that when works were being selected in Ji'nan for the forthcoming national exhibition, Yuntian had done his best to support Bai Ye, and Sui Yi knew nothing about this. As for whether Yuntian had seen Bai Ye at the opening of the exhibition in Beijing, she didn't know, and he didn't say. If he'd told her all about it when he came back, then nothing would have happened. But if he was deliberately keeping her in the dark, that was hard to understand. Was there something going on? Especially after Sui Yi had met Bai Ye herself that time, she turned out to be a woman of rare beauty with an outstanding temperament. She liked her very much, but she was also aware of what kind of woman Yuntian liked. At that time, it was just a feeling, a feminine instinct, and she did not think too much about it. She was not the kind of person to become jealous and suspicious for no good reason.

After that, Yuntian went to Shanghai to attend Bai Ye's seminar, as was originally agreed. It was an exchange project between the two academies of art. Yuntian said he would take her with him, but she couldn't go because she caught a cold just before leaving. But when he came back, he seldom mentioned Bai Ye. When she asked him about her, he was evasive, as if deliberately avoiding the subject. The real reason for all this was that there had indeed been a brief passionate encounter between the two of them, which had nearly resulted in an actual affair. After he came home, he still remembered that strange episode from time to time. There was one occasion when Sui Yi accidentally rubbed his ears, which startled Yuntian; it seemed that she had witnessed him and Bai Ye kissing. At that moment, Sui Yi seemed to understand something was wrong from his frightened air. Later, she saw the text of Yuntian's speech for Bai Ye's seminar in the new issue of *The Artist*, sent over by Xiao Shen. She felt that his evaluation of Bai Ye was overblown – he was deliberately talking her up. Yuntian had always upheld the principle of being objective in evaluation, so why did he suddenly negate these principles when it came to Bai Ye?

In fact, these were all psychological issues. It was an important recent discovery that really put her on the alert.

They lived in a typical old British colonial house, with three rooms on each floor. A large south-facing room in front was the living room, with a floor-to-ceiling door leading out to the garden; a dining room faced the rear, connected to the kitchen behind; and a study was off to the side. One wall of the study was covered in teak bookshelves, carved with an exquisite floral trim from top to bottom. During the Cultural Revolution, a leader of the Revolutionary Committee lived here. He always used this room as his office, so the bookshelves were well-preserved. Now, Yuntian had this room as his studio, and the bookshelves were full of large and small art books. One day, Yuntian was not at home, and as Sui Yi tidied up his studio for him, she happened to notice several volumes jammed together on the bookshelf. There were several books, thick and thin, about Bai Ye. Some she had looked through before, others she was seeing for the first time. Two of these books were very thin.

They were reproductions of her collected works. They were the volumes she had given Yuntian when he first met her, at the time of his exhibition 'Autumn Whispers' in Shanghai. After he came back, he showed these two small picture books to Sui Yi, and she remembered them well.

The other two volumes there she had not seen before. One very thick and heavy book was the catalogue from the national art exhibition. The page with a light blue label marking it showed Bai Ye's painting. The title page bore her signature and a line in her handwriting: "Eternal thanks". This catalogue was proof that he'd pushed for her inclusion and then later met her in Beijing.

The other volume was a book specially printed after Bai Ye's seminar in Shanghai. On the title page, there was another message from her, which Sui Yi didn't understand at all: "You won't lose it, will you?" Not lose what? What was she talking about? This sentence seemed to be a hint – there must be a story behind it.

Also, why was she addressing Yuntian so informally? Why was she calling him 'you'? She and Yuntian belonged to two different generations. What relationship could exist between them to justify her intimate form of address?

However, although much of this was just speculation, step by step she was getting nearer to the truth.

Sui Yi was afraid that a second Tian Yufei was about to appear.

If that were the case, she would be alone. She didn't have a Luo Qian on her side any more, let alone a Luo Fu. She made up her mind: if they were having an affair, she would not quarrel with him or let outsiders know of their private troubles. She would go abroad to join Yiran. No matter how many billion people there are in the world, there are only one or two in this life that you can truly rely on.

She didn't show or even hint at her distress to Yuntian, not to mention their frequent visitors such as Xiao Shen and Yu Changshui, and kept her mouth shut around Little Xia. She also didn't say a word to Yiran for the moment; her daughter cared most about the two of them. If there was a problem between her parents, Yiran would suffer double.

The crack really opened one evening when Yuntian came back and Sui Yi was at work in the garden with the lawnmower. Sui Yi always mowed the grass herself. She liked the refreshing fragrance of freshly cut grass. Yuntian held an album tucked under his arm, and when he passed he greeted Sui Yi and entered the house. After a while, Sui Yi also came in. Yuntian was sitting in the living room, drinking tea, but the book was not lying on the table. The next day, when he went out, Sui Yi went to the shelving in his studio and saw, just as she had expected, there was a new album of paintings next to the other books about Bai Ye. When she took it out for a closer look, the cover was in Chinese and Japanese. The title was *A Rainbow-Like Bridge*, and the subtitle was *A Collection of Works By Young Chinese Artists Exhibited in Japan*. A small light-blue label was sandwiched in the middle. When she opened it on that page, she was struck by the beautiful, gentle and romantic atmosphere. A kind of deep feeling that spreads gracefully in tranquillity, rippling vividly. Looking more closely, the painting depicted a large bunch of flowers – gypsophila in full bloom! Weren't these the flowers Yuntian brought back from Shanghai more than a year ago? Now, this bunch of dried flowers was still in the black vase in the corner. The bunch of flowers in the painting was undoubtedly the same as the one that currently stood in the vase! Did this mean something? When she saw the title of the painting – 'True Love' – she understood everything.

At this moment, she lost her old style of doing things. After such a shock, she became a little irrational. She ran to the living room, grabbed the phone and called Fei Liang. "Let me ask you something," she said. "You must promise me that you will never tell anyone about this, not even Chu Yuntian!"

He was silent for a long time. It seemed that it could hardly be Sui Yi on the other end of the line. She had never been this impulsive. However, Fei Liang was an honest man. "Ask away," he said. "I promise I won't tell anyone."

"Last year, when you came back from Shanghai, who gave you the bunch of gypsophila that Yuntian was holding?"

"Bai Ye. Apparently, she'd brought them round to the hotel the night before. Before leaving, she wrapped the bouquet in paper and asked me to give it to your husband." Having said this, Fei Liang asked in surprise: "Why? Is something the matter?"

"What time did Bai Ye come to the hotel?"

"I don't know. Xiao Shen and I were staying somewhere else. We weren't in the same hotel," Fei Liang explained.

Everything was now quite clear. Sui Yi already understood exactly what had happened; she was not imagining it – she knew by instinct and her sixth sense. Her world collapsed again. Although she didn't have all the facts, she knew there was a great deal going on that she had not been told. This was just the tip of the iceberg, the slipping of the cover hiding the cloven hoof. What kind of 'True Love' needed to be eulogised with these noble, meaningful, brightly erupting gypsophila flowers? Did she really need to extract all the shameful details? Did she have to destroy this web of lies to reveal the truth?

Sui Yi didn't want to repeat the story of Yufei all over again. It was time to determine her future. Thinking of her next step, Sui Yi's usual calmness, stability and thoughtfulness returned to her.

At dusk, Yuntian came back. He couldn't find Sui Yi anywhere. He asked Little Xia: "Have you seen Sui Yi?"

"She said she felt sleepy and went for a nap in Yiran's room," Little Xia explained.

After Yiran went abroad, her mezzanine room was kept just as she'd left it, for use when she came back for New Year's or the summer holidays.

"Why not sleep in our bedroom?" Yuntian asked.

Little Xia said with a smile: "She said that you snore at night and then she gets woken up again in the morning by the birds' dawn chorus. She can't get a wink of sleep. She said that from now on, she's going to be sleeping in Yiran's room and you can have the bedroom all to yourself."

"Whatever she wants," Yuntian said with a smile. "Sleeping isn't a conversation – it's quite all right to want to be alone." He didn't think anything of it.

At dinner, Sui Yi sat there quietly, with a gentle smile, a calm manner and the same measured consideration as usual. In fact, in her calmness, there was desolation and indifference in her heart. She had made up her mind, but she would not let him see it. She kept her secrets just as he kept his. This might have constituted a kind of revenge, but she believed that it was something he deserved to suffer.

Yuntian told her that a gallery agent had come from Dalian and wanted him to sign an exclusive contract. He said that he would make his paintings rank among the top three in the domestic market within two years. He said it had taken him quite a while to get the man to give up." Sui Yi smiled and said: "You should have told him that if you wanted to sell paintings, you would have asked Xu Dayou and Tian Yufei."

He didn't realise it, but she was deliberately bringing up Tian Yufei's name. She was using the knife of the past to cauterise her wound today.

Then they discussed sleeping in separate rooms. "If you prefer it, do as you like," Yuntian said. "We slept in that room after we got married if you remember. It's much quieter."

"Those azure-winged magpies make such a racket," Sui Yi said. "They wake me up every morning. I've endured it for too long. I can't stand it any more."

In fact, her last words were a kind of psychological venting, but Yuntian simply did not recognise it and laughed it off.

Then Sui Yi continued: "Yiran doesn't want to come back for the summer, because it's too hot here. She wants me to go to her, and we'll visit some ancient towns in southern France."

"That sounds great," Yuntian said. "Why don't I go too? I'd love to see Aix-en-Provence. That's where Cezanne had his atelier in the last years of his life. Cezanne was lonely in his old age and painted there all by himself."

"Why don't you come next time?" Sui Yi suggested. "I want to spend some time with Yiran. You have so much to do here. You won't be able to stay abroad for any length of time…"

This was a surprise to Yuntian. In the past, whenever she travelled, she always wanted him to come with her, and they'd hold hands with each other, chatting away. That was how it had been when they were a young couple, when they were teenagers, even when they were children. Why did she want to go by herself this time? However, Yuntian didn't think too much about it. He decided that Yiran must be missing her mother now that they were thousands of miles apart and wanted to spend some time with her. After all, Yiran wasn't even twenty when she went to live abroad, and she was all alone over there. She didn't even have a boyfriend.

He said of course that was OK.

Once Sui Yi had made up her mind, she arranged everything quietly. It didn't take long for her to get the visa for France, but she even kept her packing out of Yuntian's way. She also did not inform him of the date of her departure. One day, Yuntian told Sui Yi something that touched on Bai Ye. Now when it came to anything to do with Bai Ye, Sui Yi felt it like a stab wound to her heart, but her self-esteem was too strong to let it show. She kept looking at him with a smile on her face.

Yuntian said that Bai Ye had phoned him to let him know that his recently published essay 'Scenes of Yesteryear' had inspired her, and she wanted to do a series of paintings entitled 'Lost Time' which would depict past scenery, past seasons, past people and past urban landscapes. With her fuzzy painting technique, the scenery in the paintings would convey a sense of passing youth and years gone by. She wanted to ask Yuntian to write a paragraph for each painting, only about five hundred words. It would be a new form of art, combining graphics and text, literature and painting. She said that if Yuntian agreed, she would like to come soon and discuss it face-to-face. She also said that she had many excellent ideas, and the more she thought about them, the more excited she became.

Yuntian was very excited when he said this. It seemed that her inspiration had aroused his creative impulse. This amounted to a hard push on Sui Yi's back. She knew that if she wanted to avoid the coming storm, she had to leave as soon as possible. From that moment on, she decided exactly when to leave, but she was not about to let him know. She was going to leave cleanly, suddenly, severing their relationship with one stroke.

Three days later, Chu Yuntian set out early in the morning for the drive to Beijing. He had business there and would be away for two days.

After Yuntian left, Sui Yi called Little Xia and said that she too would be away for a few days. She didn't say where she was going but instructed her on what needed some attention about the house. When she said "My husband's blood sugar has been a little high recently, so you should remind him to take his medicine when eating," she choked a little. Little Xia didn't understand what was going on. Then Sui Yi went upstairs to the top floor, stood there for a while and slowly came down. She walked around the building, room by room until she had visited every corner of her house. Then she went into the garden and sat on a rattan chair. She liked the broad white rattan chairs out on the grass under the big trees. She asked Little Xia to make her a cup of tea. She looked at the old building covered in ivy, ancient and quiet, a little tired, and unconsciously opened the door of memory. Decades of feelings overwhelmed her, and she burst into tears, which made Little Xia feel quite at a loss. Then she wiped her face with a tissue, stood bolt upright, slung her coat over her arm, hugged Little Xia, lifted her little suitcase and walked out. There was a taxi waiting for her outside, as she had ordered.

Chu Yuntian came back at noon the next day. When he came through the door, he shouted happily for Sui Yi. This time, he had bought a kind of tough leathery paper in Liulichang, very absorbent, in a long, wide roll, which would be perfect for the paintings he was planning, to be entitled 'Treasuring the Four Seasons'. After a few shouts, there was still no response. Little Xia came running and said: "Your wife left yesterday." The expression on her face then was most peculiar; it was hard to say whether she was more surprised or confused. She must have been thinking, Sui Yi has gone away – why don't you know that?

"I have been calling her since yesterday, but she never answered," Yuntian said. "Where has she gone?"

"She didn't say," Little Xia said, "but I think she must be going on a major trip. She took two suitcases, one big one in the car and the other was hand luggage."

. . .

Chu Yuntian felt at that moment that something bad must have happened. Why didn't she tell him where she was going? Why did she leave without saying goodbye? He dropped his things and ran around the house, upstairs and down. She hadn't left any letters or notes. In his hurry, he noticed one clue. On the chest of drawers in their bedroom, a frame containing photos of the two of them when they were young had been placed face down. When he ran to his studio, he was stunned by what he found there: all the answers were there at first glance –

On the painting table, there were five volumes arranged in a row. Of course, they all contained reproductions of Bai Ye's paintings. The catalogue from the exchange exhibition of young Chinese and Japanese artists was placed in the middle, open wide on the page with 'True Love'. Behind the catalogue was a large bunch of fluffy and tender gypsophila in a dark vase. The light penetrated through the window, and the scattered flowers and shadows were vague and confused, shadowing both the painting table and the volumes lying on top of it… Sui Yi had arranged all the irrefutable evidence of his infatuation right there and then left him – she was making way for him to be with Bai Ye!

He picked up the phone; he wanted to tell her she was wrong! It was all a misunderstanding… they were just coincidences… there was no need for her to be suspicious. But how could he explain away this bunch of gypsophila he'd brought back from Shanghai and the painting in the catalogue, 'True Love'? Was that also a misunderstanding, a coincidence or her overthinking things? How could he lie to her again? Did he have the heart to deceive this kind and good woman who had always loved him so much? He couldn't face it.

Sui Yi's phone remained off. He dialled Yiran's number. Yiran didn't wait for him to speak, she just said: "Mum is here!" Then she continued in a reproachful tone: "Mum's even told me about the girlfriend you had before I was born. How could you treat her like this? Who could possibly be better than Mum? You know she's loved you so much all her life! I know all about Bai Ye, and I don't care whether she's a good painter. I also don't care whether she's good-looking! What I know is that she's my number one enemy! All of us studying here in France have heard about how she uses people. I can tell you that sooner or later she'll find someone more useful to her than you are, and she'll dump you just like that!" Yiran seemed to be spitting flames!

Yiran had always been Yuntian's darling. When his daughter shouted at him so angrily for the first time, he realised that he was going to lose not only Sui Yi but also the other person he loved most in the entire world! Yuntian said: "Yiran, I'm going to apply for a visa tomorrow. I'm coming to France. We'll talk face-to-face... this is all just a terrible mistake..."

After hearing this, Yiran became even more determined. "Don't bother," she said. "Even if you come, it'll achieve nothing. We're going to Spain tomorrow, and I'm moving out of here right away anyway. I won't be answering your calls from now on!" With that, she slammed down the phone.

As soon as their call ended, it seemed like he'd lost everything – he felt empty. He shouted: "Who is this Bai Ye anyway? Go to hell!"

He threw the vase filled with gypsophila into the living room, and shards of black porcelain and white flowers scattered all over the floor.

Little Xia came running from the back kitchen. She didn't know what was amiss and was scared out of her wits. She had never seen the elegant Yuntian lose his temper like that and thought he must be going crazy.

For many days, Yuntian made countless calls to Sui Yi and Yiran. His mobile phone needed to be charged three times a day, but no one answered. He sent countless text messages without any response. He knew that Sui Yi had made up her mind to leave him this time, and in the short term it would be impossible to make her come back. During the past twenty years, he had twice betrayed her, and he must have almost destroyed her. He remembered the old affair with Yufei. Thanks to the help of two friends, he saved his marriage. He still remembered that at Luo Qian's home afterwards, he had told him about his own terrible past and said: "To hurt a person who really loves you is to put out all the flames and turn her heart to ash!" This time, had he really quenched the flames in her heart again – could he even have put out her will to live? There were only ashes in her heart.

His greatest pain now was the absence of anyone to talk to. He thought of Luo Qian. Could he bear to tell him that he had done something so stupid? How could he get involved in a passionate emotional affair with a younger woman? However, he always wanted to find someone trustworthy to help him analyse whether she really loved him... Even if this came at the cost of being shouted at!

One day, Chu Yuntian couldn't stop himself any longer, and he went round to the small street behind Diantai Avenue to find Luo Qian. When he got there, he couldn't find the gallery. He thought he must have gone to the wrong place. Then he realised that Luo Qian's Backstreet Gallery had closed down; now, it had become a barbershop called 'The Elegant Gentleman'. He pushed open the glass door. The barber was a thin, capable man, of whom he made enquiries. The barber was very talkative and gave him complete and reliable information. He said that the former owner of the gallery – that was Luo Qian – had closed down about six months earlier because he didn't make enough money, and he'd offered him the shop. Mr Luo was a painter himself, but people in Tianjin don't hang oil paintings in their houses. He'd gone to Guangdong to join a community of artists, where they had an oil painting collective, selling wholesale, that was making a lot of money. He also said that Luo Qian was long gone, and he'd cut all his ties with this place. He'd even sold his house in Yangliuqing.

Yuntian listened and felt like a whole volume in his history had now had the last page turned and the book closed. No one knew what was written below.

CHAPTER 9

Before he had even reached the age of sixty, Chu Yuntian felt the desolation of life. Just like the trees in autumn, when the wind blows, the leaves rustle and fall, and what remains is but the sparse fragments of yesterday.

He had resigned as vice president of the academy long ago and recommended Xiao Shen to take over from him. He also resigned from the Artists Association. The main reason he left these positions was the fact that the art world had been engulfed by the rising tide of commercialism. As predicted by Mr Yu from the auction house so many years earlier, no one cared about the quality of painting any more; they focused only on the price. When elegant calligraphy and fine paintings are transformed into worldly goods, they are defined by their price. Yuntian didn't sell his paintings, so they had no market price. Naturally, no one took his work seriously. In the end, the public only cared about his fame and status. His influence, talent, prestige and all kinds of extraordinary experiences had turned into brightly coloured, intangible assets, which were then put to full use by other people.

It bored him more and more. He stood on all manner of platforms and stages, under the spotlight and in full view of the public – he was at once an indispensable part of the proceedings and about as much use as a decorative vase. He began to hate himself.

Now he had sloughed off these positions and achieved immediate results. Fewer and fewer people came looking for him. Who would bother to come and talk to him about painting now? Instead, he was able to concentrate on studying painting theory in his studio, pondering over his brush and ink, and living as calmly and tastefully as if he had returned to the lonely 1970s, before everyone had to think about money all the time. Now the only thing missing was a few friends who would drop in occasionally, and Sui Yi to talk to all the time.

Only he knew how dreadful life was without Sui Yi.

Even Yu Changshui no longer came to see him. Yu Changshui had moved to Shenzhen and married his girlfriend; they now lived in a beautiful apartment. He was also doing good work, employed as a professor in an academy of fine arts. Since arriving in Shenzhen, more people had come to him to buy his works. He was the envy of some of the students at the academy, and they were only the more convinced that selling paintings for lots of money was the route to happiness.

Before leaving for Shenzhen, Yu Changshui took his girlfriend to say goodbye to Chu Yuntian. Yuntian remembered all the years that this young man had followed him around, talking with him about art, how they had trusted and helped each other, and left many beautiful memories. He liked the kindness and understanding of this young man. After he left now, it might be that they would never see each other again. With a sudden surge of emotion, he took out one of his favourite paintings and gave it to him as a souvenir. At the same time, he said to him: "Money is important, but there are more important things in the world than money. Everything that money can't buy is more important than money. For example, friendship, health, true love and the pursuit of art." Then he said in an even more serious tone: "You should be very clear in separating the paintings you do for money, from those of personal exploration."

Chu Yuntian's words were really important for Yu Changshui. He kept them constantly in mind. Although he could not live without selling his work because he needed the money to live, he had learned from Yuntian over many years that real art has nothing to do with commerce. He would always remember what Yuntian told him, and he thanked him from the bottom of his heart. At the same time, he thought that when he left there would be even fewer people around Chu Yuntian that he could talk to and would understand him. Especially after Sui Yi left, he had been very lonely, and he seemed to have aged a great deal. At that sad thought, he started to cry.

He went out of the door, but he could not bear to turn around and wave goodbye to Chu Yuntian, who was standing there to see him off.

Two years later, Yuntian had become used to not trying to call Sui Yi only to hear the dialling tone. But he and Yiran gradually restored occasional contact. A daughter will miss her father. On his sixtieth birthday, he received a beautifully printed catalogue of works of the Barbizon school in the collection of the Orsay Museum sent to him by his daughter. He turned over the leaves in this volume for three days. He didn't know whether to look at the paintings or to touch the past through the scent of paper and ink permeating the book. However, his daughter kept silent about Sui Yi's situation, which must be in accordance with her wishes. This also made him indirectly feel the depth of the damage Sui Yi had suffered.

How could he tell her that he had no contact now with Bai Ye? He could not tell her that he was now suffering from the pain of breaking up with her.

Within any social circle, there is no such thing as a secret. Gradually, it became common knowledge that Sui Yi had left him. Yuntian was a celebrity, and anecdotes and gossip about celebrities can while away the idle hours for others. Fortunately, Yuntian had always maintained a good reputation and there was not much malice in the rumours. It was better now. He had less contact with the outside world and so heard less gossip.

After Sui Yi left, two things happened. First, Bai Ye sent him three text messages in a row, wanting to come to Tianjin to see him. He wrote back putting her off, saying that he was too busy. She then sent him a further text message:

> I am spring; winter cannot stop me.

Yuntian sent another message saying that he was just about to go to France to see his daughter, and after that there was silence. Bai Ye seemed to have vanished. This made him feel very puzzled.

The second thing that happened was even more outrageous. One day, Hao Jun came to visit him, dressed up to the nines. He hadn't heard from her since the day of Luo Fu's memorial service. So where had she sprung from? She said that after Luo Fu's funeral, there had been a big fight with two of his cousins, which ended in her winning the lawsuit and pocketing every penny that he'd left. She was very rich now, but she still lacked a good friend. Yuntian understood exactly what she was hinting at but pretended not to. He told her that she was still young, with all her future ahead of her. Her true partner would come to her sooner or later. He did not expect Hao Jun to make her intentions clear. "I'm glad to hear you say that," she said loudly. "I don't care how long I have to wait for you. I've thought the whole thing through – we'd make the perfect couple! You have what I lack, and vice versa. Your ex-wife was a wonderful woman, but she wasn't the kind of person who could really help you make something of yourself. I can not only make you comfortable but also bring your paintings to life. Look what I did for Luo Fu over the years – I made him rich, but sadly he didn't get to enjoy it. For example, although your house is exquisite, it's been out of repair for a long time and needs to be renovated. You need someone to take care of these things for you…" She kept on and on, and suddenly Chu Yuntian's eyes were full of anger. He looked a bit like the God of Thunder as depicted on the walls of the Temple of the Queen of Heaven over in the old city. It was quite terrifying.

"Out!" Chu Yuntian roared. "How dare you! Get out now!"

Little Xia, who was pouring a glass of water for the visitor, was scared silly. Hao Jun had never seen Chu Yuntian get so angry, and she didn't understand why.

Afterwards, there was a rumour going around that Chu Yuntian had proposed to Hao Jun, but she turned him down. However, before this annoying gossip reached Chu Yuntian, another piece of bad news occupied his every waking thought.

Gao Yuqi was dead. He'd been killed in a car crash in the Taihang Mountains.

Zheng Fei was the first to call Chu Yuntian to tell him about it.

His mind went blank when he heard the news. Zheng Fei was sobbing and incoherent, unable to explain anything about what had happened. Less than an hour later, Xiao Shen rang the doorbell and ran in, his face streaked with tears. Anxiety, grief and despair were written on his features. He said: "Yuqi died last night. The car came off the road and fell into a ravine, and it hasn't been recovered yet. There were only two of them in the car – he and the driver. They were both killed."

Yuntian was appalled. He listened in silence.

Xiao Shen continued: "In the last part of his latest painting, it depicts the old farmers and children left behind in the countryside. He thought the image of people living in the Taihang Mountains would be most evocative. He often went there to collect figures and make sketches… The Taihang Mountains are too dangerous, the roads are so narrow and they aren't properly surfaced, there are no barriers, and accidents often happen. Just when they were turning a corner, they hit a boulder and went off into the ravine…"

Yuntian stopped Xiao Shen with a gesture from his hand. He couldn't bear to hear any more. At the same time, he felt as though the huge pillar supporting him was broken. After sitting in silence for a long time, he raised his face and asked Xiao Shen: "When will they be holding the funeral? I want to attend."

"They won't be holding an open coffin event," Xiao Shen said, "because the body has been so badly crushed. And right now his wife still won't accept that he's dead – she keeps trying to call him on his mobile."

The next day, Xiao Shen told Yuntian that the people in Luoyang had decided not to hold any kind of memorial service. Very few people had heard of Gao Yuqi or seen his paintings; holding a memorial service would simply be an empty formality. The publishing company he'd once worked for decided to open his studio to visitors from the art world – his studio being the large workshop in the garment factory – to let everyone see his masterpiece, 'Migrant Workers'. In addition, they were hoping to transfer this immense piece to the Beijing Art Museum for exhibition at the end of the year, holding a seminar at the same time.

"That's a wonderful idea. Who's thought of that?" Chu Yuntian asked.

"Zheng Fei," Xiao Shen replied.

Chu Yuntian said thoughtfully: "He's been a good friend to Gao Yuqi. He was lucky to have someone like Zheng Fei." Then he said to Xiao Shen: "On the day they open the studio, let's go and remember him. Tell Zheng Fei that I'll do whatever it takes on the Beijing side to arrange the exhibition and seminar."

Three days later, Chu Yuntian and Xiao Shen flew to Luoyang. It was a sunny day, but their hearts were dark. Zheng Fei came to pick them up and cried when he saw Yuntian. Zheng Fei had lost his most beloved friend. What Yuntian had lost was someone who put his art above all other considerations. Both of them knew how much Gao Yuqi meant to the other, which was irreplaceable. "Why did it have to be him that died?" Zheng Fei said. "It's so unfair!"

Chu Yuntian thought about this many times. He could not answer, nor did he understand it. He could only say that it was the will of heaven. But why does it always have to be so cruel?

Zheng Fei still used his strange old car to drive them out to the studio in the factory. After entering the workshop, they found that everything remained the same – the paper on the ground, the painting tools and materials piled on the table, pots of ink, buckets of water, colour plopped on plates and bowls, a large number of sketchpads and books, painting catalogues, as well as lunch boxes, spoons, chopsticks, thermos bottles and the small fold-up camp bed piled with blankets, quilts and clothes… All maintained the original state of the artist at work. Only a single black-and-white photo of Gao Yuqi had been added to the front wall of the room. However, the artist was not gone, because he lived among the thousands of energetic migrant workers in his painting. Yuntian once again saw this masterpiece that he had kept in his mind for so many years. Today, looking at it afresh, he could see that it was more complete, fuller, more natural, more vivid, more filled with tension and impact – an even greater expression of the liveliness of an era. No one else had contemplated taking up such a theme, no one paid any attention to this huge group of blue-collar workers, and no one placed them at the very centre of life. No one else could depict them with such all-encompassing love, such profound human care, such vast and majestic artistic talent.

Chu Yuntian suddenly said to Zheng Fei: "I have a request to make. Could you ask everyone in the room to go out for a while? Give me some time to be alone with him. I don't need long, just seven or eight minutes."

Zheng Fei whispered to the dozen or so people in the room. They all understood and went out silently, leaving Chu Yuntian alone with the unfinished masterpiece. Suddenly, Yuntian knelt down in front of the painting, unconsciously shed tears, moved his lips and silently said what he thought. At that moment, he believed Gao Yuqi heard every word he said.

After a while, Yuntian stood up, opened the door and kept saying "Thank you, thank you, thank you" to the people standing in the corridor.

Only Zheng Fei noticed the two dirt marks on his knees. He knew in his heart what had happened in the room just now. He was deeply moved.

Originally, Chu Yuntian and Xiao Shen had planned to fly back the next day. Then, they heard that Zheng Fei and some of Gao Yuqi's other friends planned to go to the Taihang Mountains the next day to hold a memorial service at the place where he died. Yuntian wanted to join them. Zheng Fei said that the place was dangerously steep and would not let him go. He said that they would offer prayers on his behalf. Yuntian insisted on going. Xiao Shen stopped any further argument by saying impulsively, with red eyes: "If it kills us too, then so be it!"

After that, they had to give in. The next morning, Zheng Fei arrived in a Japanese Mitsubishi off-road jeep borrowed for the occasion, and for safety's sake he had also hired a driver who specialised in mountain roads. Zheng Fei said to Xiao Shen: "You won't have to return to Luoyang after you're done. I've asked the driver to take you across the Taihang Mountains, leaving the range at Pingshun in Shanxi Province. That'll take you out on the motorway to Taiyuan, and from there you can take a plane back."

This arrangement was very thoughtful. Xiao Shen thanked him

again and again. In this way, early in the morning, they drove north and entered the Taihang Mountains at Xinxiang in northern Henan Province.

As soon as the car drove into the Taihang Mountains, it entered another world. This range that stretched across Hebei, Shanxi and Henan was full of high mountains, crags and cliffs, quite different from any other mountain range. The rocks were all bare, precipitous and rough, exposed to the full force of the elements. Every mountain peak and rock was like the face of a huge old farmer who has gone through all manner of hardships, looking old, suffering and patient.

Zheng Fei's car took the lead, and Chu Yuntian's followed. As they travelled, at one moment they were heading straight to a mountain peak, at the next they were diving to the bottom of a valley; here they were winding through circuitous and steep slopes, and there they were carefully crawling along a bare ridge above the clouds and mist, with a vast abyss on either side. Xiao Shen was afraid to even look out of the window. He felt cold in his lower limbs. Yuntian was unusually calm, but his eyes looked confused and empty as if he were in the world depicted by Gao Yuqi.

The car stopped at the corner of a high, dangerously steep hill. There was indeed a boulder sticking out there. Zheng Fei pointed to the deep valley below the road and said: "This is where it happened."

Looking down, the deep blue valley was cold and empty, as if bottomless. Anyone would be frightened at the sight. The roadside was covered with undergrowth, and some of the small trees were broken. It was easy to imagine the terrible, heart-stopping moment when Gao Yuqi's car went over.

Facing the deep mountains and empty valley, they lined up and stood carefully.

Zheng Fei spoke to the vast valley below: "Yuqi, we are all here. Chu Yuntian and Xiao Shen are here too. This is where you went to heaven, and we will always be your good friends!" With that, he bowed, wept, took out a bottle of wine and a cup, and then each of those present filled the cup to the brim and poured a libation. At this moment, Yuntian felt the magic of the scene before them. He had painted landscapes for most of his life, and seen countless valleys, beautiful, empty, clear, distant and profound. But for the first time, he felt that this vast and misty valley contained a person's soul.

They lingered there for a long time before going their separate ways. Zheng Fei and his companions retraced their steps and returned to Luoyang. Yuntian and his companion still had to travel onwards to Jinzhong. They told each other's drivers to drive slowly and cautiously, and then shook hands and hugged each other. The mountain wind blew their tangled hair and clothes. They waved goodbye to each other, got into their respective vehicles and headed in opposite directions.

The driver, surnamed Gu, was a native of Henan Province. He was a middle-aged man, strong and steady, and he drove competently. He wore a small jade Buddha tied with a thin red thread around his neck, which he'd received in a consecration ceremony on Mount Wutai many years ago. Mr Gu did some thirty to fifty trips a year to the Taihang Mountains. He'd memorised all the valleys and twists and turns within this great mountain range. He said he'd never had any issue driving in these mountains, but he had to keep both hands on the steering wheel, and he couldn't be distracted for a moment. The Taihang Mountains were very dangerous – there were countless places where it was all too easy to give up the ghost. Many locals spent their whole lives in these valleys, never once going outside. Now the younger generation was leaving for work and often they wouldn't come back. Life was too hard in the mountains, and it was too difficult to get in and out of the range. Now the mountain villages were at least half empty, and there were some with only a few households left. In the past, if Mr Gu forgot to bring food and drink into the mountains and was thirsty and hungry while driving, he could get something to fill his stomach in any of the villages. Now, there was no one there. Every time he entered the mountains, he had to bring sufficient food and water with him, or he'd be in trouble. "What happens if it pours with rain?" Xiao Shen asked him. "Do you have to stop? Where do you sleep?"

"That's a good question," Mr Gu said. "In case of heavy rain, slippery roads or mudslides, you can't go anywhere. In the past, you could find a nearby house and ask for a place to sleep. Now…" he laughed and said, "things are better. I'll show you in a moment."

After driving for a little while longer, they came across a fork in the road. Mr Gu turned his car and immediately they saw a small village. There were no large villages in these mountains, just tiny, scattered communities. They stopped to have a look. The village was empty and uninhabited, but some of the stone houses were still solid and intact. When the mountain people left, they took all the things they needed, and just left the things they didn't need or couldn't take, such as water tanks, stone mills and farm tools. A small stone-carved Mountain God was sitting in a hole in an old locust tree, which had also been left behind here. All the doors were open. Mr Gu led them into a house. The only thing in the empty building were piles of dry leaves. "These houses have been empty for many years," Mr Gu explained. "The leaves are blown in by the wind. Once they've been blown in, they will not be blown out again. These houses are all abandoned, and I can stay in whichever one I want. It's very soft and comfortable to come in and sleep on the dry leaves."

Along the way, they saw some other mountain villages. Occasionally, there were old people basking in the sun, smoking or at work. Their grandchildren were playing at their feet. Their sons and daughters had left to find work while they stayed at home, farming the land and looking after the next generation. They were the subjects that Gao Yuqi collected and sketched.

"We'll soon have to cross a mountain," Mr Gu explained. "It's very steep, with lots of cliffs. Fasten your seat belt. I come and go often, so you don't have to worry. Once we've got past this mountain, we'll not be far from Pingshun." Then he continued: "You should have a look at the mountains on both sides. They've been built up layer by layer. Since it's nearly dusk, these mountains are really beautiful when they are illuminated by the sun."

Sure enough, just as Mr Gu had said, when the car came down the next section of the road, it was obviously highly dangerous. Both sides of the road plunged straight down into the abyss – it was quite terrifying! Mr Gu drove the car to a very high promontory and parked it on the edge of a bare cliff. The clifftop looked like a platform cut by a huge blade. It was wonderful! Mr Gu invited them to step out of the car and have a look. The mountains on all four sides looked like vast clouds, rolling upward. At this moment, the sun was setting, and the rock cracks and gullies were as dark as ink. The stone was dyed red by the glow, just like the healthy blush on a man's face, vigorous, strong, tough and rough. This boundless, majestic, sublime and heroic scene affected Yuntian deeply. Although the five sacred mountains were beautiful and famous all over the world, they did not have this primitive wildness, such natural purity. He could not help saying: "The Taihang Mountains are so wonderful, so special and so unique that to fail to include them among the five sacred mountains shows that our ancestors never appreciated them properly." When he said this, without knowing quite why, he felt a spasm of emotion, a kind of pity for the genius who had just died, a great painter who was still unknown at the time of his death. It was so sad... so unfair! These feelings were suddenly integrated with the uninhabited but incomparably magnificent landscape that lay in front of him.

An emotion and a scene became one!

A purely artistic impulse and a natural landscape became one!

A strong spirit and a strong life force became one!

A kind of human beauty and a kind of natural beauty became one!

He was overcome by the urge to paint. He could not wait to get home and rush into his studio. At this time, his hands could almost feel the pools of thick ink and heavy colour in which his large brushes were dipped, before being swept across the broad sheets of rice paper. After returning home, within a very short time, he produced a number of fine works better than anything he'd done in the past decade. He felt that he was connected with the spirits of Jing Hao, Fan Kuan, Guo Xi and other masters who'd painted the Taihang Mountains a thousand years before. During this period, he went to the Taihang Mountains in Hebei and Shanxi several times to sketch.

That same winter, he and some painters, together with Zheng Fei from Henan Province, held an exhibition for Gao Yuqi's 'Migrant Workers' in a newly built art museum in Beijing. A huge exhibition for just one painting was unprecedented. As soon as it went on show, this painting shocked the art world. Many artists from all over the country travelled to the capital to see it. Seeing the crowds pouring in, Zheng Fei said to Chu Yuntian: "It's a pity that Yuqi never got to see this."

"Well, we saw it for him," Chu Yuntian exclaimed.

It was sad for Gao Yuqi who never knew how many people came to admire his work, but it was a great source of satisfaction for Yuntian. This satisfaction came from the faces of the crowd, moved and shocked by the exhibition.

This was a victory for a real artist in an era of rampant commercialisation.

At the seminar, Chu Yuntian made a speech entitled 'Artistic Purity Standing Against the Tide of Money Worship'. The title spoke for itself. He said: "This painting will be as an unfinished symphony in the history of art, and the fact that it remained unfinished is a tragedy. The hero of this tragedy was an unknown painter before today, but from now on he will have his place in the history of Chinese painting. What he has left us is not only a painting of eternal verities marked by the defining characteristics of this era, but also the memory of his lifelong sacrifices for the sake of his art. Someone once asked me, how much money is his painting worth per square foot? This is the most vulgar question it is possible to ask. I told him that art is a kind of nobility of spirit, and as such it is priceless."

That day, when he spoke, his emotions were hard to control, and his blood was boiling. After speaking, he felt that his underwear was as sodden as if it had just been washed, and his heart felt as bright and clean as if it too had been washed.

Of course, he thanked Gao Yuqi from the bottom of his heart for sending him back to his art so much revivified and purer.

CHAPTER 10

Over the past few years, Yu Changshui's career and life in the south had gone smoothly. But he took as his motto what Chu Yuntian had said that day when they said goodbye, and he strictly separated paintings for sale from those of personal exploration. Clear and turbid ran the two different streams, never to be mixed together. He took a stand as an artist. Even when working on decorative pieces, he would not pander to the market; they were never kitschy, and he always adhered to his own aesthetic principles. This made him stand tall and climb higher, step by step.

In the early summer of this year, an art museum in Paris invited Yu Changshui to hold a solo exhibition. He prepared forty of his paintings for this show – not many, but all were exceptionally fine, exquisite, top-grade works. Not one of them was intended for sale. They were not only exquisite in brushwork, but each possessed unique qualities and rare technique. In all of Europe, the French seem most attuned to the taste of Chinese art. Just after the opening ceremony of the exhibition, many French people surrounded him and asked questions. However, he couldn't speak French and his English was only average. A bearded Frenchman who had studied Chinese painting asked him: "There is a saying in Chinese painting that 'ink is divided into five colours'. Why five? Why not six or seven colours?" This question puzzled Yu Changshui, and he didn't know how to answer it.

Just at that moment, someone handed him a letter. He was too busy to open it until lunchtime. The letter was written in Chinese: "Mr Yu, I know you will be very busy today, so I will wait for you at a red-fronted café opposite the entrance to the art museum at three o'clock tomorrow afternoon. I hope to see you." There was no name signed below. Who could this be? He only knew a very limited number of people in Paris. He could not think who it might be.

At three o'clock the next afternoon, he came out of the art museum, went to the eye-catching red café opposite and pushed open the door. The café was dark, quiet and elegant, and the aroma of coffee filled the air. It was obvious that the furnishings were intended to suggest a nostalgic mood. Among the numerous flowers and plants, there were many old photos of Paris from the nineteenth century and theatre posters on the walls. The stars of yesteryear featured in these advertisements could still be named by every Parisian.

He was looking around for who could have invited him there when he noticed a woman getting to her feet in front of the window and waving to him. When he walked over, the woman stood up with a smile and said: "Mr Yu!"

The woman was about thirty years of age, quite tall, elegant and gentle-looking. There was no need to wonder more about who she might be. Just looking at her fine, smiling eyes, he recognised her immediately and asked in surprise: "You're Yiran, aren't you?" Yu Changshui used to know her very well. At that time, he often went to Chu Yuntian's house, when she was a lovely and intelligent girl. However, after she went abroad to study, he hadn't seen much of her at all.

The woman nodded and said: "Yes. Thank you for coming." Then she ordered him a cup of coffee.

Yu Changshui asked: "I thought you lived in Bordeaux?"

"After I graduated there, I came to Paris for postgraduate study," Yiran explained. "Then, I was hired by a museum here to organise and research their Chinese collection. They have a large number of Chinese artworks, all piled up in a warehouse. Nowadays there are not so many Sinologists in Europe, and fewer and fewer people know about these things. I have been living in Paris for several years now."

"Is your mother all right?" When Yu Changshui asked this question, he regretted it immediately, because he thought Yiran might find it inappropriate. Unexpectedly, she didn't seem to mind. She answered him honestly: "It was very bad for a while. She had a major operation, but now she has recovered. She has been living with me, in the Latin quarter."

Yu Changshui knew about the split. He was not aware that Sui Yi had suffered such an ordeal after leaving. Was it something to do with the affair? His heart suddenly darkened.

Yiran sensed this, and she said to Changshui: "It's all over now. It's OK. Don't worry."

Yiran didn't take after either her mother or her father. Frank and open, her generation was less psychologically burdened.

Yu Changshui told her something about himself.

"I know all about it. Bartok, who organised the exhibition for you, is my friend. I've also been to see your paintings. They are magnificent. Chinese ink painting has a certain abstract quality, and the French like this very much. There were so many people at the opening ceremony yesterday, you didn't see me. If I hadn't asked you to come, you wouldn't have recognised me." Then Yiran said frankly: "Mr Yu, I invited you here today to ask you something. It's about our family and the past. I don't want you to feel uncomfortable, so if you don't think this is appropriate, I won't ask. Is that OK?"

Yu Changshui spoke without the slightest hesitation: "I will tell you everything I know. I owe a great deal to your family."

"OK, thank you. Did my father really have an affair with Bai Ye?" She spoke very frankly.

"I can tell you without a shadow of doubt that the answer is no," Yu Changshui assured her. "To begin with, your father was really attracted to her. Her paintings were very fine. Your father likes talented people, you know. In addition, she went to great lengths to attract your father's attention." He paused and then continued: "Frankly, she was a very manipulative woman. I could see that clearly because I wasn't involved, but your father may not have been able to see it. Your father understands art, but he doesn't understand people."

Yiran smiled faintly and said: "If you like someone too much, you will overlook all their faults. But Bai Ye always was the kind of person to make use of others. Some of her fellow students that I've met hate her for that!" She said this with some anger.

"Well, now everyone can see just what she's like," Yu Changshui said. "She's only interested in others to the extent that they are useful to her. She'll worm her way into relationships with several people at the same time, but she doesn't really have feelings for any of them. She wants you to believe that she's in love with you, so you will help her. She was having an affair with Lü Chi back in the day, and he helped her a lot – it caused a massive scandal when that came out!"

"Does my father know about that?" she asked.

"Lü Chi lost his job and got thrown out of the Shanghai Academy! Of course your father knows!"

"Does my father still associate with her?"

"As soon as your mother left, your father cut all contact with her. After Lü Chi was dismissed, there was no communication between the two academies. For a while, there was some gossip about Bai Ye and your father. Your father was very depressed and shut himself away. Later, I heard that Bai Ye married a rich guy from Hong Kong, so the gossip ceased."

"What? She married some rich guy?" Yiran was very surprised.

"That's not surprising, surely? The only thing that she was ever really interested in was money. With money, she wouldn't have to work hard getting her paintings sold."

"Does she still paint?"

"She's in Hong Kong – who knows? I haven't seen her paintings anywhere for years now. She was never a real artist, so it doesn't matter whether she paints or not."

Yiran sighed and said: "My father was such a fool!"

They sat in silence for a moment. The coffee in their cups became cold, so they had to order fresh again. After a while, Yiran asked Yu Changshui: "Is my father all by himself now?"

"Alone and lonely! Now Luo Fu is dead, and I've moved away, Xiao Shen is the only one who goes to see him regularly. He used to have a good friend named Gao Yuqi. Have you heard of him? He was an artist your father very much admired, but he died in a car accident a few years ago."

"I read my father's speech given at the seminar on his work in a magazine. But no one here has heard of Gao Yuqi. Europeans regard themselves as the centre of the world, and we hear little news of Chinese art. How is my father's health?"

"It's OK. I went to Beijing last year for work and made a special trip to Tianjin to see him. To be honest… he's not in high spirits. Who can he talk to in that big empty house? I think he is a little… a little aged."

Yiran lowered her head, her tears falling onto the tablecloth.

They didn't continue their conversation. Originally, Yu Changshui wanted to ask after Sui Yi, but seeing Yiran like this, it did not seem right to touch a wound that still hadn't healed. When they said goodbye, Yiran didn't leave him her phone number. He thought that she would not contact him again, but the day before the end of the exhibition a staff member of the gallery handed Yu Changshui two bags. They were accompanied by a letter of only a few lines:

Mr Yu

I'm giving you two bags. One is for you and your wife, a little memento of the occasion. The other is for my father. Please give it to him. I know you're very busy, so just put it in the post once you get home. Please take care of him. My mother said to say hello. I wish you a safe journey, and I hope you are happy with the success of your exhibition.

— YIRAN

After reading the letter, Yu Changshui was filled with emotion. When he calmed down, he took a message from this short letter: Sui Yi asked him how he was but did not ask him to convey anything to Chu Yuntian. That day, when he had met Yiran at the café and told her about Bai Ye and her father's current situation, would that not go some way to atone for the past tragedy? Why is it so difficult to heal rifts, whether due to mistakes or misunderstandings?

After returning home, Yu Changshui posted the package to Chu Yuntian. A few days later, he sent a text message on his mobile phone. It was only a few words. It couldn't have been shorter:

I got it, thank you.

He didn't so much as ask a single question.
Their history remained frozen.

For many years after his daily siesta, Chu Yuntian would go and sit on one of the big rattan chairs under the tall fir trees in the garden, reading letters, newspapers or books. In recent years, as mobile phones became ubiquitous, there were fewer letters. He missed the old way of using words. He put away all the letters he received once he'd read them. He still drank green tea, which he said was his last hobby.

In this house, his favourite place was sitting in the white rattan chairs under the big trees. This was where he talked with his friends, and also the place where he had once chatted with Sui Yi. Now he would often just sit here by himself, the other chairs empty.

An empty chair is desolate; leaving it there is a sign that you are waiting.

The sunlight from the gaps in between the trees shone brightly, making the light patches on the grass as beautiful as a painting. The plants were full of life in the sun and sleepy in the dark. Yuntian now suffered from high blood sugar, and he was prone to fatigue. From time to time, he would fall asleep in the rattan chair, and his book or newspaper would drop to the grass.

Little Xia still looked after him. She was kind-hearted and had lived with the family for many years. She shared his feelings with him, knew his pain and took care of all manner of daily tasks like a daughter. The last two years, Little Xia had a boyfriend in the city, a delivery driver. His family name was Sun, and he originally came from Nanpi, in Hebei Province, which he'd left to spend some years in the army. He was a simple and trustworthy fellow. He'd been in the logistics corps in the army, and now he drove a long-distance lorry for some company. He'd be away for three days at a time.

Whenever he came back, Yuntian would make sure Little Xia could spend time with him. Her boyfriend was very grateful to Yuntian for being so understanding, and he would help Little Xia with her chores whenever he was free. Yuntian enjoyed this; it brought some life into the house.

Last year, Chu Yuntian did an important thing that had long been on his mind, that is, donating his best works to the local art museum. He knew that his paintings like 'The Thaw', 'The Yellow River', 'The Great Wall' and 'Eternal Taihang' ought to be in museums so that they would not be scattered, and nor would they fall into the hands of the mercenary trying to make more money. Another thing he donated was Luo Fu's painting 'Ploughing Deep'. This was a witness to Luo Fu's contribution to the history of contemporary painting. It was his final act for his friend, and it was also the culmination of a long-cherished wish. Yuntian said nothing of this at the donation ceremony arranged by the art museum. All the fine words that could possibly be said are inferior to action. At this time, everyone realised that he'd quietly saved one of Luo Fu's greatest works, but he never even knew. The event made many people in the art world sigh, and there were even some who wondered whether Chu Yuntian, who was visibly growing more feeble, was arranging his final dispositions. But this was just vulgar speculation, and out of respect for him, no one put it into words.

Yuntian was accustomed to painting or writing in the morning. In his youth, he felt that when he got up in the morning, his body was full of sunshine and light – this was the time for inspiration. Recently, he had been moved by Tchaikovsky's *The Seasons* to write twelve essays, each expressing the customs and tastes of a month in a year. On the surface, he was describing his feelings about nature, but really he was writing about life. Every time he wrote, all kinds of images would naturally flit through his head. This made him come up with the idea of turning his words into paintings. From January to December, there was one painting for each month, and he called this 'A Year in My Mind'. In this way, the ups and downs of nature would be integrated with his experiences of life, which would be emotional, exhilarating and joyful. He suddenly thought: Isn't this the kind of modern literati painting I discussed with Mr

Hirayama at Tokyo University of the Arts? He also thought: Are 'The Thaw' and 'Eternal Taihang' not modern literati paintings, too? Modern literati have both a small and a big persona; they are both the brass and the strings in an orchestra. The combination of the two is the life and art of modern literati.

Xiao Shen hadn't been to see him for many days. He had been in a bad mood lately. Nobody seemed to be trying to achieve anything; the critics had done nothing, and no one listened to him. *The Artist* had become almost a vanity publication. Every year, Chu Yuntian would be sent a painting or two by Yi Liaoran. He was getting older and didn't rush about so much, spending most of his time in Huangshan. He would get up in the morning at cockcrow and return in the evening with the clouds, living like an ancient sage. He sent his paintings to Yuntian simply because he remembered him. In this era, paintings were valuable commodities; who else would just give paintings away like that? He answered with poems and paintings of his own. Recently, Yuntian had suggested several times to Xiao Shen that they should go to the mountains together to see Yi Liaoran – in a few more years it would be too late. Especially in the past year, his knees had been getting a lot worse, and he could no longer climb high steps. Was he really beginning to fail?

His old house was decaying fast. Originally, the roof had to be repaired every two years before the rainy season began. The dark purplish tiles, which had been imported from overseas all those years ago, were solid, thick and rarely cracked. However, the tile ridges had to be repaired and caulked every year. The lead guttering was also blocked by fallen leaves and needed to be cleared. The chimney needed cleaning. But all these things would be a major undertaking, and he was afraid of being put to any bother, so he postponed them. When it rained heavily that summer, the roof leaked badly. Little Xia was in a panic as she ran up and down the stairs with basins, buckets and cans. Sometimes it rained all night and the whole building resounded with the drips. He said it was like living in a clock shop. This year, the roof was not only overgrown with weeds but a small elm tree with a trunk the thickness of a finger was growing on the east corner of the roof. When Sui Yi was at home, she used a lawn mower to cut the grass in the garden every ten days. She did it all by herself since she liked the smell of grass filling the house when it was freshly cut. Now in some places, the weeds reached waist high.

The sun had just turned to the west, and the garden was already getting a little cold. Little Xia brought out for Yuntian the thin blanket Yiran had given Yu Changshui to bring him. The colour of the blanket was his favourite olive-green. Although Yiran had given it to him, only Sui Yi knew what colour he liked and what he needed. He understood that perfectly well.

Then someone knocked at the door.

Little Xia went to open the door, and someone came in. Yuntian was wearing reading glasses and could not see far. But a figure appeared that made his heart beat faster. Even in a crowd of ten thousand people, even at a distance of several hundred metres, he would recognise her right away. He had watched her all his life – he had seen her walk towards him thousands of times. But at this moment, he could not believe it, he did not dare to hope, or even imagine it could be true.

Had she come back? Surely he was dreaming! But in an instant, how could it be? Sui Yi was standing in front of him! Still so elegant and quiet, still with smiling eyes, but what had happened to her? Why was she so thin, so aged, her hair white, and her eyes lined with crow's feet? Had she suffered so much? He had no idea that she had been seriously ill abroad, had undergone surgery and had very nearly died.

He had already smelled her unique perfume and knew that it was true. Of course, it was unexpected, unimaginable and joyful. She came back to him from far away.

He seemed to have no strength to haul himself to his feet. His shaking finger pointed to the empty rattan chair beside him and said: "That's your chair, sit down. You must be tired."

Little Xia stood not far away, wiping her tears away with the back of her hand.

She sat down and looked into his old, haggard face. After a long time, she said: "I've brought yesterday back to you."

A feeling of understanding and forgiveness enveloped him tightly and warmly. The corners of his eyes sparkled with tiny flecks of light. "What you've brought back to me is tomorrow."

First draft completed 30 April 2020
Final revisions completed 18 June 2020

ABOUT THE AUTHOR

Born in Tianjin in 1942, **Feng Jicai** is a contemporary author, artist and cultural scholar who rose to prominence as a pioneer of China's Scar Literature movement that emerged after the Cultural Revolution. He has published almost a hundred literary works in China and more than forty internationally. He is proficient in both Chinese and Western artistic techniques, and his artwork has been exhibited in China, Japan, the US, Singapore and Austria. He has had a major influence on contemporary Chinese society with his work on the Project to Save Chinese Folk Cultural Heritages and his roles as honorary member of the Literature and Arts Association, honorary president of the China Folk Literature and Art Association and adviser to the State Council, among others. He is also dean, professor and PhD supervisor at the Feng Jicai Institute of Literature and Art, Tianjin University.

ABOUT THE TRANSLATOR

Olivia Milburn is a professor at the School of Chinese, Hong Kong University. She completed her undergraduate degree in Chinese at St Hilda's College, University of Oxford, a master's in Oriental studies at Downing College, University of Cambridge, and a doctorate in classical Chinese at the School of Oriental and African Studies, University of London. She has authored several books including *Cherishing Antiquity: The Cultural Construction of an Ancient Chinese Kingdom*, *The Spring and Autumn Annals of Master Yan* and *Urbanization in Early and Medieval China: Gazetteers for the City of Suzhou*. In collaboration with Christopher Payne, she has translated two spy novels by Mai Jia, including the bestselling *Decoded*, from Chinese to English. In 2018, Milburn's translation work was recognised by the Chinese government with a Special Book Award of China, which honours contributions to bridging cultures and fostering understanding.

About **Sino**ist Books

We hope you enjoyed this story on the pursuit of creativity amidst the commercialisation of art.

SINOIST BOOKS brings the best of Chinese fiction to English-speaking readers. We aim to create a greater understanding of Chinese culture and society, and provide an outlet for the ideas and creativity of the country's most talented authors.

To let us know what you thought of this book, or to learn more about the diverse range of exciting Chinese fiction in translation we publish, find us online. If you're as passionate about Chinese literature as we are, then we'd love to hear your thoughts!

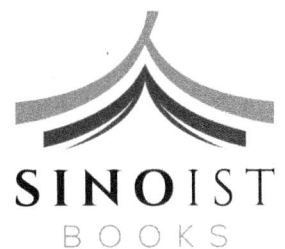

sinoistbooks.com
@sinoistbooks